ALL YOU NEED TO KNOW™ ABOUT THE CITY

2009/10

Christopher Stoakes

LONGTAIL

Christopher Stoakes has been a City insider for 25 years, as a financial journalist, partner in a City law firm and a management consultant.

Chris was a scholar at Charterhouse and at Worcester College, Oxford where he read law. He qualified as a solicitor at Freshfields (now Freshfields Bruckhaus Deringer). He subsequently edited *Global Investor*, *Risk Financier* and *International Financial Law Review* among other finance publications and for eight years wrote the 'Financial Lawyer' column for *Euromoney*. He has been by-lined in more than 30 business magazines and in most of the quality nationals.

Chris was the marketing partner in a mid-sized City law firm, the head of legal training at an international law firm and a founder of Sherwood PSF Consulting Limited. He is a qualified teacher and has held senior visiting positions at Nottingham Law School and the College of Law. Chris is the author of *All You Need To Know About Commercial Awareness*, also published by Longtail.

" As the marketing partner in a City law firm I discovered that our new staff had no understanding of how the financial markets work. So I started telling them about it, based on my knowledge as a City lawyer and a former financial journalist. These talks turned into training courses. I've written this book because there aren't any good basic guides to the financial markets – either they get too technical too quickly or they are monumentally boring. This book is designed to be a quick read: it gives you enough to ask questions without feeling stupid, and it tells you what else to read next if you want or need to. I've had to cut corners, leave things out and simplify a bit in the interests of getting the message across quickly and simply. But what's in here is all I've ever needed to know in 25 years of working in and around the City. "

WARNING

This book is a simple and concise guide to a complex, multifaceted market that is changing all the time. Given the need to simplify an inherently complex subject, this book is not comprehensive or definitive. Readers must not rely on this book except as a general, schematic overview. Accordingly neither the author, the publisher, their agents, consultants nor employees accept any liability for any loss (direct or indirect; immediate or consequential; contractual or tortious) however caused from use of this book or reliance upon it.

LONGTAIL

First published 2005 by Four by Four Publishing Limited. Second Edition published by Longtail Publishing Limited February 2007 Second Impression February 2008 Third Impression April 2009
Tel: 020 7938 1975 Fax: 020 7938 3861 Email: info@longtail.eu
Web: www.allyouneedtoknowguides.com

Publisher:	James Piesse
Deputy Editor:	Sheenagh Nixon
Sub-Editor:	David Sanders
Typesetting:	Louise Downer
Art Director:	Andrew Debens
Photos:	© Grant Smith/View (30 St Mary Axe)
	Author photo © Fraser Deeth & Dion Lucas / Kingston College 1st Diploma Art & Design – many thanks to Patricia Ayre

Written (2004) and revised (December 2006, January 2008 and February 2009) at Scripto, Kingston and Studio, Wendover.

ISBN 0-9552186-3-2
ISBN 978-0-9552186-3-7
Printed in the UK by Clays Limited

For AFS in memory of FS

CONTENTS

– corporate capital – reinsurance – alternative risk transfer – cat bonds
– weather derivatives

INTRODUCTION

It's your first day at work. Your clothes are starchy new. Your shoes are stiff and pinch your feet. You don't know what you're doing or where you're going.

But you hazard a smile. After all, this is the zenith of all that hard work and all those ambitions. It's what your parents and Gran have always wanted for you. You've started work, it's your first job and you're working in the City.

Only everyone else seems to be so much more knowledgeable and confident. Everyone must be looking at you. There goes that new bug, they must be thinking, new to the City.

Whatever you do or say you don't want to look an idiot: you don't want to torpedo your career before it's even got under way.

If this is you – and, don't worry, we've all been there – then this book tells you all you need to know to avoid making a fool of yourself. And, crucially, it gives you the confidence to ask questions to find out more.

ROCKET SCIENCE MADE SIMPLE

What's in this book is what I've pieced together from almost 30 years of working on the peripheries of the financial markets, from reading stuff about them, writing about them and talking to people in them.

The financial markets are full of really clever people with PhDs and rocket-science minds – and that's problem: they start explaining something and, three sentences in, you're lost.

This book isn't like that. It's written by an ordinary joe for other ordinary joes. Once you understand enough about the financial markets to move on to more serious, weightier (and, dare I say it, more boring) books, you won't need this one any more. But it will have got you started. And that's often the most difficult thing in life.

For that reason this book doesn't purport to be the gospel truth or the last word, but rather the first word. If it's your 'first word' to understanding the financial markets, then it's as good a start as you'll get anywhere. It's also (I hope) short and light and quick to read.

At its heart it tells you two things: who the players in the City are; and what financial instruments they trade and transactions they do. The analogy with a fruit & veg market (Chapter 1) tells you who they are. The diagram just before the Afterword tells you what they trade.

Thousands of readers before you have found them a great way of getting to grips with the City. But, of course, something has happened since the last edition: the sub-prime credit crunch, and in its wake the global recession.

CREDIT CRUNCH

Who would have thought that in the past couple of years so many big banks would go bust or be nationalised? Or that the financial meltdown would be so bad that it would drag the rest of the world's economy down into the hole with it, in a depression that loomed as bad as that of 1929? And that interest rates in the UK would fall to levels never seen since the Bank of England started in 1694?

No one.

Now, supposing you're a new bug or would like to be a new bug but you're wondering, post-credit-crunch, whether there's much of a City to work in. What good is this book?

Answer: quite a bit of good.

Those two models (fruit & veg market; financial instruments and transactions) still stand. But what you need to understand is that everything – and what in fact led to the financial meltdown – has become the trading of risk, slicing and dicing it and selling it on. The old idea that the financial markets were a means of channelling capital (a pompous word for money) to the most deserving companies and investments became just that, old hat.

It was superseded by the idea that everyone in and around the financial markets is a risk-taker, betting his or her capital (or, even better, someone else's – the City has always been very good at letting people take risks with other people's money) on which way a market or instrument would move.

So the world went trading crazy. I explain this throughout. In Chapter 1 I give an overview of the credit crunch and how it was caused by the ability to sell on home loans. When talking about private equity (in Chapter 2) I mention the idea that long-term investment (inherent in venture capital, private equity's diminutive dad) was turned on its head by the 'quick flip' (buying a business, restructuring it and selling it on within three years).

In Chapter 6 when looking at what a bank is, I mention the use of proprietary (the bank's own) capital to take large stakes in risky positions – which led some commentators to carp that Goldman Sachs, aka a leading investment bank, was actually no more than a collection of stakes in other businesses and piles of risk or, in other words, a private equity fund or even a hedge fund.

In Chapter 9 I explain how hedge funds (which bet on short-term high-risk, high return strategies) cast the boring old, long-horizon pension funds into the shade. I also discuss short selling (selling something you don't own in the hope you can buy it back later more cheaply) which was blamed at least in the UK for runs on the banks that had to be bailed out by government. And in Chapter 13 I discuss derivatives which have had a large part to do with all of this risk-taking and market instability or, as Warren Buffett, the most successful investor in the world, dubbed them 'weapons of mass financial destruction'.

So the trading of risk became the heart of the financial markets. Whether it will remain so when we emerge from this mess, who knows.

Financial speculation has always been about risk and reward: you take on more risk in the expectation of greater reward. Each bank and financial institution thought its own risk management systems were OK. But when there is systemic failure (that is, when the whole financial world collapses as one) it doesn't matter how watertight your own particular little boat is, the credit crunch tsunami sweeps all before it.

MYSTIC MEG

Will things get better? Oh, sure they will. They always do. The question is: when? How long will we have to wait?

It took Japan ten painful years to start climbing out of its era of deflation (constantly falling prices, so no one buys anything because it'll be cheaper tomorrow, so depressing prices further, and so on) and the prediction is that Iceland, which has effectively been bankrupted by the credit crunch because its financial services sector dwarfed its economy, will take 70 years to emerge from destitution.

So will things ever be the same again? In many respects I hope not.

If the City and the financial markets are about risk and reward, then it seems to me that too much risk was taken on by people who simply pocketed the reward for themselves by way of big bonuses. And when things went south they simply let their institutions pick up the tab and, when they couldn't, relied on governments to step in with taxpayers' money and bail the banking system out.

Yet in the good old days, banks were there to help businesses raise money, by lending to them and by helping them issue shares and bonds (all of which is explained in these pages).

To my mind a lot of the recent slicing and dicing of risk which led to the financial meltdown was too clever by half. It never achieved much except to earn big fat fees and take a lot of supposedly clever people in. So with any luck that won't happen again, at least for a while. But there's nothing new under the sun in the financial markets. So the good times will return and, no doubt, with them some of the egregious (that means bad to you and me) behaviour that greed seems to breed.

WHO THIS BOOK IS FOR

I originally wrote this thing for young professionals: young bankers, brokers, fund managers, lawyers, accountants, insurance brokers, surveyors, PRs and actuaries, among others. But also for support staff: secretaries, PAs, business managers, people in Accounts or HR or Business Development; in other words, people who are specialist in their own jobs but need to understand what the 'fee-earners' in the business do in order to help them perform their roles. You are all professionals in my eyes.

But it turns out many others have read it too. I have given courses on which this book is based to a roomful of City magistrates. And to people outside London who still need to know what goes on in the City because it affects their company or their clients.

In fact, I reckon that everyone these days needs to know about the City, not least because the City looks after your savings and pension.

But that aside, the City is a fascinating place. The dark, narrow alleys that link the streets which radiate out like spokes from Bank tube station (where the Bank of England is) can't have changed much in 300 years. And the street names – Bread Street, Wood Street, Milk Street, Cheapside – are where actual markets used to take place.

So, if you've ever wandered around the dark alleyways of the City, looked through an office window at people behind screens and wondered what they were doing, this is the book for you. Ditto, if you've ever craned your neck up at the tall towers of Canary Wharf in Docklands and wondered who worked there and what they did. Or if you've found yourself chatting to someone at a party and been unable to maintain the conversation after they've revealed that they're 'an investment banker' or 'a fixed-income trader'.

EXCLUSION CLAUSE

Now, a word of warning. Although the City, and what it does, is enormously exciting, the details can be dull, boring and complex. After all, we're talking about vast sums of money: people don't fool around with those things lightly. However, I've left most of the dull stuff out. In almost 30 years of working in the City I've not needed to know it, so I doubt if you do either.

But that means this book does not purport to be comprehensive nor, because things change so quickly, correct. This may be a strange thing to say about a book on the City written by a lawyer. But the truth is that in trying to make things simple to understand, I run the risk of distorting them. To tell you the truth, I don't care.

What I am trying to do is to give you a simple map. It won't tell you exactly the way things are on the ground but it will give you enough of an approximation to help you find your way. You see, I reckon it's better to be roughly right than precisely wrong.

REGULATION

So, for example, one area I have deliberately omitted is regulation. It's too complex, technical and boring. To my mind it's like describing life in a village by detailing the parish council rules.

Regulation has two purposes: to stop financial institutions like banks harming themselves by going bust; and to stop them from harming others by defrauding them or manipulating markets on the basis of inside information.

So one reason for leaving it out is that it can hardly be said to have worked. And it needs to be subjected to a massive overhaul.

But if you do need to know about it it's because you're either a regulator or else work in compliance. In either case, ask a colleague.

THREE THANK YOUs

Speaking of asking colleagues, I have some acknowledgements to make:

1) Viola Joseph for spending her evenings and weekends casting an eye over this to make sure it's not complete tosh and for giving me the encouragement and support to carry on.

2) The many people who read previous editions of this thing and took the time and trouble to tell me how much they liked it (and to point out mistakes) – especially the young professionals who say it helped them decide to work in the financial markets. I hope it helped you find jobs and hang on to them in these troubled times.

3) James Piesse, my publisher, who saw the potential when I first suggested the idea of this book to him and whose ceaseless work since has propelled it to the market position it now enjoys (as any rock star knows it's not the music but the marketing that matters).

Christopher Stoakes
London
February 2009

Chapter 1

THE CITY AS A MARKET & THE GLOBAL CREDIT CRUNCH

SPEED-READ SUMMARY

- Think of the City as a market where customers (companies) buy the use of money

- There are four main players in the City: companies; banks; institutional investors; and brokers

- Money is a medium of exchange of value

- The foreign exchange market is the single biggest money market in the world – and 'follows the sun'

- Liquidity is a measure of how easy it is to buy and sell financial instruments; if liquidity is poor, trading in a market may move prices against you

- There are non-financial markets in the City such as insurance (Lloyd's of London) and shipping (Baltic Exchange)

- The sub-prime credit crunch was caused by over-aggressive lending to poor quality borrowers in the US real estate market

- When the market turned, these loans became worthless and banks stopped lending to each other, which meant they suffered a cashflow crisis and many went bust

- Governments stepped in to bail out the banks and restore consumer confidence, but banks had effectively ceased lending to business and the global financial meltdown became a global depression

Think of a typical market selling, say, fruit & veg. It's an exciting, noisy, messy place. It starts early. The people who work in it have a sense of purpose. They all seem to know their jobs. There are a few nefarious-looking people lurking round the fringes. They may not actually be crooks, but you wouldn't put it past them.

The City is exactly the same.

The difference is that when you go to the City you don't buy fruit & veg or meat. You buy money. Or, more accurately, the use of money. This may seem a bit weird. After all, when you go to a market or a shop, you use money to buy the goods you want. So how come you buy the use of money in the City? And what do you use to pay for it? (Answer: money.)

I have a very simple mental picture for explaining the City and whenever I come across someone in the City, I slot them into this framework. Here it is.

A SIMPLE FRAMEWORK

Companies are the City's *customers*. They're the ones who come to the City for advice on how to raise funds and (often) what to do with those funds.

More often than not they will go and see a *bank*. Now the term 'bank' is much wider than the bank in the high street where you keep an account, as I'll explain. But, for the time being, imagine banks as the market's *stall-holders*. These banks can be commercial, investment or merchant banks.

Behind the banks are the *wholesalers*, the people who provide the market with its produce to sell. They turn up in vans and lorries loaded with the stuff; in the case of the City, with the money that companies want. These are *institutional investors*. They provide the money that companies need.

Finally, there are the *porters* with trolleys who go racing around, moving produce from the wholesalers' vans to the stalls, transferring produce between stalls and putting some of it back in the vans. These are the *brokers*.

So:
- Companies are the customers
- Banks are the stall-holders

- Institutional investors are the wholesalers
- Brokers are the porters

Now, this isn't a very sophisticated picture and in some respects it's a bit wonky, but it's a good starting point and by the time you've worked out its shortcomings you'll know enough about the City to be able to discard it if you want to. But I'm going to stick with it for now and in this book. It still works for me.

HOW MONEY STARTED

But before we go any further, let's look at the idea of money itself. Imagine a primitive world without money. You have to barter for what you want. Let's say you grow grain but what you want is salt (to preserve meat and fish over winter). Instead of getting on with farming your crop you have to spend time finding someone who not only has salt *but who wants grain in return*. This is what economists call a 'double coincidence of wants'. And that's not the end of it. Having found that person you will only conclude a successful exchange if you can agree a price (how much grain for how much salt). One other problem: most activities don't allow the stockpiling of value. If you kill mammoths, those surplus to requirements would go off before they could be eaten. Even if you grow grain, you'll not be able to grow enough to tide you over in retirement, so you won't be able to stop working.

As society developed, people used popular commodities such as sheep to pay for whatever they wanted to buy. But sheep are difficult to carry, don't last forever, can't be divided (try ripping off a leg of mutton to provide change) and some are bigger and healthier than others. Salt was also used – Droitwich salt (from Birmingham) was a unit of currency and the word 'salary' comes from the Latin for 'salt money' – which had the merit of being transportable, durable, divisible and standard. But it can still get wet, not everyone wants it all the time and you need to agree the exchange rate.

Then people switched to precious metals such as silver and gold as currency. Currency provides a medium of exchange (in place of barter), a liquid store of value (it doesn't go off so you can stockpile it for the future), a unit of account (whereas sheep don't come in a standard size) and stability (it doesn't go out of fashion or die). It provides, therefore, a standard of deferred payments (you can buy now and promise to pay later). But gold isn't that portable and it isn't so divisible.

People entrusted their gold to goldsmiths who gave them a receipt. When a depositor wanted to pay someone else, he wouldn't bother to go and get the gold: he'd simply hand over his receipt to the other for that person to claim the gold off the goldsmith. In practice it was much easier to leave the gold where it was and just exchange receipts. This is how money (paper notes) started. And the goldsmiths, knowing the gold would stay where it was could 'lend it out' by issuing further notes in respect of it, which is how banking started. This is the 'multiplication' effect of paper money. (Incidentally, in some parts of Africa salt used to be worth more than gold. It's certainly more useful.)

Nowadays we use coins and notes over gold because they are portable, uniform (which means that money is *fungible* – when you lend a friend a fiver, you don't expect that identical note back), divisible, acceptable (in the old days, some people didn't want sheep or salt) and durable (you can replace old coins and notes).

In fact the old idea that paper money should be backed by reserves of gold has disappeared. So, when you think about it, we use coins and notes because we have *confidence* in their value, not because they are a substitute for gold. Confidence (the sense that your money has value and you will get it back if you stick it in a bank) is critical to financial markets. Money is a funny thing when you think about it: a confidence trick.

FINANCIAL MARKET OR MARKETS

I started by talking about the City as a market. And it is. Whether you call it a financial market or markets in the plural doesn't really matter. It is both: a market where money and financial instruments are traded; and a series of linked markets specialising in different types of instrument. I'm going to mention a few right now just to give you a feel.

Most people associate financial markets with stock exchanges where stocks and shares are traded (a note on language: terms in the financial markets are notoriously fuzzy: 'stocks' in the old days meant government debt issued as stocks or bonds while shares are the equity that companies issue – yet nowadays stock exchanges are called stock exchanges even though the bulk of the trading activity is in company shares. So the terms 'stocks' and 'shares' are synonymous). Certainly if you see a picture of a market with a trading floor (that is, an actual place where brokers meet) the chances are that it is a stock market, though precious few of them have trading floors any more (the London

Stock Exchange doesn't; the New York Stock Exchange is one of the few that does).

This is because a lot of markets these days are virtual, that is, they exist in cyberspace with trades done between brokers on screen and over the phone or net. Once when I was a rookie financial journalist starting out, I went to see a senior City banker in a big bank whose job title was something like 'Grand Vizier of Financial Engineering' or 'Financial Engineering Evangelist' or 'Money Markets Messiah' or something of that order – you get the idea – and he asked me what the market was: 'What's the market?' he said. I had no idea (the great thing about being a journalist is that you can be really thick and they still have to waste their time on you and be nice to you because they know you're going to write about them). Actually it turned out to be a rhetorical question because he answered it himself by moving his hand through space and as he moved it he clicked his fingers – once – and said: 'That's the market. The last trade is the market.'

Anyway, I cover stock exchanges (more particularly the London one) in Chapters 3, 10 and 11 but I wanted to mention here a couple of funny things. People often think stock exchanges are owned by the government. But actually they are businesses in their own right. In fact the London Stock Exchange is itself a public company that is listed on, wait for it, the London Stock Exchange. Weird or what? It's like an infinite regression. And, second funny fact: stock exchanges are places where takeovers happen as companies buy each other's shares to take each other over; but stock exchanges in recent years have been taking each other over. This is to increase their market share through enhanced liquidity (I deal with that later on in this chapter).

Now, the stock exchange may be the most visible part of the financial markets – and, by the way, there's nothing that says you can't have more than one in a country (in the UK in Victorian times Manchester had its own stock exchange serving local industrial companies and wealthy investors, and in the US the Philadelphia stock exchange still thrives). But there are plenty of other things that are traded in the financial markets: bonds for example (see Chapter 5), which are basically tradable loans; gold and silver (examples of hard commodities); oil (where the unit of measure is a barrel); coffee and cocoa (examples of soft commodities). In London there are two other markets which are border-line financial. One is the shipping market which, for historical reasons when London's docks were the centre of international trade and there were strong ties with the Hanseatic states like Hamburg, is called the Baltic Exchange. And Lloyd's of London, the insurance (or to be pedantic the reinsurance) market and which has nothing to do with the Lloyds banking group. Lloyd's I cover in Chapter 15 but I want to say a couple of things here. Shipping and insurance are intimately linked, which is why both markets are in the east end of the City – towards the historical docklands (now dominated by Canary Wharf, a sort of City East if you like).

The shipping market is not about the buying and selling of ships, but the buying and selling of ship cargo carrying capacity (called 'charterparties') which is significant given that four-fifths of the world's goods are transported by ship not air. So economists regard the Baltic Exchange as a bellwether for the global economy – if the market is rising it means manufacturers worldwide are expecting increased demand so are booking space on ships in anticipation. And the link with insurance is that 300 or so years ago, coffee houses in the east end of the City became the meeting points for ship owners and captains, people with cargoes to be transported, and wealthy individuals prepared to provide insurance by underwriting the risk of loss of ship and cargo for a premium. Shipping news was chalked up on the boards of these coffee houses, amongst which Edward Lloyd's was the most famous. Hence Lloyd's of London. Paris café society? Starbucks? Eat your hearts out.

And by the way, the money markets are not, actually, where money is traded. The term 'money markets' is the short-hand for the cybermarket where short-term bonds and overnight deposits are traded and placed and where government in the guise of the central bank interacts with the financial markets (for more on this see Chapters 11 and 12).

But the one market that is a real money market where different currencies are traded is the forex or foreign exchange market, which I'll cover now.

FOREIGN EXCHANGE MARKET

The forex market is where currencies are bought and sold. When you go on holiday you need to change pounds (sterling) into the currency of the place where you are going. When you come back you change back whatever is left over. Usually you do this by going to a bank or a currency changer like Thomas Cook. In exactly the same way, companies, banks and institutional investors need to change currencies.

Direct investment

Companies need to change currencies when they do business overseas. For instance, if a company has a customer in another country who pays in his local currency, the company needs to change that money back into its home currency. It might go further and set up a subsidiary in another country (or, for example, build a factory there). To do that it needs the local currency in order to pay the local builders to put up the factory. So it needs to change its money into the local currency. Then, when that local business starts to generate profit for it (in local currency), that profit needs to be changed back into the company's home currency (called its currency of account) so that it can tot up its profit and loss at the end of the year. This sort of investment in another country by a company is called *direct investment.*

Indirect or portfolio investment

The other big users of the forex market are institutional investors (insurance companies, pension funds and asset managers – discussed in more detail in Chapter 9). One of the things they do is invest in companies all over the world, by buying their shares on a stock exchange. This is called *indirect investment* (also known as *portfolio investment*). So when a UK institutional investor buys, say, shares in a Chinese company, this is called indirect investment in China. The Chinese company's shares are likely to be listed in Shanghai or Hong Kong, so the UK institutional investor needs to change sterling into the Chinese or Hong Kong currency in order to buy those shares locally. And when it sells those shares, it needs to change the money back.

So, companies that go in for *direct investment* abroad and institutional investors that go in for *indirect investment* abroad use the forex market.

Virtual or OTC market

But the biggest users of the forex market – in fact they *are* the forex market – are banks, because they operate all over the world and make loans in many different currencies. The reason I say they are the forex market is because – and this may seem a bit strange at first – *there is no actual forex market as such.* There is no single place where currencies are traded. All forex trading is done over the phone and on computer screens. Forex traders in companies, banks and institutional investors call each other up to trade. Most trades are between banks, or between companies and banks, or institutional investors and banks. In other words, banks act as intermediaries – they stand in the middle of most transactions. This sort of market that does not have a central exchange or market place is often called an *over-the-counter* (OTC) market because those in it trade directly with each other, often using what are called 'online trading platforms' which are like websites.

Central banks

Governments are also big users of the forex market. Each country through its central bank (the state-owned bank that acts as regulator of that country's interest rates) amasses reserves which it will hold in a combination of currencies including its own and those of the leading economies: the US dollar, for example, is the most widely held currency in the world. Governments may use those reserves, for instance, to buy their own currency in the market if it weakens. When they do this they are said to *intervene* in the forex market or to make an *intervention*. For more on this see Chapter 12.

You may be thinking, *but who says whether someone can trade forex or not?* The answer is: anyone can trade forex provided someone else is prepared to trade with them. No bank, company or institutional investor is going to trade with anyone else unless they think they are *creditworthy*, in other words, unless they consider them big enough and safe enough to keep their side of the deal and pay over the money they've agreed to exchange. So if I claim to be a bank, no one is going to trade with me until they have heard of me and checked me out. And if they do that, they'll discover I'm not a bank and won't deal with me. In this way, the forex market is said to be *self-regulating* because no single government or regulatory body is in control of it.

Quicker, smarter?

It is easy to think that the City today is far more sophisticated than it used to be. Not necessarily so. If you were a banker in the City in the 1870s, you could send a letter 'by hand' to another bank at 7.30 a.m. (they started early even then) and expect to have received a reply by 11 a.m., and there were at least six regular mail deliveries a day. So you could have several exchanges of correspondence in just one day.

When Barings, the merchant bank, went bust in 1995, the first thing the board did was to get the archivist to look through the bank's archives: Barings had gone bust almost exactly 100 years before and directors wanted to know how it had been bailed out then. (Usually the Bank of England steps in and organises a 'lifeboat' with all the other banks chipping in to bail it out.) So it's nice to see that money and the people involved with it haven't changed that much over the centuries.

Trading book

The forex market is also said to *follow the sun*. This just means that it stays open all the time – it's a 24/7 market. What happens is that all the major banks who make up the forex market have offices in London, New York and Tokyo.

You'll know that New York opens for business in the early afternoon London-time and by the time London closes for business, New York is in full swing. So as London winds down for the day, each bank transfers its 'book' (imagine it as a big, Dickensian ledger in which the forex traders write down all their deals – everything they have bought and sold) to New York. Then as the sun begins to go down over Manhattan and is starting to rise over Japan, the banks move their book across to Tokyo. And as Tokyo closes, London opens and so it goes on.

For this reason it is termed a *continuous dealers' market* and the Dickensian ledger is actually a computer-based electronic record that is updated every second (in what is called 'real time') so no book actually gets transferred as such. But bankers still use the term 'book' to indicate where the bulk of their trading is happening at any particular time. Contrast this, where prices are established by the millisecond with each successive trade, against the old 'fixing' ritual in the gold market, where the price of gold was 'fixed' twice a day by a group of six banks. Each would send a bowler-hatted representative round to merchant bank Rothschild at 11 a.m. and 3 p.m. each day, armed with their customers' buy and sell orders. In front of each representative was a little flag to raise or lower until equilibrium between buys and sells had been reached, at which point the price was fixed until the next fixing session.

Final point: forex traders specialise in particular trades. The most common one in London is the $/£ trade (exchanging sterling for dollars or vice versa) which is known as 'cable' from the days of the first transatlantic cables.

Trading in the forex market may be for immediate delivery (buying and selling currencies now) which is called the *spot or cash* market, or for delivery at an agreed price at a later date, called the *forward market*. As we shall see in Chapter 13, forward contracts are the basis of the derivatives market.

The forex market is huge, like a massive sea – which is a good analogy, because people who operate in the financial markets talk about the 'liquidity' of markets. The 'deeper' a market, the more 'liquidity' it is said to have and the easier it is to move into or out of that market by buying and selling.

LIQUIDITY AND PRICES

When markets seize up, they suffer from a lack of liquidity. *Liquidity* is a measure of how efficiently you can execute a trade in a market or (to use the London Stock Exchange definition) 'a measure of tradeability of a company's shares'. Liquidity determines whether you can trade at all and, if so, whether you can trade efficiently, i.e. at a good price. Imagine you are a whale. Your idea of the good life is being able to swim at the bottom of the sea, minding your own business. If you're in the Atlantic, no problem. You swim around and the Atlantic is so big and deep that you're not making any ripples on the surface and no one knows you are there.

Now imagine you are a whale in the local lake. The lake may be deep enough so that no one standing on the bank can see you. But whenever you swim around, people can see the ripples. They know where you are. In other words, the depth or liquidity of a market determines how easily and invisibly you can swim in it. The reason why this is important is because an institutional investor can, by its very activity in a market, *move the market against it*. What does this mean?

When you or I go shopping, we expect to get whatever we want at the price that's marked on the packet or the shelf. Not so in the financial markets. What happens there is that the price of everything is changing all the time, depending on how much is in stock and how many buyers want it. Imagine a baker's shop where the number of loaves available and what they cost is forever changing, depending on how many people are in the shop at that moment and what they are ordering. It's straight out of Diagon Alley in *Harry Potter*. A nightmare! Well, that's how the financial markets operate. In other words, your very act of slipping into the baker's to buy a loaf may move the price against you. This is why market liquidity is so important. And the term 'efficiency' is simply a function of how little a market moves against you when you move into or out of it. So if I go into the baker's and whenever I go in they have a very limited selection and it all immediately becomes expensive, then that's a pretty *inefficient* market. And after a while I may not go there any more. So in time that market may dry up and die.

CREDIT CRUNCH

Talk of markets drying up and dying brings us neatly up to date with the credit crunch which, while I've been gassing on about the City as a market, has been the elephant in the room. All this time you've been sitting there thinking: 'Yes, yes, OK, OK, but what about the credit crunch? What about the recession, depression, whatever? What about whether there is ever going to be a market again? What about whether it's going to be an I-Am-Legend-Mad-Max world out there?'

All right. There's been so much on TV that you probably know as much as I do about it. But in case you've been on Mars I'll keep the following short and sweet.

Picture if you will (as they say in the States) a solitary wooden shack standing alone in fields of cotton for miles around. Maybe next to it there's a grain hopper and a nodding donkey or one of those windmill things that gets water out of the ground. This is the starting point for *A Painted House*, John Grisham's elegiac account of life in the 1950s in Mississippi, where he grew up. The cotton farmers are dirt poor. Most don't own the shacks they live in, let alone the land they farm. Few manage to do more than break even year-in, year-out. Few can afford to paint the bare clapboards of their houses (hence the title of his tale).

Originate-to-distribute

Now, let's say you're a banker. Want to lend good money to these sharecroppers scratching about in the dirt? They need it, to buy seed, to buy a tractor, to hire labour at pickin' time, and you're in the business of lending. So how about it?

If you're a good banker, prudential, with a long-term view of advancing credit (that's to say: if I lend it now, I want to know I will get it back in ten or twenty years' time), the answer is probably a polite thanks-but-no-thanks. Sure you can take a mortgage on the land, but the land's the problem. You can only use it for farming and there's too much land to farm and not enough profit to be had. So, if you have to foreclose who are you going to sell the land to?

Now, suppose someone comes along – let's call him an investment banker (in other words, the devil incarnate) and says: 'Guess what? You don't have to keep the loan. You can sell it to some suckers who don't even know where Mississippi is – and you won't have to look your borrowers in the eye ever again. How about it?'

Now this is a completely different proposition and it sounds good to you, because once you've made one loan and sold it off you can make another, and another and another and each time earn a big fat arrangement fee for doing so and you don't have to give a damn whether the loan is ever repaid because it will be repaid to someone else, not to you. This is called originate-to-distribute. You originate the loan, then distribute it to someone else.

Securitisation

Around 25 years ago in a suite of offices high above Wall Street, the seeds of the world's recent financial meltdown were sown. In an investment bank called Salomon Brothers (now part of Citigroup) – at the time one of the top financial institutions in the world – a bunch of the very best banking brains set about creating a financial mechanism that would change the world's capital markets for ever. Their mission was simple to express but almost impossible to achieve: in short it was to package up bank loans and sell them to institutional investors. If they'd been astronauts it would have been the equivalent of aiming at Mars with a Meccano kit. How they did it is set out in Chapter 14. All we need to know here is that securitisation turns loans – which in those days were not easily sold on – into bonds which are, because they are designed to be traded.

Securitisation was helped in the US by the existence of federal agencies whose purpose is to guarantee certain types of loan. These agencies had weird and wonderful names like Sally Mae, Fannie Mae and Freddie Mac (guaranteeing student loans, home loans and business loans respectively). These agencies themselves adopted securitisation as a way of selling on loans in the form of bonds in return for money which they could then lend, and so on and so on, as above.

All of this led to a perfect storm: low interest rates in the early 2000s which fuelled a real estate price explosion in the US; a tradition of federal guarantees and securitisation of home loans which meant investors were happy to buy them; plus the concept of originate-to-distribute. Only it wasn't loans to poor rust-belt farmers. It was loans to people with poor credit histories – the so-called sub-prime market.

Sub-prime lending

'Sub-prime' is an American euphemism for borrowers who are less than ideal. If 'prime lending' means lending to borrowers who are going to pay you back, then sub-prime means lending to borrowers who maybe aren't.

Somehow 'poor credit lending' doesn't have the same quasi-scientific or at least rational ring to it as 'sub-prime' – I mean, show me a self-respecting banker who's willing to lend to 'poor credits'. But, as I say, if you're not going to hold on to the loan and are going to make a fee just from arranging it, why not?

Lending criteria became so lax that certain types of loan got tell-tale tags, such as the ninja loan (no income, no job, no assets), the liar loan (the borrower self-certifies his or her income without the lender checking), the stretch loan (more than half the borrower's pre-tax income will go on mortgage payments), the piggyback loan (a second mortgage provides the deposit for the first), the teaser loan (an initial artificially low level of interest) and so on.

And why would anyone want to buy such loans?

Three reasons. First, federal insurance of home loans (as mentioned above) had acclimatised the market to these securitisations. Second, the US real estate market was going gangbusters in the early 2000s after the Fed (the US central bank) eased interest rates in the wake of 9/11 to encourage people to borrow and spend and so keep the economy buoyant. This meant that if a loan went bust you could foreclose on the mortgage (fancy name for a loan secured on a house) and sell into a rising market, which meant that all of the amount outstanding, interest on interest, foreclosure fees, etc, would be more than covered, turning foreclosure into a lucrative sideline in its own right.

Third, mutualisation of risk. Buy one of these loans and it goes bad and your investment could be wiped out. Participate in a pool of ten and you lose a tenth. Participate in a pool of 10,000 and the default statistics favour you. Banks encouraged this by dividing these pools into tranches or slices with the best credits in the top slices and the real rubbish at the bottom.

Toxic tranches and SIVs

The top slices sold, no problem. The bottom ones tended to stay with the originating banks and in time came to be known as 'toxic tranches' – they were so bad they were like kryptonite and glowed in the dark.

Banks were also sticking these securitised loans into funds called structured investment vehicles (SIVs) and selling off participations in those, which meant they could argue that these loans were no longer theirs.

(Stay tuned because toxic tranches and SIVs make a rather unwelcome reappearance a couple of pages on from here.)

This wasn't happening in a vacuum. This was happening at a time when – as I said in the Introduction – the financial markets were gripped by trading frenzy. It was like sharks feeding. This was spurred in large part by the prevalence of derivatives (see Chapter 13) and the explosion in securitisations (Chapter 14): the two converge because you can achieve a securitisation by a swap which is a derivative; but this won't make sense to you till you've got through those chapters.

So everyone around the world was going crazy for this stuff. They couldn't get enough of it. Then there was the 'wall of' theory. At any one time there is a part of the world that is creating a trade surplus – in the 1980s it was Japan, more recently China, at other times Middle Eastern oil money, plus the odd quirk like Russian oligarch roubles – and this money is likened to a wave that is seeking markets to invest in (except, of course, when you're in a recession, depression, whatever).

And this was another factor: these securitised home loans marbled (to use a wonderful phrase I've ripped off from *The Economist* newspaper, as it likes to style itself) the financial system. It was like dry rot shot through an old house – even that clapboard joint we mentioned at the top.

A tsunami in US real estate

In the scramble to buy their own piece of the American Dream the demand created by poor borrowers inadvertently contributed to driving property still higher till no one wanted to be left out. It became a self-reinforcing spiral and led to what are called inflated asset values, like the dotcom bubble in the early 2000s; like the South Sea Bubble in the 1730s; like all sorts of bubbles in the tulip market from the 1600s onwards when the Netherlands was the trading centre of the world.

But in the meantime, interest rates had started to tick up as policy makers around the world tried to keep these inflationary pressures under control (for more on inflation see Chapter 12). Which in turn brought this incredible rise in property prices to a halt.

But as soon as the property market turns and the value of that property collateral declines and you are a lender, you are in deep trouble. More people will default if they think the property they have bought is declining in value – why bother to keep paying interest on an asset that's declining in value? Just walk away.

And if you auction off the foreclosed property and all around you other lenders are doing the same, the market starts to fall steeply because of the over-supply and this becomes self-reinforcing. And that in turn means that your other loans – which at one point looked so great because you made them in rising markets where the underlying collateral was going up in value – start to look shaky too.

And on top of that as potential mortgage customers see the property market decline they savvy up and decide they don't want to buy property after all, so they don't want a loan and your new business starts to dry up. And since you're in the business of originate-to-distribute, your failure to continue originating means your core business has stalled.

And as the property market starts to shut down you have another problem: you can't put a value on the loans you've made (this is called 'marking to market') because you don't know how much the underlying property will be worth if you do have to foreclose. So you don't know how much your business is worth. Which means it could be worth as little as... nothing. You may not think so, but others will.

And if this is happening to you, you can bet your bottom dollar that it is happening to all the other banks out there. And as soon as banks start to smell a whiff of panic – as soon as they start to think that other banks may be in as much trouble as they are, they stop lending to each other.

This became a major issue for banks stuck with toxic tranches and those which – like Bear Stearns – felt obliged to bail out the SIVs that hitherto they had treated as arm's length vehicles (this is what ultimately did for Bear Stearns).

As banks ceased trusting each other they stopped lending to each other. This may not sound a big deal but the inter-bank loan market is a critical source of short-term money for banks.

When you think about it, banks have only two sources of money: us, the depositors; and each other. And both sources are short-term. But banks lend long-term (a mortgage loan can be for as long as twenty-five years) and support these loans by rolling over their positions in the short-term inter-bank market (which involves renewing their existing inter-bank borrowings as often as daily or monthly or quarterly). But as soon as banks stop trusting each other they stop lending to each other and these three month loans are not rolled over (that is, renewed).

The sad, sorry saga of Northern Rock

Now let's move our camera eye from the wide rolling prairies of the States across the pond to sleepy old England – specifically the north – and focus on Northern Rock, a UK building society. Northern Rock was as simple and direct as the people it served. People up north like things to be simple and direct. And Northern Rock was. It was based in the North and it was safe as a Rock. Northern Rock. Geddit? It even sponsored the local football team (Newcastle United) which ended up being as much of a basket case as its sponsor.

Now if you're a building society your principal customer base is people in your part of the world, in your regional locality. You take money in from the locals and lend it out to them to buy the property they live in. This is an unspectacular and solid business and as safe as, well, houses.

But this was too boring for the bigwigs at Northern Rock. First they turned themselves into a bank: instead of their depositors owning them they now had shareholders and, presumably, were able to reward themselves with share options and the usual trappings of corporate success.

Next they looked to grow the business as big and fast as possible. Why? Obvious, really: the bigger the business the more you can pay yourself for running it. Anyway, the NR senior management incentivised themselves by paying themselves bonuses based on 'gross' loans made, in other words the total volume of mortgages they lent, not taking into account those that were redeemed, refinanced or went bust (which would have been the 'net' figure: the total less the ones that didn't last). Since they dominated the local market, which was mature, they weren't going to be able to expand their depositor base much. So instead of funding themselves just by deposits they turned to the wholesale banking market.

In other words, they borrowed on the inter-bank market and used that market to provide mortgages throughout the UK. They also securitised their mortgages but strangely enough this wasn't what came back and bit them on the bum. It was the fact that they were funding long-term mortgages in the short-term inter-bank market.

When that market closed down, Northern Rock faced its own credit crunch. It couldn't borrow to save its life and went bust. Well, actually the UK government stepped in and took it over. Why? Because if Northern Rock had defaulted on its obligations to depositors, no one with money in a UK bank would have felt safe, everyone would have queued to get their money out and all UK banks would have been bust: the end of life as we know it.

Banks stop lending – and are bailed out by government

As we now know, Northern Rock was only the start. In fact none of us (me included) read the tea leaves and really understood what was happening out there.

Gradually banks went bust and were either taken over by other banks or were nationalised. In the States, big names like Lehman Brothers and Bear Stearns disappeared. Merrill Lynch was subsumed into Bank of America. Investment banks Goldman Sachs and Morgan Stanley quickly converted themselves into bank holding companies (which is what US banks that take deposits are called) so that they could get the advantage of the US government deposit guarantee. This meant other banks were prepared to go on trading with them. In the UK, HBOS was taken over by Lloyds which itself went cap in hand to the government, as did RBS, owner of NatWest.

Iceland, an economy dominated by its financial services sector, effectively went bust when its major banks failed. This was felt in the UK, when for a while internet depositors with Icesave (including a whole lot of local authorities with money on deposit there) thought they weren't going to get their money back. Meanwhile, UK businesses with Icelandic owners, from Karen Millen to football club West Ham, faced an uncertain future.

The Bank of England, like central banks the world over, slashed interest rates to encourage the economy by encouraging borrowing. But this didn't get banks back to lending. They didn't pass on the interest-rate reductions to borrowers.

Instead they used the lower interest rates to rebuild their own balance sheets (in other words, use this cheap money on themselves first before making it available to their borrowers) and suddenly what had seemed like an isolated meltdown of the international financial system spread to the wider commercial world: businesses routinely have overdrafts to tide them over when their cashflow is thin (for instance when they're waiting for a customer to pay but have outgoings to meet in the meantime). But now perfectly sound businesses found their overdrafts (which are technically 'on-demand' loans repayable at any time) being withdrawn without notice. Result: lights went out all over the country.

So, just as everything had been spiralling upwards – especially property – everything started heading like a rollercoaster back down. Governments started guaranteeing banks' toxic assets, buying those assets up in exchange for fresh money (called 'quantitative easing' as it seeks to inject more money into an economy's money supply to get that economy going again) and taking banks over.

For people of my generation this is unprecedented. We have never seen anything like it.

Where to next?

The UK Labour government has said that this is the worst recession, depression, whatever for 100 years. That's going way back before the Great Crash of 1929 and the Depression that followed it when currencies such as Germany's deutschmark became valueless and people needed wheelbarrows of notes to buy a loaf of bread (which led in part to the 1939-45 World War). This is bad, bad news not least because it comes from the particular UK government that is credited with creating spin (making bad news sound good). Great.

Will markets recover? Eventually. But at what cost? Governments have abandoned their use of interest rates to control inflation (see Chapter 12 for what this is about) and in their desire to stimulate any sort of demand have cut interest rates and thrown money at public sector employment and projects. But the cost of this is being stored up to be paid in the future. In Iceland they estimate it will take 70 years for every man, woman and child to pay off their part of what the banking collapse has cost that country.

Chapter 2

WHY COMPANIES NEED MONEY

SPEED-READ SUMMARY

- Companies need funding for their fixed assets (which they need in their business) and to meet their outgoings (working capital)

- Without working capital, profitable companies can go bust through lack of cashflow

- Two types of money are available: debt (loans) and equity (shares)

- Venture capital is a source of equity funding for young and fast-growing companies

- Venture capitalists have four exit routes: trade sale, IPO, recycling and buy-back

- Private equity is raised from institutional investors to fund MBOs and MBIs

- Before the credit crunch, leveraged buyouts of big public companies were a feature of the private equity market

This chapter is going to be a bit frustrating. Having introduced you to the City and talked about the credit crunch, I am now going to take you away from the financial markets. We're going to look at the City's customers – companies.

Imagine businesses of all shapes and sizes flocking to the City for money and advice – and not just from the UK but from all over the world. These are the market's customers. But what do these businesses want money and advice for? If you grasp this, a lot of the City's activities will become clear.

Imagine you set up a corner shop. You are a *sole trader*. You aren't a company. You are simply a person (or, if there are more than one of you, a partnership) opening a shop. What do you need by way of cash?

FIXED ASSETS / WORKING CAPITAL

The answer is you need two types of funding. The first is *fixed capital* or long-term funding ('capital' just means a chunk of money; 'funding', like 'financing', just means the provision of money). You need this money to buy the shop, fit it out and maybe buy a van for deliveries. These are assets of the business (in the jargon, 'fixed assets') without which you simply can't be in business at all.

But you also need money to buy stock, pay the staff and pay overheads like rates, electricity and so on. This is short-term, daily outlay and is called *working capital* (this is a confusing expression because it's not what most of us mean by 'capital' which we think of as having a long-term, under-the-mattress connotation). Working capital is the money that's needed to keep the business going. As customers come in and buy the stock, you start to recover some of that outlay, but there will be times when you need more working capital, for instance if you decide to expand the amount of stock on your shelves or if there's a time – for instance over the summer holidays – when customers are away and you're still having to pay the regular outgoings. Working capital is critical to a business. Without it, a business runs out of money and has a *cashflow* crisis. We saw in Chapter 1 how Northern Rock went bust and had to be bailed out by the UK government because – though profitable – it had a cashflow crisis.

DEBT AND EQUITY FINANCE

So, where do you get this money from? At this stage there are really only three sources: yourself (savings); your friends and family; and the bank. Let's assume you've put your savings into the business. You then go to the bank.

Debt finance

The bank will *lend* you money. It will make you a *loan*. In return for using its money, you pay the bank *interest* and you have to pay back the *principal* (i.e. the sum you have borrowed) either in chunks during the loan or in one go at the end of the loan when the loan *matures*. This is called *debt funding*. The bank may also want *security* (like a mortgage lender which takes a *charge* or *mortgage* over your house – 'charge', 'mortgage' and 'security' mean the same thing, but 'securities' means something different – tradable financial instruments like shares and bonds).

Equity finance

But what about your family and friends? Some may offer a loan, like the bank. Others may say: 'We think you'll make a go of this and be successful. We'd like to share in that success. We'd like to *invest* in your business.' What they want is to *share* in the success of your business. One way of doing this is for them to come into *partnership* with you. But they may not want to be involved in running the business. They may want to be passive investors. And they may all want to invest different amounts and have different shares of your business.

The easiest way of achieving this is for you to set your business up as a *company*. A company is simply a legal entity which has *shareholders* and *directors*. Your family and friends will become shareholders and you will run the business as a director. So the company is formed and issues shares to your investors in return for their money (the more they invest, the more shares they get). In return for putting money into your company, your friends and family get shares in the company.

Now, we know what a bank gets in return for making a loan: interest and return of the principal. What shareholders get is *dividends* (when the company makes sufficient profit to pay them dividends on their shares). So your friends and family will hope that the company will pay them dividends out of its profits (although initially most small, growing companies will reinvest their profits in the business to expand – in order to maintain their cashflow and support their working capital requirement).

Your shareholders will also hope that, as your business grows, so the value of their share of your business will grow too. They will also eventually want to *realise* their investment – sell the shares in order to make a profit on their investment. When they come to sell those shares, they hope they will get much more back for them than they originally invested. In other words, their investment will have appreciated (got bigger). This is called *equity* investment. It's like having equity in a house (the bit the bank or building society doesn't effectively own).

This is how all businesses start. What your family and friends have provided is *equity capital*. What the bank provides is *debt finance*. To use City jargon, your family and friends have provided an *equity injection* or *seed capital* or *early stage capital* (used to describe the capital in a company that is growing from nothing). It is also called *risk capital* – because if the business goes bust, they get nothing back (whereas the bank, having security over the business's assets, will be able to sell those assets to try to recoup its loan).

Now, what I am about to say is really important: there are only two types of money available to businesses: debt (provided by lenders) and equity (provided by shareholders). So when someone is talking about money or capital, ask yourself this question: is it debt or equity?

Let's say the shop does well and you want to open another one. Your family and friends may want to invest but may simply not have the money or may not wish to risk it all in your business (investors like to *diversify* their risk rather than concentrate it). And the bank (typically) may not want to lend you too much in case it gets *overexposed* to your business, unless and until your equity base is larger. Where else can you go? The answer is that you need *venture capital.*

VENTURE CAPITAL

Venture capital is seedcorn capital provided by businesses that specialise in providing equity capital to small, fast-growing companies that need it.

They are called *venture capital providers or venture capitalists*. Investing in small businesses is risky (which, I guess, is why it's called 'venture' capital, as in an 'adventure' or 'venturing forth'). The majority of businesses that go bust do so within their first five years. It's like growing plants from seed: many – often the majority – just don't make it. Most venture capitalists reckon that one in three or even two in three

Why cashflow matters more than profit

Ask yourself these two questions:

- Can a business be profitable and still go bust?
- Can a business be unprofitable but still keep going?

The answer to both is, believe it or not, yes. Whether you make a profit depends simply on whether your cost of production is less than the price at which you sell your goods. It has nothing to do with how quickly you have to pay those costs or how soon you get paid for the goods. This is why a business may look profitable on paper but can run out of money before it gets to generate that profit.

Businesses are different from you and me. By and large, individuals don't like debt. We may have a mortgage and we may have credit card debts and overdrafts. But while a mortgage is considered OK – it's a way of funding your home which, with luck, will be a long-term investment – overdrafts and credit card debts are things that most of us try to avoid or reduce. To paraphrase Mr Micawber in *David Copperfield*:

'Annual income £20, annual expenditure £19.99p, result happiness. Annual income £20, annual expenditure £20.01p, result misery.'

By and large, that's how individuals behave. But businesses are different. They like to borrow – in fact, they're encouraged to because the cost of borrowing reduces their taxable profit (and therefore the tax they pay), which makes it cost effective. For them, it's more important to have positive cashflow than it is to make a profit. If they run out of cash and can't pay their debts, they will have to close before they have ever had a chance to make a profit. In fact, provided a business has good cashflow it may not have to make a profit for some time.

If you're in business and have annual income of £100, outgoings of £101 and savings of £20, you could stay in business for 20 years, no problem.

Turn the above figures into millions and you'll begin to see why businesses with strong cashflows are able to continue for years on end, regardless of their profitability. In fact, in many respects banks prefer lending to businesses with strong cashflow and marginal profitability than businesses which are profitable but have unpredictable cashflow. It's also why banks lend to, and investors invest in, businesses on the basis of their *future* prospects. It's also why businesses borrow all the time, and come to the City to do so.

of their investments may go 'belly up' (go bust). So they usually want two things: (1) a large share in the company – often as much as half; and (2) a seat on the board so that they can have a say in how the company is run.

A lot of small businessmen baulk at these terms. They feel they are losing control of a business they have worked long and hard to nurture. So they decide to go it alone. But the risk is that they may run out of money or be overtaken by competitors who themselves have expanded more quickly through, for instance, venture capital and steal customers and markets away. In short, staying small in business usually doesn't work. Others will copy your idea, service or product and try to outdo you. This, by the way, is another weird thing about the world of business: companies can never stand still; they are either going forward and expanding or stagnating and, in relation to their competitors, shrinking.

This is why, bizarrely, a successful company is expected to make not just a profit every year but a *bigger profit than last year*. And if its profit starts declining, investors (who, as mentioned earlier, invest in a company on the basis of its future prospects) may want to get out. And

Business angels

There are people – ordinary individuals – who are crazy about the theatre. They put modest sums of money on a regular basis into West End productions. Some shows do well; others close after the first night. But the reason these 'angels' (as they are called) do it is not so much for the money, but to get invited to the opening night, to meet the cast and so on.

In the business world there are business angels, wealthy individuals who are often successful entrepreneurs. They take a stake (a large shareholding) in a company, join its board as a director and help it grow and succeed. In their case, they do expect to make money out of it – after all, in business, making money is a way of keeping the score. But, because they are already rich, they mainly do it for enjoyment, satisfaction and fun. It's what they're good at which is why they like to do it. It's what gets them out of bed in the morning.

Examples of business angels include John Madejski who founded *Autotrader* magazine and bought Reading football club (its stadium is named after him) and Julian Richer who owns the hi-fi retailing chain Richer Sounds – his first, tiny shop, which is in the *Guinness Book of Records* for the highest sales per square foot of any retail outlet in the UK, is still going strong in its original location, just outside London Bridge Station.

this is so even though the company is still making a profit (not even a loss), albeit a smaller one.

However, successful businessmen tend to put emotion to one side and see that it's better to own part of a big business than all of a small one. So they welcome venture capitalists and the money and expertise they bring.

However successful the company a venture capital provider (VCP) has invested in, the VCP will sooner or later want to sell its stake. This isn't because the VCP thinks the company is a poor investment but because the VCP's expertise lies in identifying and investing in small, fast-growing businesses. So the VCP wants to realise its successful investment in order to plough those funds into other, smaller businesses in the hope that they too will be as successful and provide the VCP with as good a return. VCPs believe that a business grows fastest in its first five years, so having got the benefit of that growth, they want to realise their investment and invest their profits in small businesses coming up behind.

Exit routes

There are four ways in which VCPs can realise their investment and each is called an *exit route*. The two most important are: *trade sale*; and *Initial Public Offering* or IPO (also known as a *listing, flotation* or *going public*).

A **trade sale** is when the company is sold to another that is either in the same business or wants to break into it. The company then becomes a subsidiary of the acquirer. **IPO** is covered in the next chapter. The other two are: **recycling**, which is a sale to co-investors or to another VCP; and **buy-back** where the management buy back the VCP's shareholding – usually with the equity backing of another VCP.

VENTURE CAPITAL AND PRIVATE EQUITY

Venture capital is about nurturing small companies: the funding of start-ups and early-stage development. It extends to the funding of *management buyouts* (MBOs) and *management buy-ins* (MBIs) of established businesses. An MBO (a bit like a buy-back) is the acquisition of a business by its management; an MBI is the acquisition of a business by an outside team of managers. An MBO occurs where a large company decides that part of its business is no longer a 'core' activity. It can sell the unwanted part to another company (in what is called a *trade sale*) or to the people who run it – its existing managers. They don't usually have the money to buy it without help: debt is provided by banks;

equity by private equity funds. MBOs often follow a takeover (see Chapter 4).

An MBI occurs where the external backers install new managers to run a business that is being bought out. They reward and incentivise them by giving them a shareholding in the business being bought out.

Now, when the MBO or MBI concerns a substantial business, it is hardly venture capital any more. Instead, it tends to be tagged *private equity.* Private equity is provided by institutional investors through private equity funds (see Chapter 9). When markets were booming, these private equity funds could be huge and were used to take big public companies private where they were broken up, bits sold off lucratively and the rump often re-floated on the stock market (how this happens is explained in the next chapter). If this was done quickly it was known as a *quick flip* and led to an almost trading rather than investing mentality on the part of the private equity funds. It's this trading mentality I touched on as contributing to the madness that helped bring on the credit crunch. Anyway, that's why the term 'private equity' came to mean the takeover of big public companies ('public to private'), whereas private equity funds that expressly invest in start-ups and early-stage development are often called *incubators.*

Funnily enough, cashflow plays a part here too. Traditional businesses with strong cashflows attract private equity interest, because they can be *leveraged*, meaning that their assets are used to support the borrowing that is used to buy them. At its height, this began to attract regulatory interest because of the level of debt buyouts were being burdened with. The 'leverage market' was where much of this debt was sourced, not just from banks but from institutional investors (see Chapter 9). If a deal was very big it might have required a consortium of banks and investors, called a 'club' deal. But these could lead to conflicts if the bank advising the private equity fund decided to take over the target itself. In any case, you'll note I've been using the past tense. As soon as the credit (loan) market dried up, private equity buyouts stopped (except of bankrupt businesses). Game over.

WELL-KNOWN NAMES IN VENTURE CAPITAL AND PRIVATE EQUITY

Over time, the distinction between venture capital (funding start-ups) and private equity (taking public companies private) has blurred with players active in both. In the UK, traditional venture capital providers almost deserted to private equity. Big names include **Alchemy**, **Apax**, **BC Partners**, **Bridgepoint**, **CVC Capital**, **Doughty Hanson**, **Duke Street Capital**, **Permira** and three investment trusts (see Chapter 9 for more on investment trusts) called **3i** (originally called Investors in Industry, hence the name), **Candover** and **Electra**. Most banks have venture capital and/or private equity subsidiaries.

The big names in international private equity are American. The most famous is **Kohlberg Kravis Roberts**, which shot to prominence in 1988 with the $25 billion takeover and dismemberment of RJR Nabisco – at the time the largest deal of its kind, since immortalised in the entertaining book *Barbarians At The Gate*. Other big names – like KKR, these players both raise money in private equity funds from institutional investors and lead the acquisition and dismemberment of the target – include **Advent**, **Almeida**, **Apollo**, **Blackstone**, **Carlyle**, **Cerberus**, **Clayton Dubilier & Bice**, **Forstmann Little**, **Fortress**, **Hicks Muse Furst & Tate**, **Lonestar**, **Silver Lake** and **Texas Pacific**. In 2005, almost £30 billion in private equity funding was raised in London, 80% coming from abroad. That probably marked close-on the peak in the private equity book. The level of leverage deals required meant, as mentioned above, that new deals stopped with the credit crunch and many highly leveraged buyouts themselves started to struggle. Those that went bust became targets – for other private equity providers.

A FINAL WORD ABOUT COMPANIES AND MONEY

This chapter started by looking at the two types of money (debt and equity) and why companies need money. Debt is appealing because it's tax deductible – but it has to be repaid even when times are hard. By contrast, equity does not have to be repaid but because dividends are paid out of taxed income and equity offers investors less protection than debt, it can cost companies more. A recent innovation is a *hybrid* form of funding. Hybrids that look like equity to the market – but debt to the tax man – allow interest payments to be deferred in times of stress and the debt repayment to be met by issuing extra shares at maturity.

Debt provides something called 'gearing' – it's a bit like buying a flat on mortgage: you can buy a much bigger flat by borrowing the bulk of the money than you could by using just your savings. Gearing (also called 'leverage') is what enables companies to expand faster than they could with equity funding alone. It also explains why the *leveraged buyout market* was such a prominent feature of the markets prior to the credit crunch.

How a private company can increase the equity funding open to it by tapping the public markets through 'floating' is what the next chapter is about.

How do private investors make their money?

People are often surprised at the enormous returns private equity generated over a short period. A case in point was the rash of deals in the energy sector before the credit crunch. Columbia Natural Resources was bought in 2003 for $330 million in a private equity deal and was sold two years later for almost 10 times that amount. Texas Genco was bought in 2004 by private equity investors including KKR and Blackstone for just under $1 billion and sold a year later for five times that amount. These are just two examples. It all comes down to market timing: energy is a cyclical industry, both businesses had been through tough times; and private equity specialists can afford to make big, risky investments. But only when there's money to borrow on easy credit terms. Sigh.

Chapter 3

WHAT HAPPENS WHEN
A COMPANY FLOATS

SPEED-READ SUMMARY

- When a company goes public, lists, floats or does an IPO (initial public offering) – all of these terms mean the same thing – it does so on a stock exchange (known as a 'public market')

- A company may have its share issue underwritten to ensure it raises the money it wants, regardless of market conditions

- Stock exchanges are keen to attract companies that want to list and investors that want to invest in them, so they require listed companies to provide a flow of financial information.

- Stock exchanges are keen to ensure a level playing field for investors by preventing market manipulation, insider dealing, etc.

- When companies list they usually raise fresh equity capital

- Flotation is a way for existing investors, such as venture capital providers, to exit

- If a listed company raises further equity capital it does so by way of a rights issue, also known as a secondary issue or, in the US, a seasoned equity issue

Now, we're firmly back in the City again. The act of floating is one aspect of what is called *corporate finance* in the City (the other is M&A, for which see the next chapter).

Floating or doing an IPO (initial public offering – originally a US term) is a big step in the life of a company. It marks the company's development from being private (i.e. privately held, which means that it has a small number of shareholders and its shares are not traded on an exchange) to being public where anyone can buy shares in it. Some companies pursue alternative strategies of seeking an IPO and a trade sale in parallel – this is called 'dual-tracking'.

When private companies come to the City to float they seek *advice* on how to do it and someone who will actually help *place* their shares in the hands of investors. These two activities of advising and placing securities (a security is a collective name for shares and bonds) are at the heart of what the City traditionally does. If you look at the City in macro-economic terms (i.e. in terms of big-picture economic implications) its role is to channel capital (money) into those businesses that will use that capital most *efficiently* to generate profits which in turn can be invested as capital in other deserving companies. The City is a machine that allocates capital where it will be used most efficiently.

So much for philosophy. What actually happens when a company floats?

First, you need to think of the market the company will float on. The most well-known one is the London Stock Exchange. But it's not the only one. There are others including AIM (the Alternative Investment Market, pronounced 'aim'). The London Stock Exchange (LSE) is called the 'senior market' and AIM is the 'junior market'. This is because the Stock Exchange tends to be the home of companies that have been in business for at least three years (an LSE requirement) while AIM caters for those that lack a three-year trading history.

There are other markets, some of which are run online by brokers, mainly for 'small cap' stocks (smaller companies, said to have a 'small market capitalisation') or which are closely-held, such as family or other businesses, where there is only a small float of shares that are freely traded. Some brewers and football clubs fall into this category. Both on the LSE and AIM you need professional advisers to help you list, called a 'nominated adviser' or 'nomad' on AIM.

Underwriting

The success of a company's flotation will depend on two things: (1) specifically, whether it's the sort of business with good prospects that investors want to invest in; and (2) more generally, the state of the market. The first is within the company's control. The second isn't: it would be a disaster if, on the day that the company floats, no one buys its shares and all of the money that it was hoping to raise didn't materialise, for reasons beyond its control.

Whether this happens will depend on what is happening in the world at the time. For instance, a war may break out somewhere significant in the world and the price of oil may suddenly shoot up. Or the Bank of England may increase interest rates. Or the government of the day may lose a vital vote in parliament and risk being voted out of office. Any of these events causes uncertainty and makes markets nervous. In short, all sorts of things could intervene to harm a company's flotation. What it wants to do is to insure against this.

What the company does is to get the issue of new shares (and the sale of any existing shares that are to be sold) *underwritten*: it gets someone (let's call it a bank for the time being) to act as the *underwriter*. For a fee, the bank will agree to buy any shares that no one else wants. This way the company can rest assured that the flotation will be a success and all the shares will be taken up.

THE STOCK EXCHANGE'S VIEWPOINT

Now, imagine for a moment you are in charge of the LSE. You are going to have two concerns.

First, you want to attract companies that want to list so that, second, you can attract investors to buy shares in them. In short you want to attract companies with shares to sell and buyers for those shares and in this way create a market (think of the LSE as a car-boot sale for companies with shares to sell and investors who want to buy them).

In order to attract investors you want to make sure that you don't list any old company. If you allow ropy companies to list on your exchange and they go bust regularly, people who want to buy shares are going to steer clear of your market. At the same time you don't want to guarantee that companies on your exchange are going to do well – that's far beyond the scope of your own knowledge and competence; buyers have to decide for themselves whether a company is going to be a good investment. All you can do is ensure that investors have as much information as possible and that this information is accurate and up-to-date.

So, you will insist that any company that lists on your exchange provides detailed financial information when it floats (in something called a *prospectus*, which is a glorified brochure) and continues to update that information regularly. Also, that whenever the company is proposing to do anything dramatic with its business, it will consult its shareholders (through things called *circulars*) otherwise they will be annoyed if the company in which they have invested, and which they therefore own, decides, say, to move into a completely different line of business without asking them.

So that's what you require of companies listing on your exchange. But, equally, you want to make sure that the investors who use your exchange to buy and sell shares don't do anything underhand. For example, you don't want some of them buying shares on information that isn't in the public domain and readily available to the others (this is called *insider dealing* and is a criminal offence); and you don't want the market to be manipulated by one or more buyers or sellers who are deliberately trying to corner the market in a company's shares or are trying to control the fair price at which those shares should trade.

So any exchange wants to ensure that (1) companies are transparent about what they are doing and how well they are doing; and (2) investors are operating on a level playing field and aren't trying to gain an unfair advantage over each other.

If you grasp these two points you will understand what is an enormously complex area: the regulation of stock markets. In the UK the principal market watchdog is the Financial Services Authority (FSA for short).

So, whenever a company comes along that wants to list on your exchange you are going to impose certain rules and standards; and you're probably going to insist that somebody whom the exchange knows and trusts introduces the company and vouches for it or, if you like, *sponsors* it (not in the sense of advertising sponsorship but in the sense of proposing it, like a prospective member of a golf club).

THE LISTING PROCESS

In practice the company appoints a *broker* (a stock exchange member firm) to sponsor it, then publishes its prospectus explaining what its business is about, how it has done and how well it is likely to do. If any of this is wrong the directors and the sponsor are liable.

The company also agrees: to publish financial information regularly (every three months); to notify the exchange as soon as anything major happens in its business that may affect its share price; and to send circulars to its shareholders whenever it wants their consent to do anything significant with its business.

DIFFERENT TYPES OF LISTING

You may be surprised to learn that there are different ways of achieving a listing.

An **introduction** to the market occurs where no fresh capital is raised. This is done by companies that already have 25% of their shares in public hands. It doesn't require underwriting because all that happens is that the company is listed on the exchange in order for its shares to be publicly traded on the exchange. No new shares are issued. This is the cheapest way of listing.

Principal players involved in an LSE listing

The *sponsor* is a bank, broker or other adviser (corporate finance house or accounting firm) approved by the Financial Services Authority (the market watchdog) which plays a central role in advising the company, e.g. on what it needs to do to meet the LSE's listing requirements which are called the Listing Rules.

The *corporate broker* acts as an interface between company and likely investors. It markets the shares to potential investors and puts in place any *underwriting arrangements.*

The *receiving bankers* handle share applications (only in a public offer). The *reporting accountants* are not necessarily the company's auditors but their job is to produce the figures included in the *prospectus*. They also report on the company's working capital position over the next 12–18 months (now you see how important a company's cashflow position is). The *prospectus* or *listing particulars* must be a coherent description of the business, its areas of activity and its prospects and include the reporting accountants' short-form report.

Any *offer to the public* requires a prospectus (which is the same as *listing particulars* except that the offeror has responsibility for it) except in limited circumstances, for instance where the offer is to institutional investors and/or market professionals, or it is a small offer (to 50 or fewer investors). The equivalent advisers on AIM are called 'nomads' (nominated advisers) and include brokers and the corporate finance arms of accounting firms. Their job includes part of the regulatory function of vetting offering documents.

A **placing** or **private offering** is where shares are offered for sale on a selective basis, mainly to institutional investors. It is often used by smaller businesses where the placing is on behalf of existing shareholders or venture capitalists. Again, the costs are low but the disadvantage is that the company ends up with a narrow shareholder base.

An **intermediaries offer** is like a placing but with shares allocated to intermediaries (stock exchange member firms) selected by the sponsor, who then sell those shares down to their own clients. The aim here is to achieve a wider spread of investors than with a placing but without a full-blown public offer.

Finally there is the **public offer** where fresh shares are offered to private individuals and institutional investors, and the issue is usually underwritten. This is the most expensive route (because the fees charged by banks to underwrite remain relatively high) while achieving the widest spread of investors and the largest raising of capital.

The types of public offer are the *offer for sale* which is of shares already in issue; the *offer for subscription* which is an offer of new shares (both of these being at a fixed price); and the *tender offer* to bidders on an auction basis above a minimum tender price, which is the price at which the issue is underwritten. There are two types of tender offer: *allocation to highest bidders* until an issue has been taken up, or a *common strike price* (average bid) with all the shares allocated at this price.

Note that in markets generally there are two types of auction: the usual one where buyers bid each other up until the highest bid is accepted; and the *Dutch auction* (dating from the tulip trade) where buyers remain silent and the seller reduces the price until it is accepted by a bidder.

HOW SHARES ARE TRADED

In most markets buyers and sellers announce bid and offer prices simultaneously and throughout the trading day, called *continuous double auction*.

Anyone who trades (buys and sells) shares that are listed on the stock exchange has to notify the exchange of how many shares have been bought or sold and at what price and this information is then published to everyone. So everyone dealing on the stock exchange knows what is happening. And if there are wild price movements (called 'fluctuations' or 'spikes') then the stock exchange will investigate to see if these have been caused by people using inside information, because this is against its rules and could affect confidence in the market. This also happens to be against the law so the Financial Services Authority, the market watchdog, will also investigate to see if a crime has been committed (the two work closely together).

THE COMPANY'S PERSPECTIVE

Now, let's go back to the company's perspective. The first decision the founder needs to take is how many shares to sell. It's always wise to sell some, to have a few millions set aside as rainy-day money. But if the founder sells all his or her shares, prospective investors will be put off: they will assume the founder lacks confidence in the future of the business or won't continue to work as hard for it as before. For this reason one condition of listing is a lock-in period during which the founder is not allowed to sell more of his shares.

The next question is how many new shares to issue. The founder and the venture capital shareholders don't just want to sell existing shares. This is a superb opportunity to raise additional equity to expand the business further. In fact, the founder probably has plans in mind that require additional funding.

So, part of 'going public' or floating is raising additional equity capital to expand the business.

THE STEPS TO OBTAINING A LISTING ON THE LSE

The key dates are **impact day** and **admission**.

Impact day is when the prospectus is published (having been approved, together with the underwriting or placing agreement and the audited accounts, by the FSA), the price of the shares is confirmed and the flotation is officially announced.

Admission is when the shares are actually admitted to the Official List (as it's called) and to trading. The company and its advisers decide the basis of share allocations, which is announced to investors. During *admission week*, applications and cash from investors are received by the receiving bankers/registrars. If the issue is *over-subscribed*, allocations are scaled back; if *under-subscribed*, underwriters pick up the unallocated shares at the agreed price. Once the shares do trade, if they rise above the issue price, they are said to trade at a *premium*; if below the issue price, then they are said to trade at a *discount*.

However, the process of preparing a company for flotation (*pre-float preparation*) takes months. In the final few weeks, *legal verification* takes place, which involves confirming every statement or claim in each document (to protect the directors who are ultimately responsible). The accountants issue their report (this focuses in part on the company's projected cashflow position) and all of the documents are submitted for regulatory approval. In the meantime, a marketing programme is launched, there is an initial review of the likely price of the offer, asset valuations of the company (from pension fund to property holdings) are carried out and the *subscription* (underwriting) *agreement* is signed.

If a company is coming to a market via a placing or public offer, it may publish a *pathfinder or price range prospectus* (also known as a *red herring*) which contains all the details except the price and is used to market to selected potential investors on a restricted basis (called a red herring because of the use of red ink indicating the prospectus is provisional). For bigger issues a *book-building* process (led by the *global bookrunner*) may be used to sound out potential investors in advance about the number and price of shares they are prepared to buy.

SECONDARY ISSUES / RIGHTS ISSUES

Although companies tend to raise fresh equity capital when they float, this isn't their only opportunity to expand their share capital. At any point they can come back to the market and raise more funds by issuing fresh shares.

These are called *secondary issues* or (in the US) *seasoned equity offerings*, and in the UK are also known as *rights issues*. This is because when a company issues fresh shares it has to offer them to existing shareholders in the same proportions as their existing shareholdings. So if I own 10% of a listed company and it wants to issue fresh shares it has to offer 10% of that fresh share issue to me. I am said to have a *right of pre-emption* in respect of them, i.e. I have first option to buy them. Of course, I don't have to buy them. I can pass up my allocation (called a *provisional allotment*) and they can be offered to people who do want them.

The reason I have this right of pre-emption is to ensure that existing shareholders do not have their percentage of the company *diluted*. I would be pretty annoyed if I owned a chunk of a company and suddenly found that in percentage terms my shareholding had just shrunk because the company had issued fresh shares without offering some to me.

Often the shares are offered to existing institutional shareholders at a big discount (*deep discount issue*) but those shares that are not taken up (lapsed securities) are called the *rump* and the broker sells them in the open market. If the broker achieves a premium, then that premium goes to the 'lapsed' shareholders. What is left over of the rump that the broker cannot sell is called the *stick* and the underwriters take up the stick.

Secondary issues tend to depress the company's share price because:
- Existing shareholders have to stump up money for the new shares just to retain their existing percentage of the company's capital
- The market fears bad news and thinks the company needs a substantial equity injection just to support the business as it is or to fund risky new projects that can't be financed out of retained earnings or borrowings.
- There is an assumption that companies only issue new shares at the top of the market when they feel their shares are overpriced.

THE ONGOING LIFE OF A PUBLIC COMPANY

The London Stock Exchange, like any market, is keen to maintain an orderly market in which:
- All shareholders are treated equally
- All price-sensitive information is in the public domain

These aims drive the ongoing regulations to which listed companies are subject, including:
- *Transaction disclosure:* Anything that is likely to have an impact on a company's share price – positive or negative – must be disclosed, whether it's a straightforward announcement of a modest deal up to publication of a circular, or the need to gain shareholders' approval. If the information is dramatic it may lead to the temporary suspension of trading in the company's shares.
- *Disclosure of price-sensitive information through an RIS:* Companies are required to make public such *price sensitive information* (as it is called) through a Regulatory Information Service which means an approved screen-based news service such as Reuters or Bloomberg.
- *Observing the Model Code:* This is a set of restrictions on directors' dealings in the shares of their company to prevent dealing on unpublished price-sensitive information – e.g. a director can't deal

during the two months before the announcement of the company's annual results.

- *Recognising the Combined Code on Corporate Governance:* Various committees have reported on the ways in which companies should run themselves. For example, Hempel (called after the person chairing it) incorporates the earlier ones (Cadbury and Greenbury) and says that companies should have, for instance, a separate chief executive officer (CEO) and chairman, non-executive directors and a qualified finance director. Pretty obvious stuff, you would have thought.

It's fair to say that some entrepreneurs never take to having their company publicly held. Sir Richard Branson of Virgin is one of these. He detested having to report quarterly on how his businesses were doing. He loathed investors who were just looking for short-term gains and didn't want to take a long-term view of his business and weren't prepared to wait while his investment in new sidelines paid off. There's also the risk that if you falter, your shareholders – who, after all, are now the owners – will either get rid of you or sell out to someone else who will (see the next chapter on M&A). So some owner-managers feel very uncomfortable as the head of a public company.

Other CEOs, labelled 'captains of industry' by the market, seem to go from one large company to another getting massive 'golden hellos' (a sum for signing on), big salaries and grants of share options (together known as the 'remuneration package'; a share option is the right to buy shares in the company at a very favourable price at a future date) and huge 'golden parachutes' (compensation for being sacked if the company is taken over) plus enormous contributions to their pension funds. They are often the CEO of one major company and on the boards of several others. Often they seem to be rewarded for failure, then pop up heading another big company. What horrifies the man in the street and gets these CEOs the tag of 'fat cats' is that they haven't built their success up from scratch. No one begrudges Sir Alan Sugar,

Corporate social responsibility

Some argue that a public company's role is not simply to make profit for its shareholders. It has duties to all its 'stakeholders' and these include employees, customers and – in the case of big businesses with extensive operations that affect the local community – those who live nearby. Environmental concerns, in particular, have been a driver in the development of corporate social responsibility – the topical idea that companies need to be good corporate citizens too.

who started by selling radios out the back of a van, from earning a lot of money from businesses he created. But people who've inherited big, established businesses don't deserve to get tens of millions of pounds just for running them (with chauffeur-driven cars and loads of perks and freebies) – especially when they get a huge pay-off for running a business into the ground and being sacked. It's a reward for failure which seems to have attracted government attention only recently in the context of big bonuses for bankers whose banks had to be bailed out by the government at taxpayers' expense. It's to stop these excesses that 'corporate governance' has become a big issue (see Chapter 9).

OK, rant over. Now, there are two major advantages to being listed: first, a listed company is able to take over other companies by buying them with its own shares (see the next chapter) and, second, a listed company is able to access one of the cheapest ways of borrowing – through the bond markets (see the chapter after that).

Chapter 4

M&As
(AND MORE ON MBOs)

SPEED-READ SUMMARY

- Once a company has listed, it can use its shares to buy other companies

- These takeovers are either agreed bids (where the target agrees to be bought) or hostile bids (where the target's directors resist)

- Public company takeovers are overseen by the Takeover Panel which applies a set of rules called the Takeover Code

- The Code lays down a detailed timetable to reduce the period of uncertainty which a bid necessarily engenders

- Companies are forever changing – taking each other over and divesting themselves of non-core businesses through trade sales (often by way of auction) or MBOs

- Companies can acquire businesses from other companies by way of share purchase or asset sale agreements

- MBOs can involve mezzanine finance

- Highly geared MBOs are called LBOs (leveraged buyouts)

Once a company has gone public, floated, listed or done an IPO (you now know that these terms mean the same thing) it is able to enter the high-octane arena of mergers and acquisitions (known as *M&A*).

In an M&A deal, a company will offer to buy all of the shares in another. It is the *bidder* and the company being taken over is the *target*. If the bidder succeeds, it will end up owning all the shares in the target and the target will therefore be its subsidiary.

M&A deals are either recommended or hostile. In a *recommended bid*, the directors of the target recommend the bid to their shareholders, i.e. they advise their shareholders to accept the bidder's offer (sometimes the bidder only retains the board's recommendation if it matches any competing offers within 48 hours – this is known as 'marching rights'). But if they don't, if they reject the bid, then the bid becomes *hostile* (or *contested*). Unless, of course, the bidder has second thoughts and just walks away.

The basics of a takeover

The actual mechanics of a takeover are really quite simple (see the diagram a few pages on). The bidder makes an offer to the shareholders of the target to buy their shares from them for a certain price. Usually it offers to pay them in its own shares (although the bidder is also required to offer a cash alternative – in other words, to allow them to accept its bid but to be paid in cash not in the bidder's shares). Once the bidder owns the target's shares, the target becomes the bidder's subsidiary and is no longer a public company since it now has just one shareholder – the bidder. If the target's shareholders accept the bidder's shares then they become shareholders in the bidder alongside its previous shareholders – in effect the two sets of shareholders now own a bigger company between them which is the bidder plus its subsidiary, the target.

HOSTILE TAKEOVERS

Let's assume the bidder doesn't withdraw its offer (in which case that's the end of the matter) but decides to persist in its attempts to persuade the target's shareholders to sell their shares to it. For instance, it may argue that the target's management are a bunch of incompetents. If it succeeds it will then sack the target's board of directors. Of course, the risk is that, if the bidder fails to win, its own management may be tarnished: its claim that it could make a better fist of running the target than its existing management will have been seen to be publicly rebuffed by the target's shareholders. For these reasons passions run high.

The first hostile takeover of the modern era was of a company called British Aluminium, in the winter of 1958–59. It was led by a banker called Sigmund Warburg. We'll be coming across him (and his bank, SG Warburg) again later.

There are two reasons why companies take each other over: (1) to move into a new market or (2) to take out a competitor. In the latter case, if a company is likely to become *market dominant* (become so big in a particular market that it can control prices) the competition regulators in the UK and the EU may step in and stop a takeover or only permit it subject to conditions (e.g. the bidder, if successful, must sell off part of the target's business).

The players in an M&A deal

Those involved include the *bidder*, whose shareholders may have to consent to the takeover (certainly if new shares are to be issued) and the *target*, whose shareholders are the recipients of the bid – its fate is in their hands. The target may recommend the offer, in which case the *offer document* will contain the target board's recommendation.

The bidder will be advised by a bank that coordinates activities, issues the offer document on behalf of the bidder, and underwrites the cash-underwritten alternative (note that a bidder for a public-company target must offer a cash alternative to its own shares). Where the bidder is making a share issue to fund the takeover, the bank will also underwrite that issue and will appoint a *broker* to arrange the sub-underwriting.

The broker monitors the market and reports back on *market sentiment* (how the bid is seen in the market; whether the target's shareholders are likely to sell to the bidder), tracks significant share purchases in the target, handles any purchases by the bidder of the target's shares and, since the bidder's shares are to be listed (the fresh ones being offered to the target's shareholders), the broker will liaise with the London Stock Exchange.

The reason why M&A activity is open to public companies is because they don't have to pay cash for the target's shares. They can offer the target's shareholders their own shares: 'You'd be much better off as a shareholder in a combined business which we, the bidder, will manage.'

However, they are required to offer a cash alternative, so shareholders in the target who want cash instead of the bidder's shares can ask for cash. Bidders don't like this: it means they have to borrow the cash from somewhere and that costs money; far better to issue their own shares, which are just bits of paper and don't cost anything.

This in turn is why CEOs are perpetually concerned about the share price of their company. If the share price goes down, their company may be exposed to a bid and they may be out of a job; quite apart from the fact that their share options are also going down in value. Of course, as soon as a bid is announced, the target's share price shoots up (because everyone knows the bidder wants the shares) so people buy those shares in the hope of selling out to the bidder at an even higher price.

The City loves these battles for a number of reasons: the media attention; the fact that this is capitalism at its rawest – with the bidder claiming that it can put the target's capital to better use; and because the demands of these transactions often tax the ingenuity of some of the City's smartest minds. But most of all because hostile M&As generate massive fees for the City advisers involved.

In a hostile M&A, neither the bidder nor the target care much about the fees involved: the target because, if it loses, the management will be sacked anyway and won't be around to pick up the tab; the bidder because its management will be heroes and because the costs of merging two businesses are so horrifically large that advisers' fees will be the least of the management's concerns, especially if the cost-savings (and these are always promised as one of the principal benefits of a bid) are achieved.

Of course, when markets are dead, so is M&A activity – especially since in recent years so much of it was *highly leveraged* (the euphemism for meaning that the bidder borrowed heavily then loaded the target with massive debt if successful).

TIMETABLE OF A TAKEOVER

One of the principles which the City Code (and the Takeover Panel which enforces it – see box opposite) is keen on is the *bid timetable*.

Hostile bids create enormous uncertainty for both companies and so the sooner the outcome of the bid is known the better; and both sides

Takeover Panel and the City Code on Takeovers and Mergers

So that bids don't get out of hand and don't go on too long, there are detailed rules about how such bids are conducted.

Takeovers are policed by the Takeover Panel which has a rule book called the City Code on Takeovers and Mergers. People often find the Takeover Panel hard to grasp. It isn't a government body. It is in fact a committee with a full-time secretariat but with experts seconded from banks, law firms and accountants in the City. Originally the Takeover Panel was a completely voluntary body without any official standing. People in the City did as it said because they preferred self-regulation to being regulated by the government. But now that the old 'club' mentality of the City has been replaced by an influx of foreign banks and given the size and importance of the deals it presides over, the Takeover Panel has been put on a statutory basis. Generally, if there is a breach of the Code, the Panel will censure the culprits (tell them off) and can insist that documents are amended or shares are sold if bought in breach of the Code.

Be that as it may, the real reason why people obey the Panel is because its aims are sensible – to achieve: equality of treatment of shareholders; adequacy of information and advice; the prohibition of any frustrating action by a target to its shareholders' detriment; the maintenance of an orderly market; and no 'siege' of the target – so bids must not be prolonged (the Panel insists that bidders have their funding in place before bidding – it can order them to put up or shut up if they take too long). And the way the Panel works is by giving behind-the-scenes advice, adjudications and informal rulings.

need to enjoy equal treatment to put their case and contradict the other side's. Hence the stringency of the timetable. Of course, a bidder usually has the advantage – it has been preparing its bid for months in advance. But targets don't want to be caught unawares so nowadays many public companies have their defence already mapped out in advance in case a bid materialises.

The bid starts when the bidder informs the target of the bid (this is usually done by an early-morning phone call from one chairman to the other – 'Look here, old boy, we've decided to have a tilt at your company. Thought I'd just do the decent thing and let you know, in the hope that your chaps will see sense and recommend the whole shooting match to your shareholders'). The bid is announced publicly and the *offer period* begins which means that the bidder must prepare its *offer document* within 28 days. The bidder will continue to buy shares in the market (subject to restrictions on stake building mentioned later) but it has to raise its offer if it now buys shares at a price higher than offer price.

The bidder must also post an announcement of the bid to its shareholders. It will also approach shareholders in the target to get *irrevocable undertakings* to accept the offer and these count towards the stake building thresholds.

Offer document

This is actually issued by the bank on behalf of the bidder and is a *contractual offer* to buy all of the shares in the target. The offer document sets out the bidder's plans for the target and the relevant financial information including details of the bidder's shareholding in the target. It must also 'sell' the bid to the target's shareholders, giving the

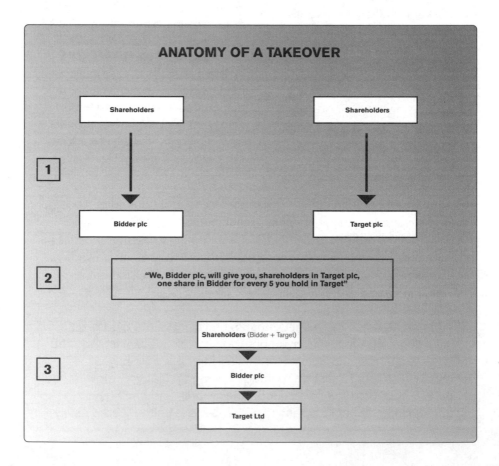

Stake building and tender offers

There are rules designed to ensure that a bidder cannot build up a stake in secret or too quickly and win the target by stealth. For example, once a bidder has 3% of the target, it must notify the target. A bidder can't acquire 10% or more of the target over a seven-day period if doing so will take its overall holding to 15% and cannot acquire more than 30% of the target (unless the bid is recommended) without making an offer for all the shares in cash at the highest price paid over the previous year. This is why some bidders stop at 29.9% and call it a *strategic holding* in the target (this large a holding in a public company does in practice give the shareholder effective control).

These rules, which change from time to time, prevent what used to be called *dawn raids* where a bidder would swoop on a target's shares and buy them up early in the day before anyone knew what was happening.

However, there is an exception where the bidder is making a *partial offer* for, say, 25% of every shareholder's holding, in which case it is done by what is called a *tender offer*. What happens is that the bidder puts adverts in the papers, specifying the percentage in the target it wants. The bidder can fix the price at which it will buy, or set a maximum. Once all the tenders (offers from the target's shareholders) are in, the bidder sets a *strike price* and all offers at or below that price qualify.

reasons why the bidder would do a better job of running the target than the target's existing directors have done. However, these claims cannot be excessive otherwise the target will complain to the Takeover Panel which will make a ruling. The offer document is a formal document so it must also comply with the City Code.

Within 14 days, the target must post its *first defence circular* to its shareholders, which sets out its reply to the bidder's plans.

Closing date

The *first closing date* for the bidder's offer (some weeks from when it posts its offer document) is the point at which the bidder can either *let the bid lapse* (i.e. abandon it), *extend* it or *declare it unconditional as to acceptances* (this last means that the bidder has acceptances of its offer in respect of at least 50% of the target's shares). If the bidder hasn't got 50% it must decide whether to extend the offer or let it lapse. There are intermediate deadlines by when the target can announce a *profit forecast* (a profit forecast is going to be the backbone of the target's defence; in effect it is saying 'Stay with us, the current management, and we will deliver') and the bidder can *revise* its offer.

After the various deadlines are up, the offer must be declared unconditional as to acceptances (the bidder has won) or, if the bidder doesn't have 50%, the offer must lapse.

ACQUISITION OF MINORITY INTERESTS

Once a bidder has 90% of the target's shares, it can compulsorily purchase the remaining 10% but on the same terms as the original offer and if the bidder doesn't want to buy them out, they can force it to. This is known as a *squeeze-out* and happens because being a minority shareholder in a company usually isn't much fun if the majority shareholder starts running the company for its benefit not yours. So either side (bidder or minority shareholder) can force a squeeze-out on the same terms as everyone else, which seems fair.

CONCERT PARTIES

One other thing: you might think that you can get round the stake building rules by getting your friends to buy shares. But that is called a *concert party* and all of the shares held by members of a concert party are aggregated (added together) to see if the thresholds are triggered.

The same applies to holdings through derivatives (see Chapter 13). If these instruments give you a quasi stake without owning the underlying shares – for instance if you hold options to acquire shares in the target – those holdings are aggregated with your actual shares held in the target for the purposes of the stake building restrictions mentioned earlier.

REVERSE TAKEOVER

This is where the bidder is smaller by *market capitalisation* (i.e. how much the company is worth, calculated by the number of shares in issue multiplied by the share price) than the target, so the target's shareholders become the majority shareholders in the bidder. A reverse takeover requires the approval of the bidder's shareholders since they will lose control of their company.

SHARE PURCHASE v ASSET SALE

So far we have been looking at share purchases – where a company takes over another by buying all its shares – in the context of a hostile bid. But not all takeovers are hostile. Sometimes, target companies agree to be taken over. These are called *agreed bids* where the target's board of directors *recommends the offer* to its shareholders.

So far we have focused on public company takeovers but private companies also do change hands – for instance when a public company sells off a subsidiary to another because that subsidiary is no longer core to the seller's business. Companies are forever fiddling around with their businesses, selling bits off, acquiring other businesses, occasionally launching a hostile bid.

They do this in the name of 'strategy' in order to outflank their competitors or to move into new business areas and out of old ones. So the corporate world is never still. It is always dynamic, and here's a test. If you look at the companies that make up today's FTSE 100 (in other words the 100 biggest companies in the UK by capitalisation, as listed in the Financial Times Stock Exchange list, which is pronounced 'Footsie') and compare it to the same list ten years ago, only about 60% or 60 companies will still be there from ten years ago. That's how quickly things change. The FTSE 100 was itself launched in 1984.

Cherry picking

These private company acquisitions and disposals can be by way of share purchase. But another technique is simply to buy bits of the company rather than the whole thing. Buying the assets rather than the shares is called an *asset purchase*, *asset sale* or *business purchase* – these terms are interchangeable. The reason for doing this is that buying the whole company can be risky: the buyer doesn't really know its history or whether it has any hidden liabilities. For instance, is it about to be sued? Does it owe tax? So the acquirer may decide just to buy the bits it wants (this is called *cherry picking the assets*). The seller may then inject those assets into a separate company in order to sell the shares in that company. This is called a *hive-down* and it has the advantage that the new company is *clean* (no risk of hidden liabilities). This is generally only used where only part of a business is being sold.

Warranties

Where the whole company is being bought the seller will give the buyer *warranties* (promises regarding the state of all aspects of the company's operations which, if not true, allow the buyer to seek compensation from the seller) and *indemnities* (under which the seller pays the buyer any unexpected losses the buyer incurs on a 'pound-for-pound' basis).

Warranties will include promises that the seller owns the business, the business is free from charge, all licences and consents to the sale have been obtained, the seller is not aware of customers that will defect, there is no litigation, infringement of legislation and no breaches of contracts. They will also cover the accounts (that they give a *true and fair view* of the state of the company) including level of debtors and creditors, as well as tax, insurance, employees and any pension liabilities.

The purpose of requiring the seller to give these warranties is to flush out information about the company: any exceptions to these warranties

Auctions

Rather than deal with a single prospective purchaser, the seller may use a c*ontrolled auction* to get a better price by trying to generate interest from a number of potential buyers (generally a *financial adviser* – a bank or, in smaller deals, a firm of accountants – will help the seller do this).

First of all, an *information memorandum* is circulated to potential bidders. This is not as detailed as a prospectus on flotation but its contents are usually subject to some *verification*. Since this is likely to reveal confidential information about the business being sold, any bidder having sight of the information memorandum is usually required to sign a *confidentiality letter* in which they agree not to reveal the information to anyone else or to use it in their own business.

Interested bidders then submit *indicative offers* on the basis of the information memorandum. Those offering the best bids are then allowed to undertake limited *due diligence* (having a good look at the business to be bought) generally by going through documents that the seller has put in what is called a *data room*.

At the same time, the seller circulates the *sales documentation* (i.e. the draft agreement) and bidders are asked to confirm their bids and submit their *proposed amendments* to the sales documentation. What matters now is not just price: one bidder may offer a high price but want all sorts of changes to the sales agreement whereas another may offer a slightly lower price with few amendments.

The seller will choose a *preferred purchaser,* chosen on the basis of price and (limited) amendments to the sales documents, and the preferred purchaser is given *exclusivity* to proceed to detailed negotiations which should lead to a completed sale.

are put in a *disclosure letter*. The seller effectively says: 'These warranties are true subject to what is in the disclosure letter.' The disclosure letter therefore brings to the buyer's attention all of the liabilities of which the seller is aware, which therefore will fall outside the warranties and indemnities. Any publicly available information that the buyer could be expected to find out for himself is called a *deemed disclosure*. These warranties and indemnities won't be as significant where the buyer is just buying the assets (asset purchase or sale).

If the deal is an asset sale, it can cover land and premises, plant and machinery, intellectual property (things like patents and copyrights, often called know-how), stock and work-in-progress, commercial contracts, debtors and creditors, the goodwill and name of the business (*goodwill* is the value that attaches to a business's reputation – what attracts customers to it). In short any or all aspects of a business.

Payment can be in cash or shares (for instance if the buyer is listed, in which case it is called a *share-for-share exchange*) and can be paid immediately *on completion* or postponed till a future date (called *deferred*) or based on the earnings of the business under new ownership (called an *earn-out*). In a share-for-share exchange there may be restrictions on how quickly the seller can sell shares in the buyer to prevent the buyer's share price being depressed. This may also involve a *vendor placing* (see Chapter 8).

MORE ON MBOs (MANAGEMENT BUYOUTS)

As you know (from Chapter 2) public companies also get rid of bits of the business they don't want through MBOs.

First of all the prospective owners (the managers) have to set up an entity to buy the business being sold (the Target). Usually this new company is often dubbed NewCo before it gets a proper trading name and is owned by the managers and the private equity providers. NewCo then enters into an *acquisition agreement* with the company selling the business (Seller). Key clauses cover issues such as: the Target's financial position; the separation of the Seller's and Target's assets and services; and warranties (the legally binding statements that the business is as expected).

The warranties, given by the Seller, are usually fiercely negotiated. The Seller will argue that because it is selling to management, it doesn't owe any warranties (since the management should know the business anyway). But NewCo's investors will want the comfort of proper warranties.

There will also be a *shareholders' agreement* (also known as the *investment agreement* or *subscription agreement*) between the management and the private equity providers (which may be one or more institutional investors). This will set out the managers' and institutional investors' respective initial investments in NewCo in terms of how much each party puts in and what shareholding they get.

The managers also give *warranties* to the investors to ensure the managers are fully committed to the business plan and have disclosed all the potential problem areas to investors.

Drag-along and tag-along

This agreement will also set out the ongoing relationship between the managers and institutional investors once NewCo has acquired the Target, including: restrictions on transfers of shares by the managers; a *restrictive covenant* on managers not to compete with the business for a period after they leave; and obligations on the managers to provide financial information on a regular basis to the institutional investors.

The investors for their part will usually have complete freedom to transfer their shareholdings to each other and outside the syndicate subject to: *drag-along rights* (if the investors want to sell, the managers can't block them or refuse to sell – any purchaser will want 100% of NewCo, so the investors can drag-along the minority shareholders on the same terms); and *tag-along rights* – if the managers want to sell, the investors are allowed to join in.

Most MBOs also need debt funding. This may be provided by the equity investors (debt, being tax-deductible is a more efficient way of funding than equity). It will also come from banks. The banks will wish their debt to rank ahead of that provided by the equity investors. This means that, in the event of NewCo going bust, the banks want to get their hands on any of NewCo's assets before the investors.

The banks are therefore said to provide *senior debt* and they are called *senior lenders*. The investors' debt funding is called *junior debt* or *subordinated debt*. They will enter into an *inter-creditor agreement* with the banks to subordinate their loans to those of the senior lenders (i.e. agree that their loans rank behind the senior lenders').

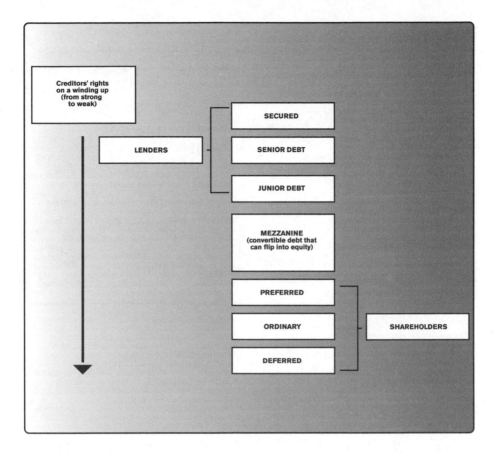

Mezzanine finance

Sometimes a lender may want the option of turning its loan (or part of the loan) into shares if NewCo does well. In return, its lending ranks behind senior debt. Such lenders are called *mezzanine banks* or *mezzanine lenders*. See the diagram above for how these different tranches fit together. Their *seniority* will depend on their respective rights if NewCo were to be wound up, from secured lenders (strong) to deferred shareholders (non-existent).

LBOs

If the Target is a substantial business that is being bought out, NewCo may even make a *high-yield bond issue*, using the capital markets. Bond issues are covered in the next chapter. An MBO that depends on a high degree of borrowing is called an LBO (*leveraged buyout* – leveraged means *highly borrowed* or *highly geared*).

Incentives for the managers...

The main incentive for the managers is their shareholding in NewCo, but this can be supplemented by:

- *ratchets* – these redistribute equity in NewCo on exit: the investors will hand over some of their shares if NewCo's expected rate of return is exceeded
- *warrants and call options* – these are like share options and allow the managers to receive extra shares at a preferential price when the business has performed better than expected
- *bonus scheme* – which will be set out in the managers' employment contracts

...and for the deal arrangers

One of the ways in which the deal arrangers make their return is through something called the *carried interest* – this is where they get an extra return or share in return for nothing (the 'interest' is 'carried' by the other investors).

Chapter 5

MY WORD IS MY BOND: DEBT SECURITIES

SPEED-READ SUMMARY

- There are two types of debt: loans and bonds. A bond is just an IOU

- Bonds are issued by public companies and governments – US government bonds are called Treasuries and UK government bonds are gilts

- The majority of bonds pay a fixed rate of interest and are called fixed-income securities

- Bond markets are among the largest financial markets in the world and the US is the single largest market

- The Eurobond market is the international bond market where bonds are issued outside the issuer's home country often in a foreign currency

- Bond issues are rated by credit rating agencies

- Bonds have maturities ranging from a matter of days (commercial paper) to more than 20 years (long bonds)

- Zero coupon bonds do not pay interest but are issued at a deep discount to their face value

- The rate of interest (the coupon) is stated in hundredths of a per cent, called basis points

- Bonds that are rated below investment grade are called high-yield or junk bonds

- A bond's yield is the rate of interest it pays expressed in relation to its market value, and is sensitive to interest rate changes

There are only two types of capital: equity and debt. And there are only two types of debt: loans and bonds. In this chapter we are going to explore bonds.

Big companies aren't restricted to raising debt through bank loans. They can issues bonds as well, and often find it cheaper to do so. It's one of the advantages of being a public company. Certainly, in the UK private companies are not permitted to issue bonds; besides, they wouldn't be significant or well enough known businesses to appeal to international bondholders.

The word 'bond' has several meanings. One is guarantee – as in 'posting a bond' to guarantee that something happens or someone behaves in a certain way. That's not what we mean here and we'll explore that elsewhere. But it also means a piece of paper that is simply an 'I owe you' or IOU. This is what people in the City mean when they talk about *bond issues, corporate bonds* and *sovereign bonds*. (Sovereign means issued by a country or government.)

BONDS v LOANS

Bonds are debt instruments (they really are IOUs). A company that wants to raise, say, £100 million (bond issues are only worth doing for substantial amounts) will issue an IOU that says: 'I will pay you 100 million pounds in ten years' time and in the meantime I will pay you interest of 5%.' Whoever buys the bond will hand over £100 million to the company and in return the bondholder will receive £5 million (which is 5% of £100 million) every year for ten years and at the end of the ten years will get the £100 million back again. It's as simple as that, except that instead of one bondholder providing £100 million, there will be thousands, each buying bonds in smaller denominations.

What makes this different from a loan is that the bondholder doesn't have to hold the bond until maturity or *redemption* (i.e. until it is repaid by the company). Instead the bondholder can decide to sell the bond to someone else. In this way bonds are tradable securities whereas loans aren't (or, at least, weren't; loans are now much more tradable than they were, partly through the use of derivatives and securitisation, discussed in Chapters 13 and 14 respectively). This still makes bonds far more liquid investments than loans and this makes them a cheaper source of funding for companies (because investors can get out of them more easily).

Bonds are also different from loans in that, with a loan, the lending bank remains in touch with the company it has lent to, whereas with a bond the issuing company never knows who holds its bonds.

Companies that issue bonds tend to be public companies, i.e. large enough to be recognised names and to want money in sufficient quantity to make the cost of a bond issue worthwhile. UK listed companies issue *debentures* which are domestic bonds issued in the UK in sterling and listed on the London Stock Exchange as debt instruments. Debentures are often secured over the company's assets so that if the company defaults on the debenture, the holders can seize the company assets that are *charged* with payment of that debenture and sell those assets in order to recover what they are owed (this is what lawyers call *security* but don't confuse it with *securities* which are tradable instruments, such as bonds and shares). But the debenture market is domestic and relatively small. The international bond markets are global and huge. Companies can usually borrow more cheaply there than at any bank.

BONDS AS BEARER INSTRUMENTS

Historically, bonds tended to be *bearer instruments*:
- 'bearer' means that there is no register of ownership – whoever holds the bond is treated as owning it (whereas debentures are registered)
- an 'instrument' means a document.

In the old days when they existed in physical form, whoever had physical possession of the bond was regarded by the issuer as the owner of it. Companies did not keep lists or registers of who their bondholders were and nowadays even though bonds are electronic entries in clearing systems and held by custodians (discussed later) the bearer principal still applies. In the past they really were pieces of stiff paper or card. Nowadays they are *dematerialised* – that is, they don't exist as real bonds but as electronic entries on computers.

In those days, physical bonds were issued with *coupons* attached to them. A coupon would entitle the bondholder to one year's interest and the bondholder would cut the coupon off the bond and present it to the issuer (the company) for payment of that year's interest. This meant the bond itself could just be kept in a safe. Whoever presented the coupon was the person to whom the company paid the interest. Hence, bond traders still talk about the coupon, meaning the interest that a bond pays. When traders ask: 'What's the coupon?' they mean: what rate of interest is this bond paying?

FIXED-INCOME INSTRUMENTS

The majority of bonds pay a fixed rate of interest throughout their life (e.g. 5%). This is why bonds are often called *fixed-income instruments* because you know that year-in-year-out to redemption, the interest payable will be the same. However, there are bonds that have a floating rate of interest (for instance, pegged to the rate of interest set by the Bank of England). These are called *floating rate notes* or *FRNs* ('note' and 'bond' mean the same thing).

GOVERNMENTS AS BOND ISSUERS

The principal issuers of bonds are companies, banks, countries (governments) and public bodies.

Governments are big borrowers in the bond markets: their bonds are called *sovereign bonds*. The biggest sovereign borrower is the United States. Its bonds are issued by the Treasury Department and are known as *Treasuries*. UK government bonds are known, quaintly, as *gilts* because in the old days when they actually existed as bits of card they had silver edges to mark them out from bonds issued by lesser credits, hence the term 'gilt-edged investment' meaning one that is safe.

Although the US government is the biggest borrower and so owes more money to the rest of the world than anybody else, it is also, oddly, the most creditworthy and is able to borrow more cheaply than anyone else. The theory is that if the US ever defaulted on one of its bonds, that would be the end of capitalism as we know it. However, this doesn't stop countries defaulting: in the 1980s Latin American countries defaulted on external debt and in 1998 Russia did.

But because the US can borrow so cheaply, its cost of borrowing is the *benchmark*, so market professionals talk about other issues being 'priced off Treasuries' or being so many per cent 'over Treasuries'. In actual fact because the amounts of debt raised in the international capital markets are so huge, bond issues are not priced in per cent but in hundredths of one per cent and each one of these is a *basis point* or 0.01 of a per cent: when you are dealing with a bond issue for hundreds of millions of dollars, whether the interest rate is 50 basis points over Treasuries (half a per cent more than the rate at which the

How the Eurobond market was born

The international bond markets have existed on-and-off for hundreds of years. In the nineteenth century, railway companies issued bonds in London to finance track-laying in South America. It was defaults on these issues that bankrupted Barings the first time round in 1890 (a *default* is the failure by an issuer of a bond or a borrower under a loan agreement to pay the interest or repay the principal when due).

In its current guise, the international bond market developed after the Second World War once countries started dismantling exchange controls, so allowing their citizens to move money freely between countries. After that war, the US started importing oil in quantity from the Middle East, paying for it in dollars. This large pool of dollars held externally was augmented by dollars placed offshore by US companies and investors to earn a higher rate of interest (the US imposed a ceiling on the rate of interest US banks could pay domestically). In addition, communist states, worried that the US might freeze their assets, started keeping their dollars in Europe.

These dollars tended to be held in the vaults of European banks and offered a source of possible debt capital. In 1963 Sigmund Warburg (remember him?) encouraged Autostrade, the Italian government agency that builds and maintains its motorways, to tap this source of money by issuing a bond outside Italy denominated in dollars. By today's standards it was a tiny issue for just $15 million. But it was a runaway success – because although Autostrade may not sound glamorous to you or me, it had the huge benefit of being owned by the Italian government. So the chances of its going bust or defaulting were minimal.

Ten years later the annual issue of what became known as Eurobonds had risen from just under $150 million a year to $5.5 billion – a 30-fold increase; and a Eurobond had come to mean a bond issued outside the issuer's home market, denominated in a currency (usually dollars) that wasn't its home currency.

In due course Eurobonds were issued in currencies other than the dollar. For instance, a foreign bond (i.e. by a non-UK issuer) in sterling was dubbed a 'bulldog', one in yen was a 'samurai', one in Spanish pesetas (before the euro) was a 'matador' and a 'yankee' was a bond issued in the US by a non-US issuer.

In this way, any international issue came to be regarded as an issue in the Euromarket and the words 'international' and 'Euro' became synonymous. In time a Eurobond may well come to mean a bond that is denominated in euros – but not just yet.

It is these bonds that make up the international bond market which in turn, when lumped together with company shares traded internationally, makes up what are called the international capital markets.

US borrows – a very fine rate) or 65 basis points is in real terms a big difference when it comes down to actual money.

RATING AGENCIES

Issuing a bond depends critically on being able to obtain an adequate credit rating.

In the world of loans, a bank will pore over a company and its accounts before lending. But in the bond markets, where traders buy and sell bonds at a moment's notice, they want to know quickly whether the issuer is likely to default. They don't have time to undertake extensive credit analysis. This is where credit rating agencies step in. There are a number but three are prominent: **Standard & Poor's; Moody's**; and **Fitch IBCA**.

In order to get a bond issue off the ground, a prospective issuer will pay a rating agency to vet its financial position and to 'rate' the issue in terms of its ability to service the debt (pay interest on it) and repay the principal. The rating agency (to which the issuer pays an annual fee as well as activity-based fees in relation to each rated issue) will continue to monitor the company's ability to meet the interest payments and repay the principal on maturity. Ratings range from 'triple A' (written 'AAA' or 'Aaa' depending on the rating agency) to 'below investment grade' ('Ba1' or 'BB+' or 'BB') and if the issuer's financial condition deteriorates or – in the language – its ability to service or repay becomes 'impaired', it may be immediately downrated.

If the rating goes 'below investment grade' many of the institutional investors that hold the issue will have to sell (pension funds in particular are usually forbidden by their trust deeds from holding securities that

---

Belgian dentists

One of the reasons for bonds' traditional popularity is that they have always been seen as useful ways of avoiding (and even evading) tax. It's tricky for tax authorities to establish who holds them, being bearer, and paying interest gross (without deduction of tax) means that it is up to the holder to declare the income they provide.

In fact, in continental Europe, individuals have tended to buy bonds rather than shares (unlike the UK) for this reason and some bonds are deliberately aimed at this *retail market* (i.e. bought by individuals) rather than just the *wholesale market* (institutional investors) to the extent that Eurobond professionals talk about the 'Belgian dentist', a fictitious symbol of the European retail market – as in: 'This issue is targeted at the Belgian dentist.'

Size of the international bond market

The bond markets are probably the largest financial markets in the world. The total value of bonds in issue is about $40 trillion, of which about a quarter trade internationally and the remainder on domestic markets.

The US is easily the largest single bond market with about $15 trillion in issue of which about $500 billion's worth are traded each day.

Some of the biggest bond issuers in the US are states and local governments. These municipal bonds – known as 'munis' – account for about $2 trillion.

---

are below investment grade). The market value of the bonds will go down as fewer institutions will want, or are able, to hold them. More pejorative terms for 'below investment grade' are *junk bond* or *high-yield bond* or *fallen angel*.

But junk bonds are not bad in themselves. There are banks and traders that specialise in buying junk bonds cheap and holding them in the hope that the issuer's fortunes will recover and the bonds will be repaid in full. Equally, some companies issue junk bonds when they are fully stretched – for instance, to fund a takeover, deliberately offering a high yield to attract funding – then refinance the issue on more preferential terms when the takeover has been successfully completed.

DIFFERENT MATURITIES

There are three aspects to any bond:
- Who issued it
- The rate of interest it is paying
- Its maturity (which tells you how long the bond has to go before it is redeemed, which is known as its tenor)

Bond maturities range from a matter of days to over 20 years. A small number of bonds in issue are 'perpetuals' – they have no redemption date and will never be redeemed unless the issuer (usually a bank, in the case of perpetuals) chooses to retire them. In this sense they are quite like shares (equity).

Bonds of very short duration are called *commercial paper* (CP). These issues are made by large, listed companies to fund short-term working capital requirements (it's that old cashflow thing again). They usually have a maturity of just 90 days and don't pay interest. Instead they are issued at a discount to their face value: at the end of the 90 days the holder is paid the full face value. So if CP with a face value of 105 is issued at 100, the company receives 100 and in three months' time pays back 105. So for three months' money the company is paying 5%, which equates to an annualised rate of 20% (a pricey and unrealistic example for illustration only). What tends to happen at the end of the 90 days is that the CP is *rolled over* – the amount owing is repaid by issuing fresh paper to replace the paper that has expired. Commercial paper is bought by banks to park short-term deposits, but mainly by other large companies to invest short-term revenues that aren't immediately needed but will be soon. CP forms part of what are called the *money markets* (see Chapter 11).

Bonds with maturities over roughly three years are called *medium term notes* or MTNs. They are often issued as part of an *MTN programme* where the company has a panel of three or four banks that have agreed to meet all of the company's debt requirements including loans and MTNs. The company decides at any point what it needs, tells the panel and the one offering the cheapest rate gets the business.

Any bond over about 10–12 years is called a *long bond*. As a general

Bond yields

Bond dealers and traders buy and sell bonds all the time. What matters to them most is not the bond's issuer (provided the rating is OK, they don't mind who it is) but the bond's *yield*. A bond's yield is the rate of interest it pays expressed as a percentage in relation to its market value (i.e. coupon divided by price of bond multiplied by 100). This is driven by interest rates.

Let's say a triple-A issuer (i.e. very creditworthy) issues a $100 million bond paying 5%. At the time interest rates are 4.5% so this is a good investment. But if interest rates move up, the 5% coupon will start to look less attractive. In fact what will happen is that the *market value* of the bond will fall until the coupon in relation to the market value looks attractive again when compared to current interest rates.

For example, if interest rates rise to 10% the bond's market value will fall until it is in effect paying at least 10%. To do that, its market value must fall to $50 million, because a bond that costs $50 million and pays $5 million a year in interest has an effective yield of 10%. Of course, the bond is still a $100 million bond (that is its *face value, nominal* or *par value*) – on maturity it will still pay back $100 million. Only it will now cost just $50 million to buy, which is its *market value*. Note: this simple example ignores when the bond matures, which will have a big impact too.

rule, the longer the maturity, the higher the rate of interest the company will pay to offset its *credit risk* because the longer the maturity, the less easy it is to predict whether the company will be able to repay the bond when the bond matures.

Zero coupon bonds (also known as *deep discount bonds*) are issued without a coupon: they don't pay interest but are issued at a discount to their par or face value; on maturity the holder receives the face value. So, for example, a five-year bond with a face value of 100 that is issued at 80 will have an implicit rate of interest of 4%.

RECENT DEVELOPMENTS

Bondholders are increasingly nervous of private equity deals which take over issuers and load them with debt to fund the takeover. So, increasingly, they are demanding bonds with 'step-up' rights. These have coupons which increase for every credit downgrade so protecting bondholders against highly leveraged takeovers.

There has also been renewed interest in hybrids that look like equity to rating agencies but debt to the tax man (meaning that payments on them are tax deductible), which allow interest payments to be deferred when times are hard and debt repayments to be met by issuing extra shares at maturity.

This has been replicated at a sovereign level by Argentina which issued $80 billion of bonds in early 2005 with a GDP warrant which pays investors a percentage of any growth in GDP over that predicted in the prospectus. These warrants were decoupled from the bonds and were traded independently when Argentina's economy did better than expected. This paves the way to a new class of variable-income security more similar to a share (where the price and dividend payments are tied to future cashflows) than a traditional bond (where the payout is fixed at the start).

By the way, when a sovereign defaults or restructures its bonds and investors lose some of their money, it's known as a 'haircut'. And that's nothing new. In bad times when the markets are flat, whether it's a sovereign that defaults or a corporate issuer (i.e. a company) that goes bust doesn't matter much to the investors. They still lose their shirt.

Chapter 6

WHAT'S A BANK?

SPEED-READ SUMMARY

- There are three types of bank: commercial, investment and universal

- Commercial banks take deposits and make loans

- Investment banks (a US creation) underwrite the issue of securities (primary market) and then trade those securities and make markets in them (secondary market activity)

- Universal banks combine commercial and investment banking – the world's biggest banks do both

- US legislation called Glass-Steagall separated commercial and investment banking after the Great Crash and Depression of the 1930s, but has been repealed – but for how long, given what's happened since?

- Merchant banks (a UK creation) helped to finance international trade through letters of credit (called trade finance) and advised companies on how to raise funds and take each other over (corporate finance)

- Most merchant banks have been taken over and are now part of universal banks

We've finished with companies now. They are the City's customers but they're not really at the heart of the City. We're now going to move on to banks. Banks and what they do lie at the core of the financial markets.

The term 'bank' is incredibly misleading. Technically speaking, a bank is any company that has a 'banking licence'. Usually a banking licence is granted by a country's central bank. This is what most books about the City will tell you and that is their starting point. They will also point out that the Bank of England, as the UK central bank, originally supervised banks in the City but that this role is now carried out by the Financial Services Authority. This is all technically correct but it doesn't tell you what banks do or why.

There are three types of bank: *commercial banks*, *investment banks* and *universal* (also called *conglomerate*, *integrated* or *bundled*) *banks* which are the first two put together.

The world's biggest banks now do both – commercial and investment banking – so what I am about to describe is a historical distinction that no longer applies. However, it helps you work out what the constituent bits of a big bank are, so I'm sticking with it.

1. COMMERCIAL BANKS

These are what you and I regard as a real bank. These take deposits from people like you and me (our monthly salary cheque for example) and they lend us money (e.g. by way of overdraft). They pay us measly amounts of interest on money we deposit with them and charge us usurious rates of interest on any money we borrow. They keep the difference (this is called the *margin* or *turn*). In the UK we call such banks *high street banks* or *clearers* (this latter because they clear cheques). They make billions of pounds a year by this simple activity. It's not hard to see why: you get 1% on any cash balances with your bank and you pay, say, 6% on any overdraft or loan. The margin or turn is 5%.

By the way, these banks don't just lend our money. As mentioned earlier, they borrow money from each other and lend it and they do this on the interbank market. The rate they charge each other is called LIBOR (London Interbank Offered Rate). For European banks that use the euro the LIBOR equivalent is called EURIBOR.

Funnily enough, from an accounting point of view, the deposits that banks have are *liabilities* (they have to pay them back to us when we ask). But the money that banks lend are *assets* (loans that are recorded in their books as assets). A bank is not going to make much profit unless it lends out the money deposited with it. So it follows that if everyone who has money on deposit with a bank went and asked for their money back at the same time, it wouldn't be able to pay them back. If this happens it is called a *run on the bank*. It's what happened with Northern Rock, hence the lines of people outside branches. When that happens, central banks step in to provide *liquidity* – money to prevent the banking system suffering *financial meltdown*. This is why central banks are sometimes referred to as *lenders of last resort*. They provide money to banks through what is called the 'discount window'.

Commercial banks lend both to individuals and to companies and governments. Lending to people is *retail banking* while lending to businesses and governments is *wholesale banking*. Incidentally, pawnbroking (lending on the security of pledged goods) was started in Italy in the fifteenth century by monks keen to combat usury (lending in return for interest). It remains an active part of many Italian banks' retail business. And while we're on things Italian, the term 'bankrupt' comes from 'banca rotta': when an Italian banker went bust in the middle ages the bench he sat on would be broken up. They came over from Lombardy, hence Lombard Street in the City.

2. INVESTMENT BANKS

The second type of bank is the investment bank. Be warned! Originally, the one thing these banks did not do was invest! In fact, they do two things:
- The underwriting and distribution of bond and share issues – this is called *primary market activity*
- The buying and selling of securities (bonds and shares) once they've been issued – this is called *secondary market activity*

Distribution and underwriting

Investment banks help companies and governments raise money. But their key role is *distribution* and *underwriting* the issue of securities. Underwriting was discussed in Chapter 3 and the mechanics are explored in Chapter 8. Distribution is the activity of finding buyers for securities – usually institutional investors and other banks. All of this primary market activity is designed to get brand new securities issued. It is, for this reason, also called *origination*.

Secondary market activity

Secondary market activity focuses on trading securities already in issue. It embraces:

- *Market making* which is the activity of being prepared to buy and sell a particular security: an investment bank may promise an issuer that, in return for getting the mandate to underwrite and distribute its bonds, the bank will make a market in them, i.e. be prepared to buy and sell them.
  This way anyone who buys the bonds knows they can sell them again – which will encourage them to buy them in the first place. And anyone who may want to buy them knows where to get them from.
- *Proprietary trading* which is where the bank buys and sells bonds for its own account, putting its own capital at risk to do so.
- *Trading* which is the generic term for secondary market activity and covers proprietary trading, market making and dealing in bonds on behalf of others (acting as a broker or intermediary).

There's no magic in these terms except that traders tend to have different specialisms so they see these as different activities whereas outside observers don't.

Investment banks are US in origin. Many of them developed their underwriting, distribution and trading expertise from acting as brokers. Imagine that in the 1850s there was massive need for capital as companies expanded across the States. At the same time, such a vast country suffered from a lack of communication. So every major city had its own stock exchange and brokers had branch offices all over the place to reach and serve investors.

Principal investment and private equity

Investment banks never used to invest, in the sense of using their own money. They do now, whether it's trading for their own account (*proprietary trading*) or acquiring big stakes in businesses (*principal investment*) which, if they do it to help a client company take over a target (by buying part of that target), is called *merchant banking*, not to be confused with UK merchant banks.

They also get involved in *private equity* where an investment bank will raise funds from institutional investors to buy businesses (and put in some money of its own). Where these businesses are public companies, these deals are called *public-to-private*.

This provided them with the ability to underwrite and distribute, by having close contact with a wide spread of investors. But those investors would only buy securities if they knew they could sell them in the future. So brokers had to provide buy-back facilities. This is why many US investment banks were originally brokers. The most famous exception is **Goldman Sachs** which used its knowledge of markets and its skill at corporate finance (especially M&As) to make its name.

GLASS-STEAGALL: WHY DIFFERENT BANKS DEVELOPED

The distinction between commercial and investment banks stems from the Great Crash in the US in 1929. Banks used deposits to buy shares. When the share market collapsed they were unable to pay back their depositors, there was a massive run on the banking system and banks went bust. The Great Crash heralded the Depression of the 1930s.

To prevent this happening again, the US passed a piece of legislation known as *Glass-Steagall*, which separated commercial banking (taking deposits and lending) from investment banking (underwriting, distributing and trading securities). Banks could be one or the other but not both. A case in point was US bank JP Morgan. Before Glass-Steagall it combined all of its activities under the one name. As a result of Glass-Steagall it split: JP Morgan retained the commercial banking activity (now known as JPMorgan Chase); Morgan Stanley was set up to do investment banking and became a separate (investment) bank; while the bank's trust activities (looking after money for investors) was spun off into Morgan Guaranty. One Morgan name: three separate banks.

This separation of banks was overseen by the Securities and Exchange Commission (the SEC) in the US. If a bank wasn't sure whether what it was proposing to do contravened Glass-Steagall, it would write to the SEC and ask it. If the SEC thought what was proposed was OK, it would reply with a *No Action letter* ('If you do this, we will take no action') and these established precedents that gradually blurred the boundaries between commercial and investment banking activities.

Glass-Steagall was eventually repealed in 1999 after lobbying by banks on both sides of the divide: investment banks argued that they needed access to more capital (which commercial banks obtain through deposit-taking); commercial banks argued that more of what they did touched the securities market (for instance through securitisation – see Chapter 14). Both argued that the financial system was now sufficiently sophisticated and regulators sufficiently close to the banks they regulated (helped by instant electronic communication and data processing) to make such impediments to banking business unnecessary, outdated and a thing of the past. Ha ha. In the last, pre-credit crunch, 2007 edition of this book, I wrote:

'This [the dismantling of Glass-Steagall] has prompted greater regulation to:
(1) prevent conflicts of interest, which has prompted the need for *compliance officers* in banks to make sure their banks remain on the right side of the regulations; and
(2) supervise bank risk-taking. Bankers – especially in investment banks – routinely use highly sophisticated computer programs to track the markets, to model risk and to safeguard their positions (this activity is called *VAR analysis* – value-at-risk analysis).

All this means that the world of banking is now more complex and regulators need to be much more responsive and flexible to market conditions.'

To misquote Bob Dylan: 'We were so much older then, we're younger than that now.'

3. UNIVERSAL, INTEGRATED OR CONGLOMERATE BANKS

These days the largest banks in the world do everything. They are commercial banks, merchant banks (see a few pages on) and investment banks all rolled into one (though usually kept as separate businesses, which is why you still need to know what each type of bank does). This has come about because:

- The distinction between commercial and investment banking has been swept away
- Merchant banks have been taken over. US investment banks overtook UK merchant banks because they had more capital (money) with which to underwrite flotations and bond issues. They also had additional expertise in the distribution and trading of securities. They were thus able to do these primary and secondary market activities more actively and more cheaply. The merchant banks were smaller and lacked capital. They could not compete.

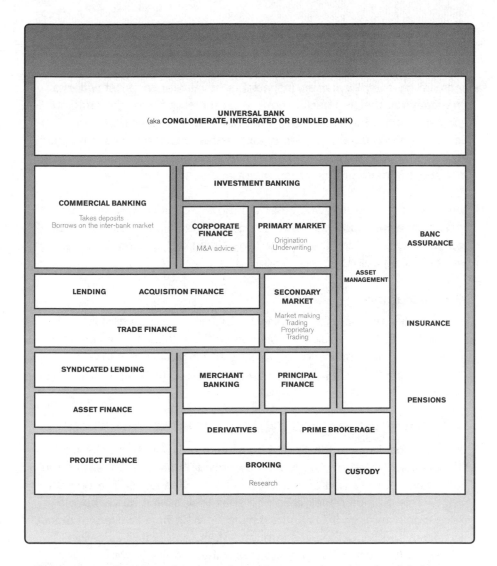

This schematic shows how a universal or conglomerate bank brings together commercial and investment banking activities with broking, fund management and bancassurance.

Universal or conglomerate banks have emerged over the last decade or so, prompted by *consolidation* in the banking industry (meaning that banks have taken each other over, leading to a smaller number of bigger banks – yes, banks are companies in their own right: why can't they take each other over?). This has been brought about by the need for *more and more capital* – the more capital a bank has to (1) lend and (2) underwrite, distribute and trade securities, the more dominant its market position will become. That in turn is a reflection of the need for *greater investment in technology* (banks are hungry guzzlers of computer systems), itself driven by the need to use computers to track and model increasingly *complex markets* (especially derivatives), to assist with *risk management* (helping banks know and understand what their trading exposures are). Big banks have achieved *economies of scale*, for instance in bearing the burden of increasing regulation. Finally, it's been enabled by *deregulation*, as banks have increasingly been allowed to engage in a more diverse range of activities.

All of which meant that when markets turned, banks hardly knew what risks they were exposed to and, being so tightly enmeshed with each other because of their trading activities, when one collapsed they all started falling like dominoes.

Bancassurance

Some banks also offer fund management, insurance and pension provision – activities usually associated with institutional investors (see Chapter 9). The combination of banking and insurance is called *bancassurance*. Leading European banks have been at the forefront of this, hence the term.

4. MERCHANT BANKS AND 'MERCHANT BANKING'

Merchant banks were the old UK equivalent of US investment banks. They helped UK exporters get paid by providing *trade finance* (through letters of credit – a sort of endorsed bill of exchange: see box on next page). This prompted their clients to seek their advice on (1) how to raise money through IPOs and equity issues, (2) how to use that money to take over other companies through M&As (both activities called *corporate finance*) and (3) how to invest their profits – which is why merchant banks such as **Flemings** and **Schroders** developed strong *fund management* arms (see Chapter 9). Flemings is now part of **JPMorgan Chase**. Schroders still exists but as a fund manager, not a merchant bank. They have largely disappeared because they were too small and lacked capital to compete in underwriting share issues. Instead they are the corporate finance arms of the biggest universal banks. However, investment banks use the term 'merchant banking' where the bank will use its own capital (money) to take a major stake on its own account in, say, an M&A deal.

Bills of exchange: the origins of merchant banking

A *bill of exchange* is an IOU under which a company (the buyer or 'drawer') agrees to pay the seller ('drawee') a given sum of money at some point in the future – usually three months ahead. It's a sort of post-dated cheque. To make it more acceptable, a bill of exchange might be *endorsed* (guaranteed) by prominent merchants. This is how merchants became merchant banks, known as 'accepting houses'.

Bills of exchange are similar to *bankers' acceptances*, which are also IOUs issued by companies to banks in return for short-term loans. The banks resell these IOUs in the market at a discount but guarantee payment.

Private banks developed by buying bills of exchange at a discount to face value and paying with their own banknotes (this was before the Bank of England obtained its monopoly to print banknotes). These bills were either held to maturity or sold in the *discount market* and brokers developed to match buyers and sellers in return for a commission. By the mid-1800s these brokers had developed into *discount houses*, which funded their holdings of bills by borrowing from banks. This was the origin of what are called, strangely, the *money markets* (they don't trade money, they trade short-term IOUs) – see Chapter 11.

Trade finance: how merchant banks began

Imagine I'm a wool grower in the north in, say, 1850. I want to export my wool. I have a buyer in New York. But I don't want to load my wool on the ship that's going to take it across the Atlantic unless I know for sure that I am going to be paid. Equally, my buyer is not going to send over the money until he's had sight of the wool. Impasse. What to do?

This is where our respective banks step in. I put my wool on the boat and give my bank the documents confirming that the wool has been loaded and that it is of the right quality (I get an independent valuer to inspect it, for a fee). At the same time my buyer puts on deposit with his bank in New York the cost of the wool. His bank tells my bank that they have the money. My bank tells his bank that my bank has the documents. All systems go! (You can see why they became known as 'merchant banks'.)

I wave the ship goodbye and my buyer's bank then tells my bank that it is holding the money to the order of my bank; and my bank tells it that my bank is holding the documents to its order. So the money is now 'owned' by my bank and the documents are now 'owned' by the New York bank. Deal done.

In practice the New York bank would issue a note for the money, usually payable in three months' time. This IOU is called a *letter of credit*. My bank could hold on to this L/C for three months then present it to the New York bank for payment. Or my bank could sell the L/C to someone else and get immediate payment now. My bank wouldn't get the full face value: the buyer of the L/C would, effectively, be giving my bank a three-month loan; and it would have to go to the trouble of getting payment on the L/C off the New York bank. So it might give my bank 95% of the face value. The remaining 5% would be three months' interest plus payment for its trouble.

The *à forfait* market

This market for second-hand letters of credit is called the *à forfait market* and this is the basis of the international market in what is called *trade finance*. It's a form of factoring. Factoring is where a bank buys a company's receivables for immediate cash: so, let's say, I sell lots of widgets but I don't want to have to wait for my customers to pay or chase up those that don't. What I want is the cash now – for instance, to enhance my cashflow. So I sell those debts to my bank for, say, 90% of their value. I get 90 pence in the pound immediately for no hassle and the bank gets the other 10% for chasing up the debts and, also, as interest on the 90% between the time it pays that money to me and when it gets paid by my customers. A lot of businesses use factoring – it's a specialist area of banking in its own right.

Just as an aside, you may well have used a letter of credit (one for immediate value) without realising it. If you go to the US and take **American Express** traveller's cheques with you, denominated in dollars, you can use them as money in many big stores in Manhattan, without having to change them into actual dollars.

WHAT DOES THE FUTURE HOLD FOR BANKING?

Bankers face their own worst nightmare. They have always tended to hate government interference on the basis that capitalism is about channelling investment to the most efficient and deserving businesses, which is something best left to the private sector. How ironic then that following the *systemic* (systemic means market-wide or universal) failure of banks (1) governments had to bail them out by guaranteeing their deposits, then taking on their most toxic assets, then *nationalising* them (taking them into public ownership) while at the same time (2) banks persisted in withdrawing credit lines (overdrafts) from otherwise good businesses so causing them cashflow crises and, ultimately, to go bust. Maybe banks will be forced to retrench to their core activities of lending (see the next chapter) and underwriting (the chapter after that) and their most egregious excesses will be subject to a new era of modesty and restraint. After all, bankers are supposed to be prudent, rather than risk-takers, especially with taxpayers' money.

DON'T BANK ON IT

As you read this it is already out of date. Before the credit crunch the big thing in banking was how big commercial banks were buying up (US) investment banks and (UK) merchant banks and brokers (see Chapter 10) to create global universal bank power houses. This table shows the current bank (left hand column) and the types of bank that were taken over or merged to form it.

Bank	Commercial bank	US investment bank or broker	UK merchant bank or broker
Citigroup	Citibank	Salomon Brothers Smith Barney	Schroders (part)
JPMorgan Chase	JPMorgan Chase Manhattan (inc Manufacturers Hanover and Chemical Bank)		Robert Fleming Schroders (part) Cazenove (part)
UBS (Union Bank of Switzerland)	Swiss Bank Corp	PaineWebber Kidder Peabody	SG Warburg
Deutsche Bank	Deutsche Bankers Trust	Alex Brown	Morgan Grenfell Phillips & Drew
HSBC (originally Hongkong and Shanghai Banking Corporation)	Midland (UK)		Samuel Montagu James Capel

But this has been superseded by the effects of the credit crunch:

US investment banks

Lehman Brothers	Went bust
Bear Stearns	Rescued by merging into JPMorgan Chase
Merrill Lynch	Rescued by merging into Bank of America
Goldman Sachs Morgan Stanley	Both became US bank holding companies (this is what US commercial banks are and means deposits are federally insured) – in order to get US federal backing otherwise no one would have traded with them.

UK banks

Lloyds Banking Group	Lloyds TSB was prompted by the UK government to take over HBOS (a previous merger between Halifax Building Society and Bank of Scotland). Doing so almost bankrupted Lloyds so the government had to bail it out and take it over.
RBS (Royal Bank of Scotland)	Had taken over UK clearing bank NatWest and was doing well but bought Dutch bank ABN Amro unwisely and posted highest UK corporate loss ever of almost £25 billion. UK government bailed it out and ended up owning roughly three-quarters. Outgoing chairman Sir Fred Goodwin infamously retired aged 50 with a £16 million pension pot paying £650,000 a year.

As big banks have stumbled and collapsed, smaller banks have emerged as unlikely heroes for doing nothing more than banks should do: being sensible. Two that stand out are: UK bank Standard

Chartered which has extensive commercial banking operations in emerging markets in Asia and Africa and by simply sticking to the knitting seemed a miraculous paragon of banking good sense; and Spain's Banco Santander which wouldn't know a toxic tranche if it was hit in the face by one. Santander was helped by two aspects of the Spanish banking regime: (1) refusal to allow off balance sheet funding (such as securitisation and structured investment vehicles); (2) the requirement to increase your capital cushion if you are expanding very quickly. Simple solutions. Why didn't the rest of the banking world think of that?

Just to show the measure of the credit crunch, banks weren't the only financial institutions caught up in it. AIG, the world's foremost insurance entity, and at one point worth $40 billion, was crippled by the credit crunch, having lost twice that amount (at the time the biggest corporate loss in US history) and had to be bailed out by the US government with plans to break it up.

Chapter 7

MORE ON
COMMERCIAL BANKING

SPEED-READ SUMMARY

- The basis of commercial bank lending is matched funding – lending banks fund themselves in the inter-bank market and charge the borrower on a cost-plus basis

- The typical terms found in a bank loan are common to many types of funding – they include representations and warranties, financial covenants, events of default and boilerplate

- A syndicated loan is one made to the same borrower on the same terms but by more than one bank, coordinated by an arranger and a book runner, with syndicate members agreeing to share payments made by the borrower

- Acquisition finance may be used by a company undertaking a massive takeover where it needs funds at short notice to complete the acquisition, with a view to refinancing subsequently

- Project finance is a tax-efficient way of funding major pieces of plant and machinery used in a business – the bank buys and owns the equipment but as lessor leases it to the business for the equipment's useful economic life in return for rental payments

- Project finance is limited or non-recourse finance where the lending banks look to the project's eventual income stream to be repaid – used to fund complex infrastructure development in developing countries (the same techniques are used in UK PFI and PPP transactions)

In the early 2000s when markets were rising inexorably, commercial banking became the poor cousin of investment banking, securitisation (Chapter 14), the trading of derivatives (Chapter 13), private equity and hedge funds (Chapter 9). Not any more. Most bankers looking for a job wouldn't mind something steady like commercial lending.

In a sense, commercial banking is not really about the City. It isn't a trading activity which requires a market. A bank doesn't have to be in the City to lend – it can be anywhere. But although shares and bonds are still considered the exciting stuff, a lot of huge commercial banking deals are going on all the time and in that sense lending is a very real part of the international financial markets.

This chapter focuses on:
- *loan basics* which are common to all types of commercial banking and to bond issues
- *syndicated loans* which are the bedrock of lending to large companies
- *acquisition finance*, used in M&A deals
- *asset finance* which isn't lending at all but achieves the same aim by a different route
- *project finance* which is the basis of PFI (private finance initiative) and PPP (public-private partnerships) in the UK.

1. THE BASICS OF A LOAN

Banks don't just lend out their deposits. They also borrow money on the inter-bank market (when it's functioning as it is in more normal times).

Matched funding

In practice, when a bank knows it is going to lend an amount of money, it gets those funds in the inter-bank market and it does so by borrowing those funds for a set period – usually three months (the inter-bank market is a short-term market; banks don't want to be lending to each other for long periods – it ties up their money). So the bank borrows short and lends long and funds itself for each loan period by a matching inter-bank deposit.

This is called *matched funding*. It means that if anything goes wrong with the loan – for instance the bank gets repaid too early or gets repaid too late by the borrower – this gives the bank a problem. If the

Common banking terms

- *Overdraft* – just like a personal overdraft and repayable on demand – i.e. whenever the bank asks for it back
- *Revolving credit facility* (called a revolver) – a more sophisticated form of overdraft, it 'revolves' in the sense that the company can reborrow whatever it has repaid, i.e. it can reutilise repaid amounts – this is called a *rollover*
- *Term loan* – a loan of a fixed amount for a fixed period
- *Letter of credit facility* – used in less sophisticated markets where the bank issues a letter of credit (a bit like a cheque drawn on the bank) that the company can borrow against
- *Drawdown* – the procedure for, and moment of, actually borrowing money under the loan

Repayment is usually by way of:
- *Amortisation* – principal repaid by equal instalments
- *Balloon* – if the amount of the repayment increases with each repayment
- *Bullet* – all in one go on maturity

If the borrower is in breach of its obligations the bank can *accelerate* the loan (demand immediate repayment).

---

bank is repaid too early, it is sitting on funds on which it is paying interest in the inter-bank market; if it is repaid too late, it isn't able to repay its own inter-bank loan. Both scenarios are painful to bankers. So a lot of the mechanics in loan agreements are about the borrower indemnifying (making good) any losses the bank incurs should either of these things happen.

What this all means is that in normal times banks lend on a *cost-plus basis* (LIBOR plus a margin) so any increased costs are passed on to the borrower (which is also why banks prefer to lend at a floating rate so that the risk of interest rate increases is on the borrower). In other words, a bank will work out the cost to it of making the funds available to the borrower and add a profit margin.

Yield protection

Given matched funding and the bank's cost-plus approach to lending, you can begin to see why a loan agreement tends to look a bit one-sided and seems to cover the bank against any eventuality. Typical terms include:
- *Increased costs clause* – the bank passes on to the borrower all of the risks associated with the bank's obtaining of funding in the inter-

bank market, including the impact of (1) increased tax and (2) increased regulatory constraints

- *Capital adequacy indemnity* – if the bank has to increase the amount of capital it must maintain with respect to the loan, that cost is passed on – viz. if any change in the bank's prescribed capital ratio reduces the rate of return.
- *Eurodollar disaster clause* – if the bank cannot get matching deposits or LIBOR cannot be fixed; this is a hangover from the days when the Eurodollar market was in its infancy and people thought it might be closed down (it's called the Eurodollar market because much of this lending is in dollars that are outside the US, in Europe)
- *Broken funding indemnity* – if the borrower prepays or pays too late so that the bank's matched funding is broken, the borrower pays any increased costs incurred by the bank

These clauses are sometimes called *yield protection* clauses because they protect the return ('yield') the bank thinks it should be getting from the deal.

Just a note on capital adequacy. On the premise that only a fraction of all depositors will want their money back at any one time, the majority of deposits made with a bank are lent out by that bank to borrowers. So, to guard against systemic (market-wide) shock, regulators require banks to carry a cushion of regulatory capital – this is money from depositors or which the bank borrows which it's not allowed to do anything with.

This is part of the global regulatory framework for banks known as Basel 2 – after the Swiss town where the central bankers' committee meets. Banks pay a lot of attention to these requirements because the greater the cushion of (effectively dead) capital they have to carry, the greater the cost of doing business. This is what prompted the beginnings of securitisation (Chapter 14).

Security (not to be confused with securities)

Commercial banks will always seek security – i.e. other sources of funds that they can tap if the borrower defaults. Security can take the form of a *charge* over the borrower's assets. If the borrower is a subsidiary of a group, there may be a *guarantor* that guarantees payment of the interest and repayment of the principal. The guarantor is usually a parent company hence the guarantee being known as a *parent company guarantee*.

Typical loan structure

The bank and borrower agree a deal. The bank goes through its internal *credit approval process*, involving *due diligence* (examining the borrower's financial standing). The borrower may require the bank to sign a *confidentiality undertaking* in respect of any sensitive information the borrower makes available to the bank.

The bank then prepares a *term sheet* summarising the deal. Both parties sign it as an agreement in principle. It isn't usually legally binding (except that if the loan doesn't go ahead the borrower agrees to pay the bank's costs). The *loan agreement* is then based on it. The bank may require *security* – a *charge* over the borrower's assets.

The loan agreement is negotiated and then signed (this is called *completion*) at which point the borrower can *draw down* the money provided it satisfies some *conditions precedent* (various *legal opinions* and *certificates* ensuring the documents are duly signed and the borrower is legally capable of borrowing).

Following *drawdown* the bank continues to *monitor* the borrower to ensure it pays the interest when due and complies with the *covenants* (promises) in the loan agreement.

Comfort letters

Where a parent company is not prepared to give a full guarantee it may nevertheless agree to confirm to the bank that, as the borrowing company's principal or sole shareholder, the parent company will keep the borrower in funds and not allow it to become insolvent. This form of assurance, stopping short of a full guarantee, is called a *comfort letter*. Depending on its terms it may or may not be enforceable.

Representations and warranties

In addition to the requirements in the box above, the borrower has to give various *representations and warranties* (statements that it promises are true). These include statements by the borrower as to its financial standing.

Making these statements forces the borrower to disclose anything untoward in a *disclosure letter* – after all, the bank is never going to be as privy to the state of the borrower's business as the borrower itself. These disclosures may affect the bank's willingness to lend. Subsequently, if these statements can't be confirmed without qualification, the borrower can't borrow (this is called *drawstop*) and, if they prove to be untrue, they allow the bank to call an *event of default*.

Financial covenants

These define the parameters within which the borrower may operate its business – especially where the loan is a *general purpose loan* and the bank doesn't know precisely what the money may be used for. They:
- enable the bank to monitor the borrower's position
- provide an early warning of financial difficulty
- enable an objective assessment *of material adverse change* (see below)
- impose a discipline on the borrower
- if breached enable the bank to *accelerate* the loan (ask for it back early)
- may be set by reference to various *financial ratios* (e.g. minimum net worth, minimum working capital, interest cover, debt-to-equity ratio, etc.).

They include (note the weird and wonderful names):
- *Negative pledge* – this prevents a borrower from pledging (i.e. mortgaging) its assets to any other creditor in preference to the bank, and so ensures the bank retains its priority over later lenders
- *Pari passu* – this is a crucial clause in a syndicated loan since it ensures that all lenders are treated the same – particularly relevant in a large syndicate (see 'sharing clause' later)
- *Restrictions on disposals* – so the borrower cannot asset strip, change its business or favour some creditors over others (by handing them assets).

Boilerplate

Finally, if that all weren't enough, there are *boilerplate* clauses, so called because you find them in all loan agreements and they provide an extra layer of safety for lending banks. They include:
- *Illegality clause* – if for any reason the bank is not allowed to make the loan (e.g. because the company is from a country that becomes off-limits as Libya, Iran and Iraq have at various times) the bank can demand early repayment
- *Force majeure* – this allows either party to suspend performance without being in breach, for circumstances (e.g. war, terrorism) beyond its control
- *Governing law* – lawyers get very fussed about this clause. It comes in two parts, one (the *jurisdiction clause*) specifying *which country's courts* can hear a dispute over the agreement, and the other (*governing law*) specifying *which country's laws* those courts have to apply when interpreting the agreement (which may not necessarily be their own). If these provisions are not included there are over-arching rules that specify which courts and laws should apply – known as *conflicts of laws*.

The above terms are common in all types of lending and the same terminology crops up in bond issues as well.

So far we've assumed that the loan is *bilateral* (i.e. two parties: the bank and the borrower). But it can also be *syndicated*.

2. SYNDICATED LENDING

When a borrower wants more than its bank is prepared to lend, the bank will rope in some other commercial banks and form a *syndicate* and the syndicate will lend to the borrower on the *same terms* using the same, single loan agreement, which all the banks sign. These terms are pretty standard and indeed the Loan Market Association (LMA) is a trade body that provides the standard documentation on which much commercial lending in the London financial markets is done. Note that we're talking international here. Most loan agreements are written under English or New York law: English because English law, like the

---

Events of default

Where a loan is not repayable on demand, the bank must have some way of (1) terminating its lending obligation and (2) accelerating repayment if the borrower fails to comply with its obligations. The *events of default* clause sets out when it can do so and is usually used to maintain its bargaining position (threatening to call in the loan, known as 'accelerating') when renegotiating. There are three types:
- *Actual default* (non-payment)
- *Non-compliance* (e.g. with financial covenants)
- *Anticipatory* (the bank thinks the borrower may become insolvent so wants to get its money back first)

Examples of events of default include:
- *Payment default* – this is an actual default – viz. non-payment of any amounts owing on the due date
- *Breach of representations, warranties, information undertakings or financial covenants* – this is non-compliance, so the bank does not have the information it needs or that information is wrong or the borrower has done something it said it wouldn't do
- *Material adverse change* (also known as MAC) – this is anticipatory and covers a significant ('material') change in the borrower's financial position, so allowing the bank to accelerate even though the borrower is not otherwise in default
- *Cross default* – this is anticipatory and is quite cunning since it says that if the borrower defaults on *any other indebtedness* (e.g. under a loan from another lender), the bank can accelerate its loan; because the likelihood is that the borrower is close to insolvency if it is in default under another agreement.

language, spread with the British Empire; New York because it is the financial capital of the world (by the way there isn't such a thing as 'American law' in the US – it is all state-specific).

There are various roles for banks to play, such as:
- *arranger* – this is the bank awarded the *mandate* (instruction to put together the loan) by the borrower. It commits to the borrower to make the loan then sells down its commitment with the help of a:
- *book runner/syndicate coordinator* (in large syndications these may be different banks) – this is the bank that actually undertakes the syndication: the arranger tells it how much exposure to the borrower the arranger wishes to retain and, therefore, what the target fund-raising is. The book runner knows which banks are interested in which types of deal, preferred size of participation and what they will demand by way of participation fees. The arranger, which has the client relationship with the borrower, may lack the book runner's knowledge of the market.

There may also be an:
- *agent* – which collects interest and repayments from the borrower and distributes them to the syndicate, monitors the borrower's financial covenants and administers waivers and amendments – for all of which the agent bank earns *arrangement fees*. Often these fees don't cover the administrative cost, but being close to the borrower during the loan may enable it to get a mandate in the future.

At the start of the syndication process there is usually an *information memorandum* which is a brochure about the borrower circulated to banks to 'sell' the borrower to them and persuade them to join the syndicate.

Sharing clause

In addition to the clauses outlined above, a syndicated loan will also have a *sharing clause* which says that if any bank receives a payment from the borrower, it will share that payment with the other syndicate members. This is to prevent the borrower from preferring one lender over another, for instance if the borrower has a separate bilateral loan with one of the banks.

3. ACQUISITION FINANCE

Before the recession, one of the growth areas for syndicated loans was in M&A transactions, where bank lending is called *acquisition finance* (acquisition finance is an example of an *event-driven* loan rather than general corporate lending).

As you now know, acquisitions are traditionally funded by the buyer's equity ('paper') such as a share-for-share acquisition or rights issue. But debt finance is often more attractive to:

- the target's shareholders (they get money not the buyer's shares)
- the buyer, since the costs are tax-deductible (whereas dividends are paid out of after-tax income)
- the buyer's shareholders, since any additional issue of equity may depress the buyer's earnings-per-share (since there are more shares in issue) which is a key profitability figure.

Acquisition finance may also be used in a large MBO. Where the level of debt is high, it is called a leveraged buyout (LBO) because it is highly geared or 'leveraged'. In an LBO the loan may be for less than a year with the intention that it be refinanced by a bond issue.

Market flex

The syndicated loan and bond markets are converging, using similar techniques to achieve syndication.

The loan market has borrowed what is called the *market flex* technique from the bond market − viz. the final pricing and structure are only determined after market soundings have been taken (rather than being fixed prior to syndication) and this is often built into the term sheet so the bank reserves the right to change the pricing and other key terms if

necessary to syndicate the transaction successfully. Indeed it may agree only to use *reasonable efforts* to syndicate, if it isn't sure there is an appetite in the market to lend to the borrower.

For example, in a hostile bid, a big decision for a bank is which bidding group to join so it doesn't lose out if the bidder it is backing fails to win. Besides which, many banks feel that merely being a member of a syndicate doesn't generate enough in fees.

Benefits of loan over bond issue

A loan can provide some advantages over a bond issue. It is easier for the borrower to negotiate a waiver or amendment with a syndicate of bankers than to try to alter the terms of a bond (since it won't necessarily know who the bondholders are). A loan tends to be more flexible for the bid stage of an acquisition, before the buyer's longer-term financing needs are ascertained (e.g. the buyer may in fact intend to sell off bits of the target).

Most syndicated loans are done on a best efforts basis, and the arranger makes this clear in its *offer letter* to the borrower. But in acquisition finance, the borrower will want *committed funds*. It's no good to the buyer for the bank to come back empty-handed and say, 'No one wanted to join the syndicate so you can't have the money.' The buyer has an acquisition to finance. So the bank advising on the acquisition may *underwrite* the syndicated loan process – i.e. it will commit to lend the full amount if necessary but can syndicate the debt to other banks either before or after signing. In short the arranger generally makes an *underwritten offer*.

4. ASSET FINANCE (FINANCE LEASING)

This is a banking industry in its own right. It's a way of funding the acquisition of an asset by getting the bank to buy the asset and 'lease' it to the company that wants to use it and which would otherwise have borrowed the money to buy it.

Imagine I'm Sir Richard Branson and I want to buy a 747 for my Virgin airline. Now, I can do one of two things. I can go to a bank and ask for a loan and the bank will take security over the plane by way of a charge (referred to above). Or I can do something smarter. I can get the bank to buy the plane and lease it to me. There are three advantages in doing the latter and they all translate into getting a cheaper rate of interest than I would on a loan.

The first is that the bank actually owns the plane so it feels safer than if it had a charge over the plane – which means that the deal has a lower credit risk which translates into a lower cost to me.

The second is that the bank knows what I am using the financing for (to get the use of a plane) so it isn't general bank lending where the bank has no idea what its loan may be used for. This makes the bank feel safer and, again, translates into cheaper funding for me.

Finally – and this is what makes the real difference – the bank can claim tax credits for buying the asset that I want to use. This is because the UK, like all developed economies, provides industry with tax advantages for investing in plant and machinery in order to remain competitive in international markets. These tax breaks are called *capital allowances* and they allow you to set the cost of the equipment against your profits over a number of years. Now, companies can have strong cashflow

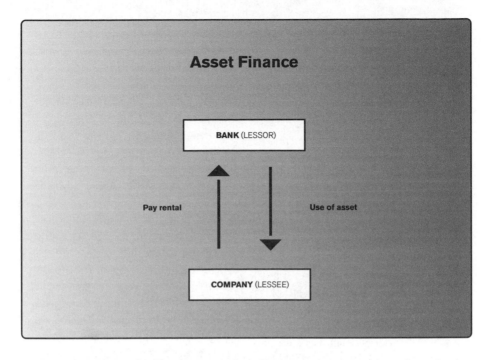

Asset Finance

BANK (LESSOR)

Pay rental   Use of asset

COMPANY (LESSEE)

without much profit. So these capital allowances may not be of much use to a company. But a bank – at least in good times – may make a substantial profit on which it has to pay tax. So spending part of that profit by buying an asset which it can then lease will reduce the taxable profit and so therefore the amount of tax it has to pay. The point is that the bank will pass on part of the benefit of those allowances which, again, reduces the cost to Branson.

Here's how it works. Branson chooses the plane, the bank buys it and then leases it to Branson under an agreement called a *finance lease*. Branson pays an amount by way of rental, every three, six or 12 months. Now this *rental* comprises two things: principal and interest – the principal being the cost of the plane and the interest being the interest on that principal. This is because a finance lease lasts as long as the *useful economic life of the asset*. In the case of a plane it's about 15 years. So the lease term is for 15 years and over that period Branson pays rental so that at the end of the 15 years the bank has been *paid out*: it's recovered the cost of the plane plus interest on that cost over the intervening 15 years. And, because of the capital allowances and the fact that the bank is the owner, it is cheaper for Branson than if he took out a loan.

Note that Branson does not actually own the plane. But that doesn't

What happens at the end of the lease

At the end of the lease term (the 15 years), the bank has been paid out and really has no further financial interest in the plane. One of two things can happen. First, Branson can continue to lease the plane for a *secondary term* (a further period) at what is called a *peppercorn* (i.e. nothing or, symbolically, a £1). Or, second, Branson can sell the plane as agent for the bank. Now whatever Branson gets for it is going to be a reflection of (1) how good a deal he makes and (2) the state of the plane (a 15-year-old Virgin 747 is probably too tatty for Branson to want to keep using, but there are no doubt several airlines who would welcome a 15-year-old 747 carefully maintained by Virgin).

In other words, whatever the plane gets on the second-hand market is down to him. So he should get to keep the proceeds of the sale – which he does. But it has to be done in a slinky way otherwise the Revenue will say, 'Ah, you, Sir Richard, owned the plane all along so we are going to withdraw the capital allowances from the bank.' This would be a disaster since the whole financial basis of the lease would come crashing down.

Instead, to avoid that, Branson sells the plane *as agent for the bank* and the bank *then remits the proceeds to the lessee by way of rebate of rental* – in other words Branson gets a reduction in the rental he has paid. Of course, he can't get 100% of the sale proceeds otherwise the taxman will say, again, that the lease is a sham. So it's usually structured so that he gets 90% of the proceeds – not all, but the bulk. It's just a form of words but can make a difference of millions of pounds.

matter to a business. What matters is that it has the sole, exclusive, economic use of the plane. That is, in its eyes, the same as ownership. Businesses are different from you and me. We like to own our stuff. They just like to use it. (Note also that when I talk about Branson here I really mean Virgin).

Now, a couple of things about the lease itself. It's different from a loan agreement because the bank (which is called the *lessor*) isn't so fussed about the financial standing of the *lessee* (Branson) since it owns the plane. In fact what it is concerned about – and these are major terms in any finance lease – is that the plane is properly maintained (*maintenance and repairing covenants*), that Branson doesn't try to sell the plane or use it as security for another loan (*covenant against assignment, sale or alienation* – alienation here means disposal) and that, if the plane falls out of the sky, the bank is properly covered by insurance (*covenant to insure*) and any *insurance proceeds* are paid directly to it. All these covenants are promises by Branson to do what is required. Failure to perform any of them is an event of default, allowing the bank to put a pilot in the plane and bring it back from wherever it is. The bank can then just sell it as the legal owner.

The availability of the capital allowances is so critical that if for any reason during the course of the lease they are withdrawn or become unavailable, the lease is collapsed and turned into a loan from the bank, with Branson becoming the owner of the plane.

Finance lease v operating lease

Finance leasing should not be confused with *operating leases*. If you rent a car when you go on holiday, that is an operating lease: it's not for the car's useful economic life and you certainly don't expect to maintain it or insure it. The hire company does that. In fact if it goes wrong you just call them up for a replacement. And once you've returned it, the hire company leases it to another holiday-maker, and so on. Funnily enough, the hire company may be paying for its fleet of hire cars by leasing the fleet of cars from a bank under a finance lease.

Double dips

Finance leasing is a huge industry that spans the globe. Clever lawyers and bankers can structure deals so that the bank is treated as owner in one country and the lessee in another, so that two sets of tax allowances become available (this is called a *double dip* and is a battleground between tax authorities and bankers; as soon as one double dip opportunity is closed, the bankers and their lawyers discover another; it's great fun).

Virtually anything can be leased provided it is used in a business context. This includes oil rigs and ships on the one hand and audio recordings and films on the other. Leasing can be complex with structures involving subleases. There are sub-industries – for instance the financing of ships (*ship finance*) and aircraft (*aviation finance*) with magazines and books devoted to the subject.

Notice to third parties

Lessors put notices on leased assets to warn others who the real owner is. This is to stop lessees from trying to sell or mortgage leased assets. These notices can be found in railway carriages and in the cockpits of aircraft. These signs are meant to give notice to any *third-party purchasers for value* (as the lawyers put it) that the plane isn't the airline's to sell and so to put them on notice.

However, in aircraft leases these notices don't appear on the engines, so the bank never gets back exactly the same engines that were on the plane 15 years before. This is because each engine is like a Formula One car: just a collection of bits of metal, nuts and bolts that spend more time in pieces than in a single assembly but which come together magically for the race or flight. So airlines operate engine pools.

5. PROJECT FINANCE

Project financings can be immensely complex deals that take years to come to fruition. What makes them different from standard commercial lending is that they are often called *limited recourse lending* or *non-recourse lending* meaning that the lenders will look only to the project to repay the loan, not the borrower. In other words, the project is evaluated on the basis of whether it alone can sustain and pay back the investment and not the assets of the borrower (which, being a special purpose vehicle established just for the project probably doesn't have any other assets anyway). This is because the governments of many of the developing countries where project financing takes place are themselves heavily in debt and banks don't want to lend them even more.

What makes a project economically viable is the cash it will generate once it comes on-stream. This alone will service and repay the debt incurred to build it. The banks, therefore, are concerned with the risks of the cashflow being disrupted – they are lending on the cashflow of a future business that consists of a single income-stream.

Project financing is used to create infrastructure in developing parts of the world, such as natural resource projects (e.g. power stations), infrastructure improvements (e.g. ports, airport, roads, bridges and tunnels) or new industrial plant projects (such as paper mills and aluminium smelters).

Who is involved

The parties include:
- a *special purpose company* – the SPC is the company through which the project is undertaken and built, which owns the project and is the project borrower

- the *project sponsors* – these are often multinational companies keen to get the project off the ground, often the contractors that build the project or supply heavy plant (such as turbines) to it. There may also be separate equity investors in the project
- the *banks* funding the project
- the host *government* in whose country the project is being built, which will either buy the project's output or guarantee the purchase of it. It may also, as part of a concession agreement, agree to provide other infrastructure support (for instance, build a road to the project)
- *export credit agencies* – every developed country has an ECA which helps to finance the sale of its exports to other markets. ECAs will help companies from their country to participate in major projects by providing financing to the project on preferential terms (called *co-financings* where funding comes from commercial banks as well as ECAs). ECAs are usually state-owned. They include **US Exim** (the US Export – Import Bank), **Jexim** (the Japanese equivalent) and **COFACE** (France). The UK's used to have the quaint name of **Export Credit Guarantee Department** but it has been part-privatised and is now **Gerling NCM**
- *multilateral lending agencies* (e.g. **World Bank, Asian Development Bank** and **EBRD** – the **European Bank for Reconstruction and Development**) – these are like ECAs but have a supranational remit so will become involved in projects that offer major infrastructural benefits in emerging markets. Their involvement (by providing finance or guarantees) often increases the willingness of commercial banks to participate.

A major source of complexity in a project financing is the time it takes to come on-stream. Funds will go into the project during its *construction* phase and will only be recouped during its *operation*. The lending banks will be keen throughout to ensure that the funds are not diverted for other purposes and that the money earned by the project once it has come on-stream is not diverted away from the lenders. This last is often achieved by having *offshore escrow accounts* (basically, trust accounts) into which the income generated by the project is paid and over which the banks have a charge, to ensure they are paid out first.

Step-in rights

During the project's construction the banks will want *step-in rights* to take over the project if it goes over budget to ensure it is finished. There may well be an *insurance policy* (called a *completion bond*) to cover

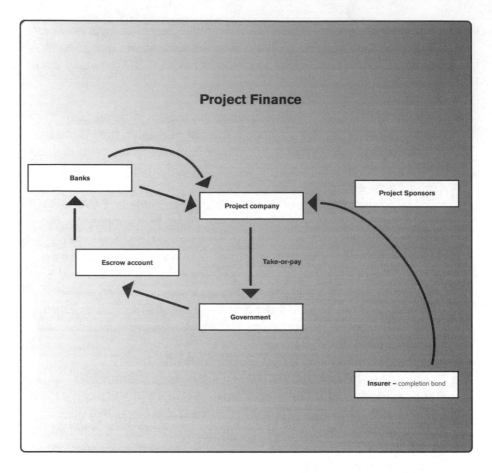

Project Finance

Banks

Project Sponsors

Project company

Escrow account

Take-or-pay

Government

Insurer – completion bond

completion risk – the risk that the project does not come on-stream at all or only at an inflated price – and *political risk* – the risk that the project may be sequestered or nationalised by the government where the project is located or by a successor government. There will be a *long-stop date* by which the project should be completed and a *drop-dead date* by when the project must come on-stream to meet the debt service and repayment projections.

Most projects are built on a *turn-kcy* basis – after the builder has finished, the project is ready to go (e.g. like starting a car) and the lenders to be repaid.

Offtake or take-or-pay

The key to the financing is how the borrowing will be repaid. This is done through an *offtake contract* where the government agrees to buy the project's output (such as electricity) to distribute to its citizens. Not all projects have an offtake agreement – for instance a motorway operating on a toll basis simply earns money from the users, while an oil project will usually have its product sold in the open market. But where the only customer will be the state or a state agency, the offtake arrangement will be critical since it will be the sole source of the project's income and, therefore, viability – which is why the agreement is also called a *take-or-pay* contract (meaning that the project output has to be paid for whether or not it is used).

UK PFI and PPP deals

In the UK, project financing techniques have been used under the banner of PFI (private finance initiatives) and PPP (private-public partnerships) where hospitals, schools, prisons and other fixed assets used in the public sector are financed privately. They are paid for by the government but the cost is spread over the next 20 or 30 years (i.e. their useful economic life). The idea is that these assets should be funded long-term and not be treated as part of the government's current borrowing requirement. In this way the costs are removed from the government's balance sheet.

Project finance – good or bad?

Project financing can attract unusual people, people prepared to devote years of their lives to a single transaction in an inhospitable part of the world. Some are driven by the belief that they are doing good, creating economic infrastructure in countries that need it. Equally, cynics say that the role of the ECAs is to ensure that industry from their countries finds new markets building projects in parts of the world that may not need them – white elephants in other words. The answer probably lies somewhere in between.

Chapter 8

MORE ON
INVESTMENT BANKING

SPEED-READ SUMMARY

- Investment banks originally underwrote and distributed bond issues (primary market activity) and then traded them in the secondary markets, as broker, market maker or for their own account

- An investment bank acts as lead manager of a bond issue, assembles a syndicate of co-managers, is responsible for due diligence of the issuer and for documenting the issue, and may also act as fiscal agent

- Privatisations through IPOs have led to a convergence between the underwriting and distribution of bond and share issues

- Bookbuilding and placings are ways of distributing securities

- Vendor placings are used to provide the target's shareholders with a cash alternative in an M&A deal

- Now investment banks do much more than securities and distribution, most involving their own capital, such as proprietary trading and principal investment – it is this which arguably has led to some of the major bank failures seen in the recession

As we saw in Chapter 6, investment banks originally did two things:
- They *arranged and underwrote* the issue of bonds for companies and governments (known as primary market activity) and
- They made *markets* in those bonds and *traded* them (secondary market activity).

USING THEIR OWN CAPITAL

Then they started to do much more. Their primary activity extended to include underwriting *share issues* by companies, and the method of underwriting share and bond issues converged. For example, a bank might undertake a *bought deal* where, as a condition of getting the company's mandate, it buys all of the company's securities on offer and then distributes them.

Since a major reason for raising money was often to take over another company (M&A), investment banks seized this *corporate finance advisory role* from merchant banks (most of which disappeared). Investment banks also provided *acquisition finance* – short-term funding for M&A deals – that might more traditionally have been seen as a commercial banking activity (see the last chapter). Bought deals and acquisition finance rely on a bank using its own capital (money).

PROPRIETARY TRADING, PRIME BROKERAGE AND PRINCIPAL INVESTMENT

This was also true of secondary market activity where investment banks bought and sold securities for their own account and not just as agent or broker for others. This is called *proprietary trading*. They would buy whole portfolios of securities from institutional investors in what are called *block trades*. They would design and sell sophisticated financial instruments tailored to a particular customer's needs. These were often *derivatives* (see Chapter 13) and were provided OTC (*over-the-counter*) meaning that these instruments are not traded on an exchange. They also provided instruments and services to *hedge funds* (see the next chapter) through what is called *prime brokerage*, which might involve securities lending and liquidity provision (this last just means lending them money short-term). All of this required capital which is why the merchant banks couldn't compete.

Investment banks didn't stop there. Apart from helping others buy businesses, they did so themselves. These elaborate buyouts were essentially *private equity* deals but, when funded by a bank's own capital, became *principal investment* (and, yes, you can argue that this is an investment activity except that banks usually bought businesses in order to merge them with others and sell them or float them – hardly long-term investment!). Investment banks also raised private equity funds from institutional investors in order to stage public-to-private buyouts.

PART OF THE FLOW

In this way investment banks lay at the heart of the financial markets. Their trading businesses – in bonds, equities and foreign exchange – were 'flow' businesses in which they might make 'buy' and 'sell' prices for clients and other market participants in order to gain an early indication of developing trends, which an investment bank can exploit by committing some of its own capital.

Committing capital is a *risk business*. Banks kept this degree of risk under constant review (remember the reference in Chapter 6 to VAR?). Even so, they were heavily dependent on the state of the financial markets and the world economy in general. It was sometimes a hairy ride, but it was a lucrative one. It was also a business that could lead to *conflicts of interest* with clients: a bank could find itself competing with clients for investment opportunities.

And then the sub-prime credit crunch revealed that many investment banks had stuffed their balance sheets full of toxic tranches and securitised home loans that became worthless. Banks themselves started to implode and become worthless in turn. A little over a year ago in this part of the book I wrote:

'Regulators – whom we'll be meeting in Chapter 12 – are concerned with both risk and rip-offs. They don't want banks to go bust, because of the chaos this would cause world markets and economies, and they don't want them ripping off customers. But so great are investment banks' principal and proprietary activities that some market observers are now describing banks like Goldman Sachs as little more than private equity or hedge funds in their own right. What these banks aim for is the 'triple play' – being adviser, funding arranger and co-investor in relation to the same deal.'

What a difference a year makes.

Whatever happens in the post-credit-crunch world of banking where most of the financial system seems to be in the (dead) hands of government, I can't help feeling that the traditional commercial banking role of lending (last chapter) or the investment banking role of underwriting and distributing securities (this chapter) will go on.

So in the rest of this chapter we will unpick the mechanics of the core investment banking role: underwriting and securities distribution.

The bulk of these issues are new issues – companies are forever making new issues, *retiring debt* and replacing it with a new issue. Although the same techniques are now used to underwrite and distribute shares, the bond markets are where these techniques originated.

UNDERWRITING BOND ISSUES

After the company (the *issuer*) has appointed the investment bank and discussed with it the terms of the issue, the company then issues the bank with a formal *mandate letter* or *term sheet* (usually drafted by the bank), setting out the basic terms of the issue and authorising the bank as *lead manager* to announce the issue and invite *co-managers* to form a syndicate to distribute the issue. The *lead manager's* role is similar to that of the arranger in a syndicated loan. It is responsible for arranging the bond issue and managing the entire issue process, advising the issuer on the structure and timing of the issue. If the issue is to be listed (see below) it acts as sponsor.

The lead manager then *launches* the issue by making a public announcement (usually via screen-based information providers such as Reuters and Bloomberg) and *syndicates* it by providing to *co-managers* (other banks) details of the likely price of the bonds, a description of the issuer and the issue timetable and asking them to confirm within 24 hours (1) that they will join the syndicate and (2) how much of the issue they are prepared to take up (the maximum value of bonds for which they are prepared to *subscribe*).

DISTRIBUTION NETWORK

Each co-manager will be aiming to sell the bond to investors, and so provide a *distribution network* for the issue. Through their contacts the co-managers will *build a book* of potential investors by selling the merits of the issue to them and getting informal indications of their likely take-up. This indication of interest will determine how much a co-manager is

Bookbuilding and the bought deal

Two methods of *origination* (the primary market activity of helping companies and governments launch issues) are *bookbuilding* and the *bought deal.*

Bookbuilding was developed in the US, pioneered in the international equity markets, and is increasingly used in the UK market for domestic issues.

In a traditional underwriting, the price is fixed only on the day of the offer and it is only then that the sub-underwriters are contractually bound. By contrast, in *bookbuilding*, potential investors are approached on the basis of a *pathfinder prospectus* (provisional prospectus) and their *indicative bids*, although not binding, show the level of likely demand and are used to determine the final issue price. The underwriter (called the *manager*) has effectively conducted an auction and *run a book* on the interested investors and the price they will pay.

The manager continues to act as underwriter in case any indicative bids don't actually materialise. But the underwriting agreement is signed after the bookbuilding process and the setting of the price, and just before the start of dealing, so the manager's exposure is much shorter than in a traditional underwriting. This method should generate a higher offer price because the price reflects the demand shown, not the (lower) price the underwriter has to fix to attract sub-underwriters.

In a *bought deal,* the lead manager, and perhaps some co-managers, agree to buy the whole issue at a given price and will then resell it through a selling syndicate.

prepared to subscribe itself. Some may only be prepared to use *reasonable efforts to sell* their allocation while others may be prepared to commit and will form a separate group of banks to provide the actual underwriting. Once the lead manager has received banks' responses and so can gauge the likely take-up, it announces how it will *allot* (allocate) the issue amongst them.

INFORMATION MEMORANDUM

The lead manager is also responsible for the *due diligence* process, ascertaining and verifying information obtained from the issuer that will go into the *information memorandum* (glorified brochure) distributed to potential investors (this is less in-depth than the prospectus for an equity issue).

LEGAL ASPECTS

The lead manager is also responsible for the documentation. This includes:

- a *subscription* or *underwriting agreement* between the issuer, lead manager and co-managers which records the basis on which the issuer will sell and the managers will buy the bond
- an *agreement among managers* in which the co-managers will agree amongst themselves how much of the issue each will take and how the fees and commissions will be allocated
- a *fiscal agency agreement* between the issuer and a bank which acts as *fiscal agent*, distributing interest and repayments to bondholders via the clearing system (which records bondholder details), publishes notices to bondholders, convenes meetings (if necessary) and holds information about the issuer which the bondholders can inspect, such as the full terms of the issue. There may be a network of agents in different countries.

BONDHOLDERS' MEETINGS – ROLE OF A CORPORATE TRUSTEE

If, for any reason, the issuer wants to depart from the terms of the issue, it needs to get the bondholders' approval. But since these bonds are bearer instruments, the issuer won't know who they are. Instead of trying to contact them, it gets the fiscal agent to convene a meeting (these are often advertised in the financial press) in the hope that enough show up or send in proxies to make the meeting *quorate*. This is nerve-racking.

If an issuer thinks this may happen (for instance if the issue is complex or novel) it may at the outset appoint a *trustee*. The trustee is a bank or specialist trustee company that is appointed to represent the bondholders present and future. Its job (set out under the *trust deed* that appoints it) is to act on behalf of all present and future bondholders to hold any *security* for the issue (uncommon in a bond issue) and to negotiate with the issuer if the issuer wants any changes to the terms of the bonds once they have been issued. So, instead of trying to get a meeting of bondholders, the issuer simply negotiates with the trustee acting on their behalf. If the issuer is using a trustee then a separate paying agent (bank) will need to be appointed under a *paying agency agreement* which will cover similar matters to the *fiscal agency agreement*.

A bond's terms: similar to a loan

There are increasing similarities between the mechanics of bond issues and syndicated loans (see Chapter 7) and the same legal terms are common to both.

However, the terms in a bond are generally fewer and shorter and they tend to be standard. The aim is to provide investors with instruments that are familiar, comparable and not complex, making them easily tradable. A bond trader does not want to have to study the minutiae of legal terminology when deciding whether to buy a bond. For example, bondholders aren't interested in the issuer's detailed business so the issuer does not make detailed representations and warranties. Instead the bondholders will rely on the information provided by the issuer in the information memorandum (or listing particulars) and on the credit rating.

Typical terms include:

- Type of bond, amounts in which issued and par value
- Coupon
- How title will pass – usually by delivery (bearer)
- Negative pledge – which says the issuer won't issue later debt that ranks ahead of this issue, but less onerous than in a loan agreement
- Payments – how made
- Redemption – on maturity and for tax reasons (when the issuer will buy them back in)
- Tax gross-up
- Events of default with a grace period
- Prescription – period during which the coupon and principal must be claimed from date of due payment
- Meetings of bondholders – how notice is given and when quorate
- Further issues (on same terms) are permitted – i.e. the issuer can increase the size of the issue
- Governing law and jurisdiction

ROADSHOWS

The prospective issue will be marketed to potential investors. This may be done by a series of *roadshows* (face-to-face meetings with institutional investors) especially where the issuer is new to the bond market or the amount to be raised is particularly large.

LISTING?

Some bonds are listed, often in London or Luxembourg. Some exchanges require the issuer to appoint an agent to communicate on the issuer's behalf with the listing authority, to lodge the necessary documents with the listing authority for approval and to advise the issuer on the listing rules.

GLOBAL BOND

The *global bond* is the actual piece of paper issued by the company as the bond. Nowadays, bonds are *dematerialised* – they are electronic entries in the clearing systems (see below). But the actual global bond is a hard-copy bond that is deposited with a *depositary* (a bank) which acts as a *safe-keeper* of the global bond, a role sometimes called *immobilisation*.

In practice, clearing systems such as Euroclear and Clearstream (bank-owned systems that keep electronic records of holders) enable bonds to be *dematerialised* so that physical pieces of paper no longer change hands.

PLACINGS

So far we have looked at the *public* offer of securities (bonds or shares) – 'public' here doesn't mean to the public at large but to a wide group of institutional investors. However, there is a different sort of offer, made to a much smaller group of institutional investors, which is very commonly utilised because it is generally much cheaper.

This is called a *placing*, where the investment bank identifies no more than, say, a dozen institutional investors that between them will take up the whole issue (either to keep or on-sell). It is similar in structure to bookbuilding.

Vendor placings and M&As

Vendor placings occur in the context of M&A deals where a target's shareholders want cash rather than shares in the bidder. They take the shares allotted to them and sell them to the investment bank which, in turn, places the shares.

What happens is that the buyer and sellers enter into an acquisition agreement which records their deal to sell the target to the buyer. One of the conditions prior to the transfer of the target to the buyer is that the shares to be placed are admitted to listing (otherwise they will be unmarketable and worthless to the sellers). The buyer appoints the investment bank through a *vendor placing agreement* (similar to an underwriting agreement).

The bank may decide to act as principal (buying the shares from the sellers) or as agent of the sellers in placing them on a best efforts basis and agreeing with the buyer to underwrite whatever isn't taken up. This is done under a *sale agreement* in which the sellers give the bank authority to place the shares.

MEDIUM TERM NOTE PROGRAMMES

So far we've been looking at bond issues as stand-alone exercises. In truth most issuers don't do stand-alones any more. Instead they go in for debt issuance programmes under which they can do a succession of bond issues. These programmes are called MTN programmes, and often called EMTNs. An MTN is a medium term note issue and an EMTN is a Euro-MTN.

Euro just means the issue is done in a currency other than the issuer's home currency and the notes (which are the same as bonds) are held by international noteholders outside the issuer's home country; in short, in the international capital markets rather than in the domestic market. Don't be confused by the term 'medium' either – issues under MTNs can, frankly, be as long or as short as the issuer and noteholders want.

Suppose you're a regular bond issuer. Instead of negotiating the terms of each issue as it comes along, you select a group of banks, negotiate the terms with them and these terms then apply to any issue of notes you want to make under the programme. This saves you a lot of time and money because the structure of each issue has been set up in advance on identical terms as part of the programme. Obviously if you establish an MTN programme and then use it once, you've gone to a lot of unnecessary additional expense; a stand-alone bond issue would have been cheaper. But if you are a regular issuer of plain vanilla debt (that is, straightforward with no complexities), then an MTN programme is the way to go. MTN programmes also provide flexibility since they allow the issuer to issue almost any type of note at short notice.

Just to confuse the innocent bystander like you and me, the market has seen fit to develop alternative labels for the participants in an MTN programme. The lead manager becomes the arranger, the banks in the syndicate that buy the notes and distribute them to investors are called dealers not managers, the information memorandum is called an offering circular or base prospectus, and so on. Sometimes an issue will be made via just one dealer in which case it's called a single-dealer drawdown.

HOW PRIVATISATION LED TO UNDERWRITING CONVERGENCE

Privatisation is a loose term that covers a number of ways in which public-sector activities are transferred to or shared with the private sector.

Project finance is one way (see last chapter). Outsourcing is another (for instance where government computer systems are transferred to private-sector suppliers).

But most commonly it means selling shares in public-sector enterprises so that they become partly or wholly owned by private-sector investors (usually partly, so that the government can retain control). Governments have different motives for doing this: raising finance, job creation, redeployment of wealth, creation or modernisation of infrastructure, encouragement of competition, developments of skills and the widening of share ownership.

Before a government-owned enterprise can be sold off, it needs to be *corporatised* (turned into a company with arm's length contracts where previously it obtained goods and services from other parts of government). In some cases (such as electricity, rail) a whole industry needs to be *reorganised* and split into new units. Then a *competitive* market needs to be created (so that what was a state monopoly doesn't just become a private one) often requiring a *regulator* to be installed.

Then the enterprise needs to be sold. This can be done by attracting a *strategic investor* – often the case in airline privatisation, where an established airline is encouraged to buy a stake and offer its expertise to help modernise what was a state airline. Or a *franchise operator* may be licensed to use a state asset such as a port.

But at its grandest, privatisation is achieved by a *high-profile IPO* or flotation aimed at the public. In emerging economies this may require a voucher scheme – where citizens are given vouchers which they can exchange for shares in the privatised enterprise (otherwise they have nothing to buy the shares with). Sometimes the industry in question is so big it has to be privatised in stages or *tranches*. This is what happened with the UK telecoms, energy and transport sectors in the 1980s.

And here's the point. Many of these IPOs involved securities distribution and listing around the world. They were unprecedented in size and scope and tested the ingenuity of bankers and the appetite of the capital markets. To ensure they were successful they were underwritten and distributed using *bond market mechanisms*, which is what we have been discussing here and was the start of how the two converged.

So, having looked at how shares (in Chapter 3) and bonds (in this chapter) are actually issued, we now have to turn our attention to who buys all of these securities – which is the subject of the next chapter.

Chapter 9

MARKET WHALES –
INSTITUTIONAL INVESTORS

SPEED-READ SUMMARY

- There are three types of institutional investor: insurance companies (casualty and life), pension funds and fund managers

- Pension funds are attached to sponsoring companies (sponsors) and invest over the long term to provide employees with pensions when they retire

- The UK pensions industry has been in crisis and pension funds are switching from defined benefits (final salary) to defined contributions (money purchase)

- Fund managers are also called portfolio managers, money managers or asset managers

- Fund managers run retail funds which can be investment trusts (closed-ended public companies that invest in the shares of other companies) or unit trusts (open-ended) or, more recently, funds that are a bit of both

- They also run wholesale money for insurance companies and pension funds

- Institutional investors invest in asset classes – bonds, shares, real estate, currencies, commodities and cash

- Investments can be made actively (stock-picking) or passively (index-tracking)

- Hedge funds are high risk funds that buy derivatives and short sell

---

If banks dominate the financial markets, it is the institutional investors – the wholesalers in my City-as-market analogy – that make the financial markets possible. They buy the shares and bonds that are issued in the market. Because of this, institutional investors are known as the *buy side* and issuers are known as the *sell side*. This is at odds with my market analogy, I admit, because in a market the customers are the buyers.

Institutional investors are the whales at the bottom of the financial ocean. Where banks are more like dolphins or porpoises – playing around on the surface, attracting attention, making a noise, showing off – institutional investors tend to remain invisible, deep down below. But without them there would be no stock markets or bond markets and much less activity in the forex market.

That's because it's institutional investors who:
- buy the bulk of all the bonds and shares that are issued
- decide the fate of targets in M&As by accepting the bidder's offer for their shares, and
- invest in private equity funds for buyouts.

Like whales, institutional investors like to glide in and out of markets without anyone noticing because (as explained in Chapter 1) they don't want their act of buying or selling to move the price against them. For this reason they are also big users of derivatives as we shall see in Chapter 13.

Institutional investors (by the way, the term 'institution' is often used to mean any established financial business, such as a bank or an institutional investor) are mountains of money. They are investment machines. And they get this money from you and me. We provide them with the money to invest in three ways – through:
- Insurance
- Pensions
- Savings

Our insurance premiums go to insurance companies, our pension contributions go to pension funds, and our savings go to fund managers (also known as asset managers, investment managers , wealth managers or portfolio managers).

Institutional investors and private equity

Apart from investing in shares and bonds, institutional investors have in recent years put money into private equity funds that are run increasingly by investment banks. These funds are used to buy public companies in M&A deals (called *taking private* or *public-to-private* and not to be confused with *privatisation* which is about selling off state-owned industry into the private sector which in turn may involve, paradoxically, a listing on the stock exchange by way of a *public offer*).

These private equity investments are commonly structured as *limited partnerships* with *feeder funds*. Limited partnerships are more flexible than companies (fewer reporting and disclosure requirements) but membership is usually restricted to 20 partners. If more than 20 institutional investors are going to contribute funds, then their money will go into feeder funds and these in turn will fund the limited partnership.

A limited partnership is used rather than a 'normal' partnership because in a normal partnership each partner is equally liable for all of the partnership's debts. In a limited partnership only the 'general partner' (usually a specially formed company) is liable for the partnership, which means institutional investors are protected.

Some of these funding structures run across Europe. They are complex to devise because they have to comply with many different regulatory regimes. But the amounts involved can be huge with a single private equity fund raising several billion dollars. The activity of raising the money to invest from institutional investors and structuring these feeder funds is often called *upstream activity*. Spending the money on deals is called *downstream activity*.

1. INSURANCE COMPANIES

There are two types of insurance company:
- casualty insurers, and
- life assurers.

As with banking, there has been much consolidation in the insurance world and the divide between the two is fuzzier than it was. There have been mergers between the two types (creating what are known as *composites*) and there are insurers that do both.

Typical names include **Aviva** (the UK's largest life assurer) which is a merger of Commercial Union, General Accident and Norwich Union, **Allianz, Axa, Legal & General, Prudential, RSA Insurance, Scottish Widows, Standard Life** and **Zurich**.

Casualty insurers provide cover against accidents or loss of assets: examples include household insurance, car insurance, holiday insurance (*casualty* here is what you and I would call *accident*). These are what people generally mean when talking about insurance companies.

Life assurers are different. They provide insurance against long-term illness and death (providing a lump sum for the dead person's dependants so they have something to live on). Since death is 'assured' – it isn't an accident that may or may not happen, but is a certain eventuality – these policies are basically savings products. They allow individuals to set aside regular amounts of money on an ongoing basis to build up a pot out of which the lump sum or regular support payments will be paid. In the past they attracted tax benefits that made them attractive means of saving.

The way both these types of insurer make their money is by investing the *premium income* (i.e. contributions) they receive. It is the ongoing investment process that provides the reserves out of which they are able to pay claims. Outside the world's main financial centres there are cities where insurance companies are concentrated: Hartford, Connecticut is one; Zurich another.

Pension provision works on the same basis: you set aside money during your working life to pay for your retirement, often with your employer contributing too. Some life insurers provide both life assurance and pensions.

2. PENSION FUNDS

There's a UK tradition that companies provide pensions for their employees after they retire. It was one of the perks of employment and dates from the days when people would spend their lives working for a single employer. With some schemes, the employee made a contribution and the employer would match it; with others, the employee might not have to make any contribution at all. Then when you retired you would receive, for as long as you lived, say two-thirds of your final salary.

Such schemes are called *defined benefits* schemes because you know what sort of pension you will be getting: it's specified or 'defined'. They used to be the standard sort of pension. Not any more. Most of these schemes have closed to new members or converted to what's called *defined contributions* (DC) where what you have to contribute is specified and what you get when you retire will depend on how well those contributions have been invested in the meantime and how they have performed.

These DC schemes are also called *money purchase* schemes because what happens when you retire is that your part of the pension pot is used to buy an *annuity* (an annual payment – 'annuity' and 'annual' mean the same thing, although in actual fact you get paid a twelfth of it each month to give you a regular income). Annuities are provided by insurance companies. How much a company and its employees put in will vary between schemes: often the employer will match employee contributions.

Pension funds rarely become household names. In fact, the largest pension funds are either in the public sector or are linked to state-owned enterprises that have since been privatised. Examples in the UK include the pension funds of what were British Rail and the Post Office (the latter was split when British Telecoms was privatised). In Europe one of the largest pension funds is that of the Dutch post office. One of the largest in the world is **CalPERS** (the California Public Employees' Retirement System) with assets of over $150 billion and 1.5 million pensioners. It is responsible for the pensions of California's retired public employees such as the police, firefighters, refuse collectors, civil servants and so on. (By the way, in the US, pension funds are called *pension plans*.)

Funds of this size invest in virtually everything, all over the world, as we shall see. In the UK large pension funds are *self-administered pension schemes* with their own in-house fund management team. But smaller funds are managed on a segregated (separate) or pooled basis by external fund managers (see section 3 below).

THE UK PENSION FUND INDUSTRY

The pension fund industry in the UK has suffered a number of blows in recent years. These include:
- **Poor investment returns** over much of the 1990s and in the credit crunch, making it hard for pension funds to keep their promises to pensioners, hence the switch to defined contribution schemes. This was exacerbated by companies taking *pension contribution holidays* when stock markets were doing well, meaning that they didn't put any money in because stock market returns appeared to be generating sufficient funds to meet pension liabilities.

- **Changes in accounting standards** which now require pension funds to account for future liabilities on a current basis: this means a fund must have assets now to meet pension liabilities in the future, no matter how far in the future those liabilities may extend and notwithstanding the investment return the fund expects to generate in the meantime. This has led to *pension fund deficits* – to the extent that some M&A deals are called off when bidders discover the extent of a target's pension fund deficit.
- **Action by the government** – in particular, Gordon Brown's imposition in 1997 of a stealth tax on pension funds by removing a tax credit they received in respect of dividends (dividend tax credit) from their investments in companies. It is the cumulative effect of this over the past decade – the fact that the money lost cannot be reinvested – that has been the real cost. Of course, at the time, only the pension fund industry complained because most people didn't understand or weren't interested in what was happening.
- **Loss of confidence** – principally through the **Equitable Life** debacle and the suggestion of regulatory incompetence. Equitable Life had for years advertised some of the best investment returns in the industry, so attracting more premium income. But to achieve these it had been running down its reserves and paying those out. In addition it promised certain policyholders unsustainable benefits. When the courts forced it to keep these promises, Equitable Life had to close to new business because it was bust. However, there have been other disasters: a number of companies have gone bust and their pension funds have collapsed too; not to mention the **Maxwell** scandal where newspaper proprietor Robert Maxwell pillaged the Mirror Group's pension funds of £400 million to prop up the group's financial position.

One response has been for individuals to stop contributing to pension funds and invest in property instead, which is why buy-to-let became so popular in the mid-2000s. This led to inflated property values and exacerbated the bust in the UK residential property market following the credit crunch.

One way government tries to encourage pension saving is through tax relief on contributions. This reduces the tax you pay when, supposedly, you're at the height of your earning powers. So that, although you are taxed on your annuity income when you retire, by then your income is much reduced so the tax you pay is considerably lower. That's the theory. In practice the cost of living is so high in the UK that people simply can't afford to save enough. And, with the effects of inflation, by the time they retire their annuity is barely enough to buy them a cup of tea.

All of this is a shame because the UK is, along with the US, one of the few countries which has had *funded pension provision* (pensions paid out of past savings, not out of current income). Many countries meet pensioners' liabilities out of the current year tax take. This is unsustainable because there is a *worldwide demographic time-bomb*: the population is ageing (birth rates in developed economies are declining) and old people are living longer. This means that the proportion of pensioners is increasing in relation to those in work so that the latter are having to 'support' the former by paying more in taxes and pension contributions. The tipping point will arrive in the next 30 years when more are retired than in work. However, many UK pension funds – scared at the size of their liabilities and uncertain returns from traditional equity markets – are moving to LDIs (Liability Driven Investment strategies) which use derivatives to match the projected pension fund liability and guarantee that it will be funded.

Asset classes – what institutional investors invest in

A major institutional investor like CalPERS (the California Public Employees' Retirement System) will invest in everything: government and corporate bonds issued around the world; shares in the world's leading companies; private equity funds; real estate (directly, by buying and developing commercial property such as office buildings and factories, as well as forests and farmland; and indirectly through REITs – real estate investment trusts); derivatives (see Chapter 13); currencies; commodities (such as oil and gold); and even in loans to companies (called the 'credit market') and infrastructure investment; as well as keeping cash on deposit in whichever banks around the world are paying the highest interest rates. Each of these is a different *asset class*. The reason institutional investors do this is to *maximise their investment return* while *minimising the risk* – by ensuring they keep their eggs in as many baskets as possible.

---

3. FUND MANAGERS

Fund managers (also known as *money managers*, *asset managers*, *wealth managers*, *investment managers* and *portfolio managers*) specialise in investing money principally in securities (shares and bonds). They occur in three guises, in:

- Independent investment firms, such as **DWS Rensburg, Fidelity, Henderson Global Investors, Invesco Perpetual** (part of the **AMVESCAP Group**), **Jupiter, Rathbones,** and **Vanguard**
- Banks:
  - many of which have investment management arms, which usually helpfully have the words 'asset management' in their names
  - which have bought independent boutiques, such as **Newton** (owned by **Bank of New York Mellon**), and **Framlington** (51% owned by **HSBC**)
  - as well some insurance companies – **Prudential** owns unit trust manager **M&G Group**; **Aviva** owns **Morley**
- In-house teams in insurance companies and large pension funds managing their employer's assets.

The money they invest comes from two sources:
- *Retail* – from individuals investing in *collective investment schemes* such as *unit trusts, investment trusts* and *open-ended investment companies* (called retail funds – see next page) or who have personal portfolios they want managed professionally
- *Wholesale* – from pension funds and insurance companies.

All three types of fund manager mentioned above manage both retail and wholesale money.

RETAIL MONEY

Individuals who want to save money can keep it on deposit at a bank or building society or – in the hope of getting a better return – may invest in a collective investment scheme, the umbrella term for unit trusts, investment trusts and open-ended investment companies. The UK has a strong tradition of individual investment in equities (shares) but nowadays individual shareholders make up less than a fifth of the ownership of shares listed on the London Stock Exchange; instead the bulk of individuals who invest in equities do so through collective investment schemes. In the past the government has encouraged this through tax credits for ISAs (individual savings accounts). In the past, banks and investment managers tended to sell their own funds but there has been a recent move to 'open architecture' where you make recommendations to investors from the universe of all available funds and not just your own.

Those who are rich enough may have a fund manager or broker to manage their personal portfolio on a discretionary basis (the fund

Trustees and actuaries: the people behind pension funds

A pension fund is attached to a company which is its *sponsor*. It's the company's employees who, when they retire, will receive a pension. But the people responsible for a pension fund's well-being are its *trustees*.

Pension funds are, legally speaking, trusts for the benefit of pensioners present and future (the *members*) and they are run by trustees who have a *fiduciary duty* to those members. Usually the company's finance director or other senior management figure is also a trustee so the sponsor and the pension fund are not completely at odds with each other.

Every pension fund is advised by an *actuary* – some of the most well known include **Hewitt, Mercer, Tillinghast** and **Watson Wyatt** – who estimate a pension fund's likely future liabilities (i.e. how many pensioners there will be in the future) and confirm whether or not it will have sufficient assets to meet those liabilities. This is critical to decisions such as: how much by way of future contributions a fund will require; how aggressively it needs to invest its assets; and the level of benefits it can afford to pay its pensioners.

Actuaries do this by using statistics applied to demographic profiles: give an actuary a group of, say, 500 people and their characteristics (age profile, how many smoke, how many have suffered serious illness, etc.) and the actuary can work out life expectations in percentage terms (how many will reach 65, how many will survive to 70 and so on). In other words they calculate the incidence of mortality. This is important since a pension fund will pay a member until they die – regardless of when that is.

manager decides what and when to buy or sell) or on an advisory basis (the manager advises the client who takes the ultimate decision). They may own individual shares directly, or indirectly through collective investment schemes.

COLLECTIVE INVESTMENT SCHEMES

Collective investment schemes, also known as *pooled investments*, are funds in which people buy shares or units. Those funds then use the money received to invest in shares or bonds.

INVESTMENT TRUSTS

The original collective investment schemes were *investment trusts*, created by Scottish solicitors in the 1860s to enable people with only a small amount of money to invest indirectly in a wide range of shares. If you only had £5, you might be able to afford one share in a couple of companies. This would be risky: if one of those went bust you'd lose half your investment. Far better to use that £5 to buy a couple of shares in a company that itself invests in the shares of 200-plus companies.

This is exactly what investment trusts do. Originally created as legal trusts they are now simply companies, listed on the London Stock Exchange, that invest in other companies. Well-known examples include **F&C** (originally Foreign & Colonial, which dates from 1868), **Witan** and **Alliance**.

To invest in an investment trust, you buy its shares in the market. It will have a finite number of shares in issue at any one time so investment trusts are called *closed-ended funds*.

UNIT TRUSTS (CALLED 'MUTUAL FUNDS' IN THE US)

By contrast, *unit trusts* are *open-ended funds*. Unlike investment trusts they are not companies and are not listed. They are funds (the legal structure is a trust) in which an investor buys *units*. These units are issued by the fund manager. Then, to sell your investment, you simply ask the fund manager to redeem (cancel) your units and pay you what they are worth. To determine this the fund manager calculates the value of the underlying investments (the shares in which the fund is invested) and divides it by the number of units in issue to arrive at a value-per-unit. This is the price at which units are bought and sold and is calculated at least once a day. The fund manager can issue as many units as there is demand, hence unit trusts are said to be open-ended.

Both types of pooled fund have a disadvantage. Investment trusts historically trade at a discount to net asset value which means that their share price is lower than the value of the underlying investments. The usual explanation is that this reflects the costs of managing the investment trust, but this isn't so because their costs tend to be low. In practice, if the discount widens (gets bigger), arbitrageurs and vulture funds (see the jargon buster) buy the shares, so narrowing the discount, then sell at a profit.

The disadvantage of unit trusts is that they have to sell underlying investments in order to redeem units (unlike investment trusts where the buying and selling of their shares in the market has no impact on their underlying investments). So, in a falling market – which, lemming-like, is when individuals often decide to bail out – a unit trust may have to sell its best investments (in order to realise the best price) to meet those redemptions.

Recent developments take the best of both – the corporate nature of investment trusts and the open-ended nature of unit trusts – and combine them. This is what open-ended investment companies (OEICs) and companies with variable capital do.

FINALLY, SPLIT CAPITAL INVESTMENT TRUSTS...

These were sold to investors as low-risk investments in the late 1990s. They were 'split' because income investors received dividends and growth investors capital appreciation. But many splits lost money and some went bust through a variety of factors including poor market conditions, offering unsustainable returns and investing in each other. Those most involved reached a settlement with the Financial Services Authority, agreeing to pay just under £200 million in compensation to aggrieved investors who were thought to have lost three times that amount.

HOW FUNDS ARE CATEGORISED

Open the personal finance pages of any national newspaper and you will see the array of funds on offer. Broadly they fall into the following categories:

- *Growth* – these funds specialise in identifying shares that will provide capital growth over the medium- to long-term; income from dividends is not a priority. They invest in companies that will grow faster in capital value than the market average which may mean that they don't pay out much by way of dividend (putting any profits back into growth)
- *Income* – these funds invest in shares with strong dividend flows and in bonds; these may be companies in mature industries that may not grow much but which pay steady dividends. They are favoured by investors needing regular income, such as pensioners; ironically, shares that provide steady dividend flows tend to be attractive and therefore go up in value, so that income funds can provide good growth as well
- *Balanced* – these funds aim for a balance between income and growth
- *Small-cap/Mid-cap* – the above funds tend to focus on large UK companies (the biggest shares are known as *blue chip*) whereas small-cap ('cap' stands for capitalisation) and mid-cap funds focus on smaller listed companies where growth may be greater but so is the

risk of a company going bust. Some are called 'penny shares' because their shares are worth only a few pence. But if you buy into a company whose shares are trading at 4p and they go up to 8p, you have doubled your money

- *VCTs* – these are venture capital trusts that invest in unlisted start-ups and young businesses; they provide individual investors with access to venture capital opportunities; they also attract tax credits
- *Index* – index funds simply track an index such as the FTSE 100, 250 or All-Share; they do so by sampling (holding representative shares) or holding every share or through derivatives; the idea is that they provide an average performance year-in, year-out whereas active funds (all the other ones mentioned here are active funds) may underperform the index more often than they outperform it
- *Sector-specific* – such as technology, telecoms, financial services, mining; these are for investors who want exposure to a particular industry
- *Country-specific* – such as Japan
- *Region-specific* – such as mainland Europe (often described as excluding the UK), North America, Asia (often excluding Japan) and emerging markets
- *International* or *global* – these give the fund manager discretion to invest in whichever markets seem attractive at the time; they often have a growth or income emphasis
- *Bond funds* – these provide steady income but little capital growth because they invest in fixed-interest instruments; good for pensioners
- *Other* – these include currency funds, commodity funds (such as gold) and property funds (investing in commercial property).

Each fund tends to be managed by a dedicated manager or team. Fund managers spend the bulk of their time looking for investment opportunities and visiting companies in which they have invested. In some of these categories there are more than a hundred funds, so fund management is a large part of the financial services industry.

Apart from the world's principal financial centres, cities famous for fund management include Boston, Geneva and Edinburgh.

WHOLESALE MONEY

This is money that pension funds and insurance companies entrust to external fund managers. They do this even if they have their own in-house investment management teams, for three reasons:

- Diversification – diversification means spreading your investment to

Investment styles, random walks and the Sage of Omaha

Investing is more an art than a science. If there were a magic alchemy that led to brilliant investment, everyone would try to find it and – of course – if everyone was practising it, it wouldn't work. For this reason markets are sometimes described as a *random walk*. No one has developed a fail-safe way to predict them.

Market professionals believe that what matters is not what the markets will do but what everyone else thinks they will do: if everyone thinks the market is going up, they will buy and it will go up – a self-fulfilling prophecy. This is called *market sentiment*.

Markets react to expectations. They are forward-looking. They are said to *discount the future* – in other words to reflect in today's price expectations of what is likely to happen in the future. Again, market professionals say that what matters is not whether a share or a bond is a good investment but whether you can find someone prepared to buy it from you at a higher price than you paid.

None of this has dissuaded people from trying to perfect the gold-plated *investment style*. There are *chartists* (also known as *technical analysts*) who map (or 'chart' using graphs) long-term market movements in shares. They use this historic data (such as moving averages and trend lines) to predict future price movements on the basis that if you know where a share is coming from in terms of price, it is easier to predict where it is likely to go.

By contrast there are *momentum investors* who try to spot market moves that reflect underlying sentiment then jump aboard the market bandwagon – and jump off it again before it collapses. There are people called *day traders* who trade from home over the internet and who buy and sell several times a day on this basis, hoping to make lots of small gains. Then there are *contrarians* who do the opposite of what they believe everyone else is doing.

Possibly the most successful style in recent years has been *value investing*. The idea is to find companies that are undervalued on their *fundamentals* (good product or service, good management, good brand, good markets with great potential; none of which is reflected in the current share price) then to buy shares in them and hold them for a long time. One exponent was **Peter Lynch** who ran Fidelity's flagship **Magellan Fund**. Another was **Sir John Templeton** who, with colleague **Mark Mobius**, specialised in emerging markets.

Another is **Warren Buffett,** who is possibly the most famous investor in the world. He runs **Berkshire Hathaway**, an investment fund, that has made many of its investors millionaires. Buffett is based in Omaha, Nebraska and is known colloquially as the 'Sage of Omaha' for his erudite views on investment.

minimise risk. The larger a fund, the wider its investments are likely to be
- Expertise – external managers may specialise in a particular market or sector that the in-house team lacks the resources to cover
- Benchmarking – using external managers provides a comparison which keeps both in-house and external managers on their toes.

Their money will be managed on a *segregated basis* (separately) or through pooled funds which are essentially *unauthorised* unit trusts. The term unauthorised doesn't mean there's anything wrong with a fund; it just means it isn't authorised to be marketed to the public at large.

BENCHMARKING

All fund managers are measured against a *benchmark*. Usually this is a market index, such as the FTSE 100. Stock exchanges, banks and consultants compile relevant indices. If a fund manager is in the top 25% he or she is said to be in the *upper quartile*. External fund managers will meet their institutional investor clients (in the case of pension funds, the trustees) on a quarterly basis to discuss their performance against the index.

The problem with benchmarking is that it is a *zero-sum game*. This is the term economists use to mean that for every winner there is a loser. So for every fund manager that is above average there must be one who is below average because indices are simply averages. Just because a fund manager is upper quartile one year is no guarantee that he or she remains so. This is because there is no single *investment style* that works all the time.

There are two consequences of this: passive investment and short-termism.

(1) Passive investment (index-tracking)

Most of the fund managers mentioned above are *active managers*: they actively seek out investment opportunities for the funds whose portfolios they manage. They buy and sell investments depending on how those investments are likely to do and in this way they are said to *turn over* their portfolios. Excessive buying and selling is called *churning* and it adds to the costs a fund carries because fund managers pay brokers commission for buying and selling. Fund managers are paid for what they do by taking a percentage of the fund's assets (its worth) – usually less than 1% – as their annual *management fee*.

Alternatives to active management

Given the inconsistencies of active management, two alternatives (popular with retail and institutional investors alike) are:

Fund of funds (FoF)

These are funds that invest in other funds. The FoF fund manager invests in other funds, buying and selecting them depending on those funds' performance. A variation is the *multi-manager fund*. The only disadvantage is the double level of fees – one lot of fees to the manager of the FoF, the other lot to the funds the FoF invests in. However, FoF structures are increasingly popular as a conduit to investing in hedge funds, to spread the risk.

Exchange traded funds (ETFs)

These have also become popular – especially with retail investors and day traders – because they are passive funds that track an index (like a passive unit trust) but, like individual shares, trade on a stock exchange. This means they experience price changes on a minute-by-minute basis throughout the trading day as they are bought and sold. So, unlike unit trusts and mutual funds, their price is not fixed just once a day after the net asset value is calculated. This makes them particularly responsive to intra-day price changes in the market.

ETFs are particularly popular in the US where they have names such as **QUBEs** (which tracks the NASDAQ 100), **SPIDRs** (called 'spiders') which track the S&P 500 and various sectors within it, and **Diamonds** which track the Dow Jones Industrial Average. Bond ETFs are also available.

Core portfolio

Increasingly institutional investors have woken up to the fact that if they are benchmarking active managers against an index and those managers are inconsistent, then they are better off 'owning the index'. In other words, if you want to track the FTSE 100, simply buy a share in each one of the one hundred companies that make up the FTSE 100: that way, when it goes up, you go up. This is called *index-tracking*. Now, you don't need an expensive money manager doing the stock selection for you. In fact you don't need anyone doing it at all: you can program a computer to do it, which is why it is also called *passive management*.

As mentioned earlier, passive management can be replicated by *sampling* the constituent stocks in an index (although stocks used to mean bonds listed on a stock exchange, the terms 'stocks' and 'shares' are interchangeable and mean 'shares') or even through derivatives called stock index futures (see Chapter 13).

Many institutional investors will have their *core portfolio* (the heart of their asset base) invested passively and then have active management around the edges, covering specialist areas like emerging markets, derivatives and venture capital.

Asset allocation

In fact what they have discovered is that the real impact on their portfolio's performance is driven by what percentage of their assets they invest in the different available asset classes rather than the individual performance of each. This decision – of how to allocate your assets – is called *asset allocation* and is driven by things like: where you are based (so which currency you should be exposed to); your liabilities; how long- or short-term they are (a pension fund with immediate liabilities should be switching from equities to bonds) and so on. Usually pension funds use external consultants to help with asset allocation and manager selection. These consultants are often firms of actuaries that have added these areas of expertise.

(2) Short-termism

Meeting regularly with their fund managers focuses institutional investors on their managers' short-term performance. In the past this pressure to achieve short-term success was sometimes transmitted to the companies in which they invested. If a company was underperforming as an investment, the fund manager would simply sell its shares. This led to complaints from companies that the City was too short-term in its outlook.

Corporate governance
(and corporate social responsibility)

However, such calls have subsided, partly because institutional investors are now taking their responsibilities as major shareholders more seriously. Instead of selling their shares – especially if the company in question is a major one in which institutional investors need to be invested because it is a major component of the index – they will sit down with the company's management and talk through its strategy and future prospects. Institutional investors have become much better at attending and voting at companies' AGMs (the annual general meeting of shareholders that every public company must convene).

Companies, for their part, have had to make their management more transparent through adherence to voluntary *corporate governance* codes. In addition, there is increasing realisation that responsible investment isn't just about maximising investment returns. There are wider issues at stake, such as the role of companies as good corporate citizens, with obligations not just to their shareholders but to employees, customers and those in the community affected by their activities. This is called *corporate social responsibility*.

In the UK something called the Institutional Shareholders' Committee (which represents the National Association of Pension Funds, the Association of British Insurers, the Investment Management Association and the Association of Investment Trust Companies) has published a statement of principles setting out the degree of involvement in, and monitoring of, investee companies. Recent developments would suggest there is greater need for this oversight. The most recent pre-credit-crunch scandal involved the grant of share options to senior management by themselves involving options 'backdating' (to ensure the options are granted at a quarterly low in the company's share price, to maximise the return when exercised), 'springloading' (granting options shortly before announcing good news, to benefit from any share price increase) and 'bullet-dodging' which is delaying the grant until after bad news has been announced (so that the exercise price is artificially low).

HEDGE FUNDS

One type of fund that has experienced an explosion in popularity is the *hedge fund*. The term 'hedge' is used in financial markets to mean the use of derivatives to reduce exposure to a risk (see Chapter 13). Hence the expression 'to hedge your bets'.

So, for example, if I am going to go on holiday to the US in six months' time and I'm worried that the dollar may have gone up against sterling by then, I might buy the dollars now to hedge my position. But that means I've tied my money up in dollars. Instead I could contract to buy those dollars at today's price using a future, option or forward so I only actually pay for them and receive them in six months' time. The point is that I am doing something sensible to reduce a possible risk.

Companies do this all the time. The term 'hedge fund' was first used by journalist Alfred Winslow Jones in the 1940s to describe funds that buy but also sell short (selling borrowed assets in the hope of buying them back later at a lower price). He himself used to take off-setting positions in shares to hedge market risk.

Use of derivatives

Now, however, hedge funds use derivatives but (paradoxically) not to hedge. Instead they use derivatives to command much bigger positions (known as 'gearing') than they could have exposure to simply by investing in bonds or shares (this is explained in Chapter 13). In other words, to make big bets on market movements, for instance in the forex markets. **George Soros** is famous for doing this in the currency markets. Hedge funds are reportedly behind the huge growth in forex volumes which at its height had daily turnover of almost $2 trillion. They have also accounted at

---

Systemic risks, secular trends, quants and betas

Investment is about *maximising return* while *minimising risk*. There are different types of risk.

Systemic risk is general *market risk*, as opposed to the *specific risk* of a particular bond or share. Systemic risk affects the whole market. Factors include interest rate rises, weakness in a particular currency, the price of oil, the collapse of a government, the outbreak of war. These are *macro-economic* variables – they affect the big picture.

Economists also talk about *secular trends*. These are equally big but tend to be long-term. For example, between the 1960s and 1980s the UK economy experienced high rates of inflation and, therefore, high interest rates – known as the boom and bust era. Since the 1990s, we have experienced low inflation and interest rates have been correspondingly low. This change from a high-inflation to a low-inflation environment is called a secular trend. All of that changed, of course, with the credit crunch.

Analysts also look at the way in which markets have behaved historically and try to use this as a basis for predicting the future. They try to identify *trends* and *correlations* – a correlation is a relationship between two things. So, for example, some shares behave historically just like the index of which they are a part; when the market moves up, they do; when it falls, they do. There is said to be a correlation between the share price and market. Using a mass of historic data and armed with a computer to crunch the figures, analysts (also known as *quants* because these are called *quantitative* techniques) try to detect how closely a share correlates to the index. This is called a share's *beta*. If a share has a beta of precisely 1, then it correlates perfectly to the index. Just in case you're wondering, *deltas* and *gammas* are to do with options pricing – options are derivatives, covered in Chapter 13. Delta is the ratio of the movement of the price of an option to the movement in the price of the underlying share; gammas are used in the valuation of options and measure the rate of change of delta in relation to a movement in the underlying share. So now you know.

times for as much as half of daily trading activity on the New York and London stock exchanges and even more in the futures market.

Different from other funds

Hedge funds differ from unit trusts and other funds in a number of ways. They are relatively *unregulated* which means that they cannot in theory be marketed to individuals (in fact they are targeted at rich individuals and institutional investors). However, this may change post-credit-crunch with those deemed to be more like banks required to maintain capital to support their trading positions. They aim to generate *absolute returns* (making money regardless of market conditions, not just relative returns against a benchmark) and some make up to 40% a year. For this reason they charge both on the basis of funds under management (like conventional funds) as well as performance fees. Hence the expression 'two and twenty' meaning two per cent of funds under management and 20 per cent of any return generated.

In order to generate such high returns they need to adopt risky strategies and can't afford to have to sell in order to meet redemptions (some of the positions they take may be too illiquid to realise quickly). So they tend not to allow investors to move in and out: instead they tend to impose a *lock-up* (you can't get your cash out) of up to five years.

LTCM – a hedge fund gone wrong

The combination of high leverage and the use of derivatives to amplify market positions can be an explosive mixture in the hands of hedge-fund managers.

Long-Term Capital Management, a hedge fund, went spectacularly bust in 1998. Its total losses were more than $4.5 billion. When it imploded it had equity of just under $5 billion, borrowings of $125 billion and a derivative position of over $1 trillion. Unfortunately LTCM had a big position in bonds and when Russia defaulted, its bond holdings collapsed in value. The risk to the markets was so great

that the Fed (the US central bank) had to step in and arrange a $3 billion-plus bail-out to prevent a systemic market failure.

Yet between 1994 (when it started) and 1998, LTCM had generated returns of 40% and it was led by some of the cleverest brains on Wall Street, including John Meriweather (ex-Salomons) and two Nobel Prize winners, Myron Scholes and Robert Merton. And – as we'll see with Nick Leeson in Chapter 13 – LTCM's underlying strategy was correct: bond values did eventually move in line with its predictions but by then LTCM was history. It simply ran out of money. Lack of cashflow, yet again.

Because of the lock-up they don't need liquidity to meet redemptions so they can take big, risky positions in illiquid markets. However, it is possible to trade holdings in hedge funds online at Hedgebay.

Hedge funds depend on the cult of the personality. A fund's success or failure is down to the individuals managing it (known as 'hedgies') who are often defectors from an investment bank. The most successful funds are in great demand and tend to be *soft-closed* (they're no longer taking in money unless a new investor is very wealthy or influential or both – hence the *soft*).

Hedge fund trading strategies

Shorting or *going short* is a favourite hedge fund activity. It means selling something you don't actually own in the hope of being able to buy it more cheaply later. By contrast, most investment funds don't short: either they are invested in shares and bonds or they have their money in cash. For this reason, hedgies call conventional funds 'long funds'. If you or I buy a car a hedgie would say we've 'gone long' in cars. Some hedge funds in recent years have been criticised for being, in effect, long funds charging hedge fund fees. However, at any one time a hedge fund is likely to have both long and short positions and a deliberate combination of the two. *Long-short* hedge funds, for example, buy shares they consider undervalued and short those they consider overvalued. They often borrow shares or bonds from banks to cover their positions (called *stock lending*).

Other trading strategies include *convertible arbitrage* (buying convertible bonds and shorting the shares into which they convert), *global macro* (exploiting shifts between markets usually by using derivatives) and *market neutral* (shorting overvalued securities and buying undervalued ones). Some, called 'fund of funds', simply invest in a basket of other hedge funds. Others, 'credit hedge funds', buy debt.

They tend also to be highly leveraged (borrow heavily). Some funds borrow 3-4 times their capital which means that lending banks can be exposed, especially since any deterioration in the underlying holdings tends to be magnified because of the gearing effect. This certainly became evident in the credit crunch because hedge funds became highly lucrative sources of income for investment banks which provided them with an array of services bundled together under the heading *prime brokerage* (there's that term 'prime' again – gives you willies, doesn't it?).

Prime brokerage

Hedge funds became popular with investment banks as customers for a wide variety of securities and services called *prime brokerage*, including stock- and bond-lending (mentioned above) and short-term liquidity (i.e. loans) as well as exotic OTC derivatives and back-office support such as clearing and settlement.

What caused banks so much trouble as the credit crunch unfolded was that prime brokers need to decide how much to lend a hedge fund against collateral (investments pledged as security) and then monitor the value of that collateral. This became increasingly difficult to do since hedge funds use more than one prime broker and invest in esoteric derivatives that are often illiquid or difficult to value. Besides, the value of the collateral isn't static since its margin deteriorates if it is popular with other investors (known as a 'crowded trade').

In fact, hedge funds' trading became a significant volume of investment banks' revenues in convertible bonds and distressed debt. They also tended to be counterparties (on the other side of deals) to banks in derivatives trades so any problems amongst hedge funds rippled out into the wider markets. Because they were highly leveraged, fund size understated their market presence. At its height, there were about 8,000 hedge fund managers globally managing over $1 trillion and many of us were exposed either directly as investors or indirectly through our pension funds (pension funds invest in hedge funds to gain out-performance on the edges of their portfolios).

So great was their impact in M&A that UK takeover rules had to be changed to tackle stakebuilding by hedge funds using long derivatives (where the holder will benefit if the price of the underlying share increases) and options, which were not previously caught in the regulatory net. They were also accused by private equity funds of trespassing into their part of the markets in the quest for higher returns. All of this led to calls for hedge fund regulation amid suspicion of possible market manipulation and that was even before the credit crunch.

Even in 2006, many hedge funds lost money – some as much as two-thirds of their assets – on exposure to commodities and energy, betting that energy prices would rise when in fact they fell.

Their impact was felt amongst traditional long-only fund managers who began to use hedge fund techniques: instead of just underweighting companies they didn't like in an index, they actively short-sold them in order to gain from their weakness. Otherwise they would simply be matching the index instead of outperforming it. This slice of outperformance is called 'alpha' by hedgies and is on top of the benchmark (known as 'beta'). Failing to outperform is known as 'leaving alpha on the table'.

Two things became clear: in an increasingly crowded market, bigger bets were chasing riskier odds; and if interest rates went up, the heavily leveraged ones would be squeezed. Certainly, as bonds were down-rated to junk, credit arbitrage funds were hit.

Hedge funds have had a torrid time. Those that profited from short-selling were banned from doing this, at least in financial stocks, for a period. Others exposed to high-risk, illiquid investments found they couldn't exit at all. Investors have had plenty to complain about: poor performance (and when hedge funds bomb they do so spectacularly); lock-ins; and, not surprisingly given all of that, exorbitant fees. The result: net assets in hedge funds fell from $2,700bn in June 2008 to $1,800bn by the start of 2009, a drop of over 30%. Add in demands from the US Treasury Secretary (among many others) for increased regulation and the continued fallout from the Madoff scandal, and it's clear that these will continue to prove testing times for hedgies. But somewhere amongst that heap of lost funds and rash investments, you can bet your bottom dollar that some financial genius – they tend to end up in the hedge fund business sooner or later – is even now turning some derivative-based, short-selling strategy into absolute gold.

SOVEREIGN WEALTH FUNDS

Another type of fund has become newsworthy: the sovereign wealth fund or SWF. These are owned and run by governments (especially Middle Eastern and Asian) and invest around the world for the future benefit of the government or country concerned (hence the term 'sovereign' even though the country doesn't have to be a kingdom). The most well-known are from the Gulf states and China, recycling petrodollars and the trade balance China has generated. Many of them have invested sizeable amounts of money in many of the world's biggest banks, especially those hit by the sub-prime crisis. This in turn has prompted concern about how they might use their shareholding to influence or steer the banks they have invested in.

Chapter 10

GOING FOR BROKE

SPEED-READ SUMMARY

- Brokers used to be agency brokers, buying and selling only on clients' behalf

- Before 1986, London Stock Exchange members were agency brokers and market-making jobbers

- Since Big Bang in 1986, brokers and jobbers have been subsumed within investment banks

- Many US investment banks were originally brokerages

- A new type of broker acting for medium-sized companies and rich individuals has emerged

- Within brokers there are research analysts whose recommendations encourage institutional investors to buy and sell

- Chinese walls within banks keep the research and corporate finance functions apart

- Broker-dealers are market makers; inter-dealer brokers act between market makers

Now for the last of my four market participants – the broker. The term 'broker' is, nowadays, even vaguer and fuzzier than 'bank'. A broker is a go-between or intermediary who enables an investor to buy or sell a security.

Most of us have come across the term 'stockbroker' and this is a good place to start.

AGENCY v PRINCIPAL

A *stockbroker* is someone who buys and sells stocks (the terms 'stocks' and 'shares' are synonymous these days) usually on behalf of a client. In other words, the stockbroker is buying as *agent* for his or her client and this is called *agency broking*.

Before 1986, stockbrokers on the London Stock Exchange were only allowed to deal as agent on behalf of clients. They were not allowed to buy and sell shares *on their own account* (i.e. for themselves). If you wanted to buy some shares in, say, Boots, you would approach a broker. (By the way, this isn't just history – it's the way the New York Stock Exchange still works, more or less.)

He (and they usually were 'he' in those days) would then go on to the floor of the Exchange. On the floor of the Exchange were people called *jobbers*. Each jobber was required to *make a market* in a number of companies' shares. This is a pompous way of saying that he had to keep a stock of shares in those companies for which he was a market maker. These jobbers stood around trading posts on the floor of the Exchange.

Now, my broker (acting on my behalf) would go round the handful of jobbers tasked with making a market in Boots shares and would compare their prices. If a jobber had a lot of Boots shares on his books he might quote a lower price (being happy to sell some) than a jobber who didn't have that many (and so was keener to keep them).

My broker would then buy the Boots shares I wanted from the jobber offering them at the cheapest price (hence the term 'offer price'). In this way I always knew that my broker would get the best deal and was acting entirely on my behalf. In return my broker charged me a *commission* and would advise me on which shares he thought I ought to be buying and selling. If I wanted to sell shares, my broker would do the same thing – go round the jobbers who made a market in those

Bid, offer, turn, spread

The *bid* is the price at which a broker offers to buy a security from you. The *offer* is the price at which the broker will sell it to you. The bid-offer *spread* is the turn the broker makes between the two (agency brokers get paid a commission; most brokers these days act as principal and earn a turn between the price they pay for securities and the price they sell them at).

The spread is a measure of how liquid the market in a security is, i.e. how frequently it is traded and in what volumes – and therefore how keenly priced it is. The less liquid a security is, the wider the spread is likely to be.

shares but this time looking for the one bidding the highest price at which to buy them from me (hence the term 'bid price').

Brokers and jobbers were *members* of the Stock Exchange. Essentially, they owned the Stock Exchange, a bit like members of a golf club who own it between them. The Stock Exchange was very much a club and they abided by its rules. These rules laid down that brokers and jobbers had distinct roles: brokers could act only as agent for clients; while jobbers could act only as market makers; and no one other than a broker or a jobber was allowed on the floor of the Exchange. This split in roles was known as 'single capacity'.

BIG BANG – LONDON 1986

In 1986 the UK government forced the London Stock Exchange to change. The government had three concerns. It said that the Exchange was uncompetitive because whichever broker you went to, and regardless of how many shares you wanted to trade, you would still be charged the same commission – called a *fixed commission*. Second, it said the Exchange was a club: an outsider couldn't join and, because brokers and jobbers were partnerships, outsiders couldn't buy shares in those member firms.

Finally, the government was concerned that the Exchange was *undercapitalised*: in short, brokers and jobbers didn't need much capital (money) to do what they did so the Exchange was actually very small in comparison with New York and Tokyo and the government was concerned that it would lose ground to other competing financial centres (since the City earns the UK an enormous amount of money in what're called *invisible exports*, the government was concerned that the City might end up earning less).

So the Exchange did a deal. It dismantled fixed commissions; in return, big investors could negotiate smaller commissions for trades in big blocks of shares. It also opened up its member firms to external membership: these brokers and jobbers *incorporated* (they turned themselves into companies) so that outsiders could buy shares in them. Finally, the old distinction between jobber and broker was removed. All of this happened in one fell swoop, hence the term Big Bang.

BANKING AND BROKING BLURRED

Big Bang changed London as a financial centre:

- **Banks bought jobbers and brokers** (so, for example, Barclays Bank bought the broker de Zoete & Bevan and the jobber Wedd Durlacher and formed Barclays de Zoete Wedd – known for a long time as BZW and now called **Barclays Capital** which is the bank's investment banking arm). Many of these early purchases by commercial banks were failures but they blurred the distinction between banking and broking.

- **Trading moved off the floor of the Exchange**. It became *screen-based*: since the distinction between broker and jobber no longer applied, brokers didn't have to go on to the floor of the Exchange, so they stopped doing so. The London Stock Exchange, which has since moved buildings, no longer has a trading floor.

- **Capital became critical**. As deals got bigger, the ability of a bank to buy an entire bond or share issue (a *bought deal*) or provide short-term funding, for instance for M&As (*acquisition finance*), determined whether it won the mandate. Poorly capitalised traditional merchant banks, used to using their wits and contacts for advisory work and underwriting, were unable to compete. They were taken over, went bust or disappeared.

- Besides, **many US investment banks had originally been brokerages** (see Chapter 6) specialising in *distributing* securities to investors. In the old days, they had offices right across the US and regular contact with retail investors who were clients of those provincial offices. This geographic reach and distribution power enabled them to underwrite, while investors demanded that they make markets in shares and bonds (i.e. if a retail investor in Hicksville, USA bought a share or a bond off his broker, he expected to be able to sell it back to the broker or via the broker in the market). This made them natural participants in a deregulated UK securities market. Those that were subsumed within universal banks were merged with the original broking and jobbing operations those banks had bought.

Some agency brokers tried to hold out, most notably **James Capel** which eventually succumbed to **HSBC** and blue-blooded **Cazenove** (broker to the Queen) that remained an independent business owned by its senior managers (partners prior to its change from a partnership to a company) until a recent merger with **JPMorgan Chase**.

MID-CAP BROKERS

However, the integration of broking, market making and investment banking has opened up a new market for smaller brokers, described as *mid-cap brokers,* who help smaller companies. One of the roles of the old broker was to act as a sponsor of companies seeking a listing. For such companies, an investment bank may be too big and expensive for their needs. So mid-cap brokers have stepped in. They also look after rich private clients who, again, may feel investment banks are too big to care about their buy-and-sell orders. In many respects they are like mini-market banks of old or small investment bank boutiques.

Well known names, past and present include: **Brewin Dolphin, Close Brothers, Collins Stewart, Durlacher, Evolution Beeson Gregory, Fox-Pitt Kelton, Kaupthing Singer & Friedlander, KBC Peel Hunt, Numis Securities, Seymour Pierce, Teather & Greenwood** and **Williams de Broe**.

Brokers with a retail focus include **Killik** (with offices in London and those parts of the Home Counties once called the stockbroker belt) and **Hargreaves Lansdown** which is a retail broker-cum-investment manager based in Bristol.

Soft commissions

Brokers reward fund managers with research. They also pay *soft commissions.* Usually commissions go the other way: a fund manager pays for a broker's services either through the spread or through paying an actual commission. But brokers reward a fund manager's flow of business by providing goods and services in return. These might include computer equipment and subscriptions to screen-based information services.

Soft commissions generate ongoing debate because fund managers derive benefits to their own business in return for buy and sell orders that are paid for by the funds they manage. The argument is that they get the benefits while their clients (the investors in their funds) foot the indirect bill. There is a move to *unbundled commissions,* that is, to separate *bundled transaction commissions* between *execution* (buying and selling) and *non-execution* (other) services.

BROKERS, DEALERS, BROKER-DEALERS AND INTER-DEALER BROKERS

Not surprisingly, the terminology has also become blurred and confused. Brokers act as agents for a commission or turn. Dealers trade on their own account and make markets. Broker-dealers do both and provide stockbroking services for clients. These days, members of the London Stock Exchange are broker-dealers – they can trade on behalf of a client (as broker) or on their own account (dealer). Many of the larger firms are also authorised to act as market makers, undertaking to buy and sell shares in a given set of companies. Inter-dealer brokers are specialists that act in trades between dealers to preserve their anonymity. Banks and institutional investors may choose to deal with a variety of these intermediaries to disguise from the market what they are doing so that prices don't move against them.

Possibly the best-known inter-dealer broker is **Cantor Fitzgerald**, which was almost wiped out by the 9/11 attack on the Twin Towers because its headquarters was atop one of them. It established its reputation in US government bonds (Treasuries). Other major players include **ICAP**, **Prebon Yamane** and **Tullett**. These brokers are also active in the *money markets* (see Chapter 11).

CONFLICTS OF INTEREST

One of the benefits of the pre-Big Bang market was that there were no conflicts of interest: brokers always acted for the client as his or her agent. But with the difference between brokers and jobbers swept away, a 'broker' could now act as principal. So a client wouldn't know whether a broker was recommending a share purchase because it was a good investment or because the broker was trying to offload shares it owned; and the client couldn't be sure that he or she was being offered the best price available. This possible *conflict of interest* was one of the reasons why the Financial Services Authority – the body put in place to supervise the new-look City – developed a detailed *rule book*.

What has happened since 1986 is that the role of the jobber/broker and that of the investment banker who trades in the secondary markets has merged. As banks bought up brokers and jobbers, so they merged them into their investment banks.

Nowadays there is still a stock exchange and it still has members who are *market makers*. But they tend to be part of an investment bank, they trade from their screens and are required to report to the stock exchange every trade they do (how many shares, in which company, at what price) and this information is then sent immediately to all members' screens so everyone knows for every share, the most recent trade at what price and in what volume.

RESEARCH ANALYSTS

Another possible conflict of interest has occurred more recently. Brokers have traditionally provided their clients with research – advice on which companies to buy and sell. This is partly a reward for custom, partly to generate business. Now that brokers are part of investment banks there are possible conflicts of interest – for example:

- If a bank is advising a company on a potential M&A deal, its corporate finance people will know the intended target. If the broking arm had that information, it would buy shares in the target in the expectation that they would go up once the takeover was announced. This is *insider dealing* and is a criminal offence but can be difficult to prove. Traditionally, banks have guarded against this by erecting *Chinese walls* – invisible barriers between corporate finance and broking to ensure such information does not leak across from one to the other.
- If an investment bank is bringing a company to market in an IPO, a helpful note from the research analysts on the broking side will help to generate interest in the shares. This happened in New York in the dotcom bubble in the early 2000s. As a result, banks have been required to spin off their research divisions into separate entities under US legislation called *Sarbanes-Oxley*.

HOW RESEARCH ANALYSTS ASSESS A COMPANY'S SHARES

There are many different ways of assessing whether a company's shares are a good investment. Here are some of the most commonly used:

- **Price/earnings ratio** – known as *the p/e* ('pee-ee') this divides a company's share price by its earnings per share (which is arrived at by dividing a company's after-tax profit by the number of shares in issue) and tells you how many years of earnings at the current rate it will take to recover the cost of the share at today's price. This varies between sectors – in some it can be as low as 4 or 5; in others as high as 25 or 30. The point is to compare the p/e of companies in the same sector. In some markets where companies traditionally do not pay out much by way of dividend – such as Japan – p/es can be as high as 50 or 60. A high p/e relative to the sector suggests a company is overpriced; a low p/e that it is good value.

- **Dividend cover** – calculated as earnings per share divided by gross dividends (i.e. as paid out) per share, this indicates whether a company is paying out all its earnings to its shareholders (i.e. failing to reinvest). The higher the dividend cover the more prudent it is. A figure of less than one means the company is paying out more than it is earning, which is unsustainable.
- **Dividend yield** – this shows the value of dividends paid to investors (income) as a percentage of the share price (capital value). When the share price goes down the dividend yield goes up, so a high dividend yield can indicate that a share is cheap – provided the level of dividend is sustainable; it won't be if the company is paying out more than it should to shareholders and is failing to reinvest.
- **Price to cashflow** – this measures the money that is passing through a company and is based on the idea that cashflow is more important (and more easily measured) than profit. So a company with a cashflow of £10 million and a market value of £100 million has a cashflow ratio of 10. Some analysts use 'free cashflow' – the cash left after tax, interest on debt and capital expenditure.
- **Price to book value** – this measures the company's share price against the value (as recorded in its accounts) of its assets as used in the business. The figure should always be higher than 1, indicating that the company uses its assets to create more value, as reflected in its share price.
- **Free cashflow** – net income after expenditure, tax and dividends, that is retained in the business. This is increasingly seen as one of the few reliable measures of worth: how much cash a business throws off.
- **Economic value added** – known as *EVA* (and developed by Stern Stewart) this is a measure of the value created for shareholders. It is positive when the return from the equity used in a business is greater than the cost of that capital.

This is a good point at which to move on to markets in general.

Chapter 11

THE MECHANICS OF MARKETS

SPEED-READ SUMMARY

- Stock markets are businesses in their own right and compete with each other – European stock exchanges have been merging and taking each other over

- There are different markets in the UK, for companies of different size and track record

- Trading systems can be quote-driven or order-driven

- Share trades are settled – through CREST in the case of the London Stock Exchange

- Most bonds are traded in the OTC market and are settled through depositaries

- Custodians look after institutional investors' securities portfolios

- Bonds are sensitive to interest rate changes – as interest rates go up, a bond's market value falls and its current yield goes up

- The yield curve is an indication of current expectations of future interest rate movements

- The money markets (where bills and repos – see the jargon buster – are traded) are a critical link between policy makers (such as central banks and governments) and the financial markets – central banks buy and sell bills to alter liquidity in the money supply and to control interest rates

So far we've looked at who buys and sells securities but not the mechanics of how these securities change hands and are paid for. This chapter is about what happens to securities once they have been issued and are being traded, and how those trades are settled. It's also about the exchanges on which securities are listed.

1. SHARES

Within the UK there are three stock markets:

- **London Stock Exchange**, known as the *main* or *senior market*
- **Alternative Investment Market** (AIM), known as the *junior market* for young companies, and
- **PLUS** for companies that are smaller still or whose shares are rarely traded.

Requirements of the London Stock Exchange

A company that wants to list on to the main market (the London Stock Exchange) needs:

- Three years of accounts
- A three-year trading or revenue-earning record
- Working capital that will last at least 12 months

and, once listed:

- At least 25% of the company must be in public hands (otherwise there will be insufficient liquidity), and
- Its market capitalisation must be at least £700,000.

About 1800 UK companies and 500 overseas companies are listed on the London Stock Exchange.

AIM – for small, fast-growing companies

Companies that can't fulfil these requirements can list on AIM. For instance a company specialising in biotechnology may have no trading history at all – it may need capital raised through AIM in order to fund several years of R&D (research and development) to create a product before marketing it or making a sale.

AIM was launched in 1995 and succeeded the Unlisted Securities Market – these junior markets have a habit of drying up after a while because they can be illiquid and, meanwhile, successful companies may shift over to the main market when they are big enough or have been going for long enough. AIM is run by the London Stock Exchange and has about 1500 companies, over 350 of which are based outside the UK. A flotation on AIM will typically raise between £1m and £10m.

PLUS (formerly known as Ofex)

PLUS Markets plc (itself quoted on AIM) is the successor market to Ofex which was started in 1995 by broker **J P Jenkins** which had previously run an OTC market in unlisted securities on a *matched bargain* basis (i.e. J P Jenkins would match buy and sell orders). In 1992 Ofex took over the running of the market from J P Jenkins but it was rebranded PLUS Markets in late 2007.

PLUS runs a primary market (i.e. it offers companies the ability to list and raise money) and a secondary market which trades in securities listed elsewhere. A PLUS listing is for smaller companies wanting to raise smaller amounts of money – although it is fighting this reputation and individual companies have raised more than £15m a time on it. PLUS has about 200 companies listed on its primary market (including Arsenal football club) with a total capitalisation of £2.3 billion.

THE STOCK MARKETS IN THE US

In the US the principal stock exchanges are: the **New York Stock Exchange** (NYSE) which still operates a floor broking system as the London Stock Exchange did before Big Bang, with jobbers who are

---

Trading and broking instructions

Day order = to be done that day or else it lapses

Open order = remains open until executed

Fill-or-kill = do it now in its entirety or else it lapses

Execute or eliminate = do as much of it now as you can and forget the rest

Limit order = do it at this price or better; don't do it if this price is never reached

Stop order = do it only once this price has been reached, but you can then do it at a different price

Block trades

Investment banks will do *block trades* for institutional investors where they buy and sell whole blocks or portfolios of securities. These are tricky deals because they can move the markets easily. The bank may act as agent for the institutional investor or actually buy the securities off the institutional investor and then gradually dispose of them in the market. This is another reason why investment banks need capital.

called *specialists*; and **NASDAQ** (National Association of Securities Dealers Automated Quotation System) which is the electronic junior market. However, some companies that originally listed on NASDAQ, such as **Microsoft**, have remained loyal to it and have not migrated across to the NYSE.

BUSINESSES IN THEIR OWN RIGHT

Stock markets are no more than car-boot sales. They are businesses in their own right and thrive or fail depending on whether they attract enough buyers and sellers. Most start as mutual organisations (owned by their members) but many incorporate (become companies) and have outside shareholders. The London Stock Exchange is listed on itself (which has always seemed weird to me) and PLUS Markets is listed on AIM.

EXCHANGE WARS

Over the past few years there has been tremendous competition between stock exchanges. As with banking, broking and insurance, there has been enormous consolidation. In Europe, the Amsterdam, Brussels, Paris and Lisbon exchanges merged in 2000 to form **Euronext**. The Stockholm and Copenhagen exchanges merged to form **Norex** in 1997. Euronext and the **Deutsche Bourse** fought to buy the London Stock Exchange, then the NYSE and Deutsche Bourse fought over Euronext. Several of these exchanges have also merged with their local futures markets (covered in Chapter 13) which have been waging their own wars with each other and against screen-based trading. Funnily enough, hedge funds (big traders on exchanges) have also been investors in exchanges, exploiting this frenetic M&A activity.

In addition there is competition from electronic exchanges, ECNs (electronic communication networks – one is **Instinet**, owned by Reuters, the market data provider) and other electronic trading platforms such as **Pipeline Trading**, **Liquidnet** and **POSIT** in the US, which enable banks, brokers and institutional investors to bypass markets altogether and, effectively, create their own. These are also known variously as *dark pools*, *dark liquidity pools*, or *dark markets* because they permit cross-trading in large blocks of securities without revealing the identity of the traders or prices.

In the US, big banks have been internalising their trading through electronic alternative-trading systems called ATSs. All of this has led traditional exchanges to merge and cut fees. In 2006 NYSE ceased to be a members' club. It listed and merged with Archipelago, an electronic trading network, which may mean its trading floor is doomed.

A big driver in Europe has been MiFID (the Markets in Financial Instruments Directive), the EU's move to create a single level playing field in financial services from November 2007 by harmonising trading and the protection of investors, removing stockmarkets' monopolies, allowing trades to be cleared and settled anywhere, and enabling banks and others to operate across the EU.

TRADING SYSTEMS

Information and communications technology is key to markets. There are different systems even within the London Stock Exchange for the trading of shares.

Settlement

Settlement is when the trades that have been executed are completed – the shares and money actually change hands. Settlement on the London Stock Exchange is through a system called **CREST** which is a paperless share settlement system.

It started in 1996 and replaced a system called Talisman (a paper-based system run by the stock exchange) and it is a requirement of listing that a UK company's shares be eligible for electronic settlement (in other words that shares are *dematerialised* as electronic entries instead of hard-copy share certificates).

Shares are held through CREST in three ways:
- *Member* – brokers, market makers and institutions that have separate accounts recording their holdings in the system
- *Personal member* – individuals with extensive portfolios who trade regularly and get notices of company meetings, etc.
- *Nominee* – shareholders appoint a member to act as nominee, so they don't get notices of company meetings, etc.

When a trade is executed, details of the trade are sent by both parties electronically to CREST which matches the messages and checks there are enough shares in the seller's account, then on settlement CREST instructs the market maker's bank to make a payment to the seller's account and CREST updates its accounts to record the new shareholder's shareholding.

As with stock markets, so settlement systems in Europe are also consolidating. The leaders include **LCH.Clearnet** (LCH was the London Clearing House) and **Eurex**.

There is **SEAQ** which stands for Stock Exchange Automated Quotations. SEAQ is a continuously updated electronic board through which competing market makers quote prices for UK equities, showing the prices at which they are prepared to buy or sell. Brokers deal with them on investors' behalf. Overseas shares are traded on SEAQ International. This is called *quote-driven* trading.

Market makers are stock exchange members who are required to offer to post buy and sell prices (i.e. two-way prices) for securities in which they are registered throughout the *mandatory quote period*, which is 0800 – 1630 for SEAQ and 0930 – 1530 for SEAQ International.

Then there is **SETS** which is the Stock Exchange Electronic Trading Service. This is an *order-driven* system based on an electronic order book that pairs up matching 'buy' and 'sell' orders for the same shares and executes them automatically (which it is why it is known as the

---

Custodians

Given the huge numbers of shares, bonds and other financial instruments that institutional investors hold, it's hardly surprising that they need help tracking their portfolios. It's made more complex by the different markets they invest in, with payment flows in different currencies and different local tax regimes to satisfy. For this help they turn to **custodians** which tend to be banks, or a part of a bank. Amongst the most well known are **Bank of New York, Chase Global Custodians** (part of JPMorgan Chase), **Northern Trust** and **State Street Bank.**

These custodians hold their clients' securities for them. They settle their clients' trades, collect the interest payable on bonds and the dividends on shares, use the forex markets to convert local currencies, and (where dividends or interest are taxed locally) meet tax liabilities and recover tax where an institutional investor is able to reclaim it. Institutional investors also *stock lend* – lending out for a fee securities they are holding for the long term to banks and brokers that need to cover short positions. Custodians deal with these transactions too.

To do this around the world, custodians either use their own offices or establish networks of *sub-custodians* which are local banks they use regularly.

This is not high-profile work – indeed, it is back-office administration – but it needs to be done efficiently, accurately and – to make money at it – in high volume. Those active in global custody have invested in staff and systems to do so.

order book). It is a fully automated screen-based market where buy and sell orders are entered anonymously and automatically executed during continuous trading. Orders are executed or lapse or are withdrawn. SETS is for larger companies, especially those in the FTSE 100 and 250, where volume is high (i.e. there is a lot of trading in their shares) and SETS is due to replace SEAQ. Then there is SETS PLUS which is a hybrid market model that combines market maker quotes and an order book. All AIM and some main listed shares are traded on it.

Stock exchange terminology includes:
- The *touch* which means the best buying and selling prices available on SETS or from a market maker on SEAQ in a particular share at any time
- The *yellow strip* which is the yellow band on a SEAQ or SETS screen that displays the highest bid and the lowest offered prices
- The *Daily Official List* which is the daily record containing the prices of all that day's share trades.

2. BONDS

Most bonds are traded OTC (over-the-counter), in other words directly between market participants (banks, brokers and institutional investors) using screens and telephones.

Bonds that are listed on stock exchanges are traded through the stock markets on which they are listed (in the case of international bonds, these are often listed in Europe on the London and Luxembourg exchanges).

DEPOSITARIES

But, by and large, the settlement of international bond trades is different from that of shares because the bond market is international, OTC and not exchange-based. Instead, bonds are held as electronic entries by depositaries such as **Euroclear** (which has merged with CREST) and is owned by a consortium of user banks and **Clearstream**, owned by the Deutsche Bourse. In the US the major clearing house for securities trading is the **Depositary Trust & Clearing Corporation** in New York.

DEPOSITARY RECEIPTS

A *depositary receipt* is where a depositary holds securities and then issues a separate security in respect of them. It's a way of enabling a company to access, say, the US market, without having to go through the formalities of issuing and registering securities that comply with US regulations. Instead it puts shares or bonds on deposit with a depositary which then issues receipts that are themselves tradable. Where a depositary receipt is set up by the issuer it is *sponsored*. Where a bank sets one up, by simply buying a company's securities in the market and putting them on deposit, it is *unsponsored*. *ADRs* trade in the US (the 'A' stands for *American*). *GDRs* are *global*.

WHAT DRIVES THE BOND MARKETS

Bonds may appear to be simple instruments but they have one complexity. They are interest-rate sensitive. In the next chapter we explore the wider economics of the financial markets. But bonds present the vital link.

There are three things that matter about a bond when it is issued: its face value, its length and its coupon (interest rate payable). Two other factors become critical: its *yield*; and its *market value.*

BOND YIELDS

As mentioned in Chapter 5, a bond's yield is the amount of interest it pays expressed as a function of its price.

A bond for $100 that pays interest at 5% has a yield of 5%. This is the *coupon yield*: the rate of interest payable expressed as a percentage of the nominal (face) value of the security. This does not change over the bond's life.

But there are other, more important yields. In particular there is the *current yield* or *interest yield* which is the interest payable expressed as a percentage of the *market value* of the bond. This is because – and this is the critical point – a bond's value will change during the course of its life even though on maturity it still pays back its face value. And the reason its market value changes is because of changes in interest rates generally.

CURRENT YIELD

For example, take our bond of $100 mentioned above. When it was issued, a coupon of 5% (in other words $5 a year in interest) was probably an attractive return because interest rates were a bit lower than that. But if interest rates soar to 10% the bond will become an unattractive investment. People will not be prepared to buy it in the secondary market because they can get double the interest payable by simply leaving their money on deposit at the bank. This doesn't mean the bondholder can't sell it; just that he or she won't get as much for it. Assuming that it's a triple-A issuer (i.e. that there is no credit risk) – and ignoring when the bond matures, which will also have a big impact – a buyer of the bond will pay only as much for it as will be the equivalent of getting a 10% rate of interest. That figure is $50, because a bond that costs $50 and pays $5 a year in interest has an effective coupon of 10%, i.e. a current yield of 10%. This is why the market value of bonds fluctuates in line with interest rates.

There is also the *gross redemption yield* which is broadly the expected return the bond will generate (taking both interest and capital value into account) over its remaining life. It's called *gross* because the effect of tax is ignored.

SPLIT-SECOND CALCULATIONS

Bond traders calculate a bond's various yields as quickly as a computer. They need to, in order to take split-second buy-or-sell decisions. That is what makes them so expert. But in addition they will be thinking about where interest rates are likely to go. There's no point in buying a bond at today's price if interest rates are about to go up. Indeed, bonds of different maturities will behave differently in the market depending on where market professionals think interest rates are heading. This is called the *yield curve*.

YIELD CURVE

The yield curve is a graph that plots interest rates for deposits of different maturities. It shows the rate of return that can be locked in now for various terms into the future – up to three months, up to three years, up to 30 years and so on. The y axis (left, vertical) shows the annual percentage yield and the x axis (bottom, horizontal) shows the period for which the investment is made. The line joining the plotted points is the yield curve itself. Generally the curve slopes up from left to right because the longer the investment, the greater the risk so therefore the greater the return the investor demands, which is why long-term money generally costs more than short-term. When the curve 'inverts' this switches round so short-term money becomes more expensive, usually because short-term outlooks are cloudy and uncertain while long-term rates (which represent in part the market's expectations for future short-term rates) are more settled looking further out. Interest rates are a reflection of expectations of inflation. So if a yield curve inverts, it may be because there is an expectation of lower inflation in the future, which is why investors are prepared to accept lower returns on long bonds.

REPO AND MONEY MARKETS

This link between bonds and interest rates is even more explicit in two key markets that link economic policy with the financial markets. These are:

- The *repo market*, which is itself part of
- The *money markets.*

The term 'money markets' also includes the inter-bank loan market (including deposits evidenced by CDs – certificates of deposit) and commercial paper markets.

REPOS

Repo stands for 'repurchase agreement'. A repurchase agreement is a simple contract under which I sell you a bond for £X and agree to buy it back in three months' time for £Y.

Essentially what you are giving me is a secured loan: the purchase price (£X) is the loan, which you will get back when I buy the bond back in three months; and the interest element is £Y (the price I will pay you in three months' time) less £X (the amount you paid me) which is called the *repo rate*. Because it is a genuine sale-and-purchase agreement, you have title to the bond. So if I fail to buy it back you simply sell it in the market, so you are completely covered. In a *reverse repo* the seller is a bank that buys securities in return for providing cash.

Repos are used by institutional investors and banks to gain short-term liquidity by harnessing long-term assets (the bonds in question tend to be government securities such as US Treasuries or UK gilts where the underlying risk of default is minimal). The amount that you will lend me on the bond is lower than the face value of the bond to cover any fall in its price over the three month period and this difference is known in the trade as the *haircut*. The benefit to you is that you are investing cash risk-free and, if you think the securities will go down in value, you can sell them in the market and buy them back at a lower price just before you need to deliver them back to me.

You can see that the repo market is very sensitive to rates and bond prices. It is also a critical source of liquidity. It is a cross between stock lending (an institutional investor activity) and money lending (a commercial banking activity).

MONEY MARKETS

Repos are one type of instrument found in the money markets, which are markets for short-term bonds also known as *bills*.

In Chapter 6, there was reference to the role of merchant banks in discounting short-term bills, *bankers' acceptances* being bills that banks have endorsed (i.e. guaranteed). The Bank of England will buy some types of bill including Treasury bills (short-term bonds issued by the government) and bankers' acceptances. It also enters into repos in respect of UK gilts (government bonds).

By buying these instruments the Bank of England introduces money (*liquidity*) into the market. By selling them, it reduces (*soaks up*) market liquidity. Doing so has a direct impact on the amount of money (liquidity) in the *money supply system* which in turn affects interest rates: tightening liquidity increases interest rates.

The money markets are thus a source of short-term liquidity (money) where short-term debt instruments are traded, such as commercial paper, Treasury bills, interbank loans, deposits (called CDs because they are evidenced by *certificates of deposit*), bankers' acceptances and repos.

The Bank of England is a central bank. Other central banks do the same for their respective economies: controlling interest rates is a key lever in controlling an economy. In this way the money markets are a critical link between the financial markets and those who make economic policy – governments and central banks, as we shall see in the next chapter.

Chapter 12

BIG PICTURE STUFF –
THE IMPACT OF ECONOMICS

SPEED-READ SUMMARY

- Governments don't like inflation (it devalues savings and encourages people to spend rather than save) but they can control it only through tax and interest rates

- The UK government sets the inflation rate target; the Bank of England's job is to achieve it through control of interest rates

- If the Bank of England fails to hit the government's inflation target, the Governor has to write a letter to the Chancellor explaining why

- When interest rates go up, the stock market goes down because bank deposits become more attractive and companies become less profitable through increased borrowing costs

- Sterling goes up (appreciates) as overseas investors make sterling deposits at UK banks, but that appreciation in turn depresses UK exports by making them more expensive in other countries

- The bond market goes down, but yields go up and, eventually, the bond market recovers as an attractive alternative to the stock market

- The reverse happens when interest rates go down

- If markets expect an interest rate rise they may have already discounted it (priced it in) and so not react adversely

---

This chapter explores the relationship between inflation, interest rates, currencies, stock markets and bonds. Once you understand this, you can become a central bank governor.

Imagine a typical TV financial news report. It goes something like this:

CUT TO reporter standing in front of the Bank of England: 'Well, I'm standing here in front of the Bank of England which today raised interest rates by a quarter of a per cent in order to damp down inflation.'

CUT TO another reporter standing on a bank's trading floor (with the bank's name prominently displayed on a pillar): 'Here in the City, the reaction to the latest increase in interest rates was immediate: the stock market fell.'

CUT TO a representative from the Institute of Directors (IoD) or the Confederation of British Industries (CBI): 'Employers will be dismayed by this rise in interest rates. It increases the cost of borrowing and will damage our exports.'

This chapter will enable you to understand what's going on. Of course, what I've talked about so far is interest rate rises. What we've experienced most recently in 2009 is the reverse – falls in interest rates to stave off a depression following the credit crunch.

1. GOVERNMENT DOES NOT LIKE INFLATION

Inflation erodes the buying power (*real value*) of money. In an *inflationary environment*, goods and services will cost more tomorrow so consumers buy them today, which itself adds to inflation. Governments don't like inflation because it erodes the value of people's savings and makes them spend rather than save. If they don't save for retirement or rainy days, government ultimately has to help them and it can only do this by raising taxes, which is unpopular with the electorate. In particular, those on low or fixed incomes such as the poor and the retired suffer badly from inflation and automatically look to government for help.

Technically, inflation is a function of the velocity of money in the money supply system. Put simply, the faster money goes round the system (the more quickly people spend the money that comes into their hands), the greater the demand for goods and services, which pushes up their price (until supply and demand return to equilibrium). It's a bit like an accelerating washing machine.

In the UK, the speed with which house prices rise is a strong indication of inflation. If people move house a lot, they buy new white goods (such as fridges and washing machines), furnishings, and so on, and all of this feeds into industry. If house prices are increasing fast, people feel wealthier and spend more on improving their houses, going out and holidays.

This is why the UK government gets worried if house prices go up too quickly – it makes people spend more money than they should, usually on credit by borrowing it, and this increases the velocity of money round the system, so increasing inflationary pressures. No surprise that, prior to the credit crunch, banks were falling over themselves to encourage people to borrow and spend, using credit cards with swingeing rates of interest to do so.

DEFLATION

Note that a little inflation is all right. It has the effect of gradually increasing asset values (e.g. house prices) which increases the feel-good factor. The opposite of inflation – deflation – is worse: consumers don't spend because they know the price of goods and services will be cheaper tomorrow – but then they don't buy them tomorrow either, because prices will be lower still the following day, so demand dries up. Industry falters and the economy grinds to a halt. Deflation is difficult to get out of. Japan was in a deflationary environment for over a decade and interest rates fell to zero – because no one wanted to borrow. The same deflationary environment has affected Germany.

This was the great fear of policy makers in the credit crunch, that unless they encouraged people to continue spending there would be a massive slowdown leading to depression and deflation. That was why they were so keen to bail out and back the banks to ensure they maintained their levels of lending – with only limited success.

2. INFLATION IS TACKLED THROUGH (A) TAX RISES AND (B) INTEREST RATES

There are only two levers to control inflation: raising taxes (which makes government unpopular); and raising interest rates. Each hits consumers in the pocket – taxes, because they pay more of what they earn over to the government; interest rates because it costs more to borrow, for instance on credit cards and mortgages. This makes people feel less wealthy so they rein in their spending.

Chancellor Gordon Brown made a clever move when Labour took office in 1997. He gave control of interest rates to the Bank of England. This meant the government was no longer responsible for the unpopular task of fiddling with interest rates. Instead the government sets the level of expected inflation – and the Bank of England uses interest rates to achieve it.

THE BANK OF ENGLAND – WHAT IT REALLY DOES

The Bank of England is not a bank in the accepted sense of the word. It is, technically, the lender of last resort, which is another way of saying that it will step in if a bank is about to go bust, as it had to do with Northern Rock and, more recently, Lloyds and RBS. This is because – as I hope you have begun to see over the course of this book – banks are critically dependent on each other: they lend to each other and borrow from each other; if one goes bust, what it owes the others will bring them down too – because of their exposures to it. So the Bank of England steps in, usually by organising a *lifeboat* – ordering other banks all to chip in to bail the unfortunate bank out and meet its liabilities. But the Bank of England's real role is economic. It sets interest rates through interventions in the money markets (see last chapter).

Strangely enough, when it started in 1694, the Bank of England was a private company. It was not part of the state at all. It helped the government borrow until the government's borrowing dominated the market to such an extent that the interest rate the government paid became the market rate: the market had to accept whatever the government was prepared to pay ('Owe a banker a thousand pounds and it's your problem; owe him a million and it's his'). The Bank of England was nationalised after World War Two, because its role was of such national importance.

Originally any bank in England was able to print its own notes (which operated like bankers' acceptances or letters of credit). By the time it was nationalised, the Bank of England had been given this lucrative monopoly, another reason for it to be in public ownership.

The Bank's traditional role of regulating banks was transferred to the Financial Services Authority so it redefined its role in terms of monetary policy: its job is to keep inflation within the band laid down by government by using interest rates to warm up or cool down the economy as required. And if it doesn't get this right, the Governor has to write a letter to the Chancellor explaining why. Doesn't sound too onerous to me.

Just as an aside, the government's handling of Northern Rock led many critics to complain that bank regulation had fallen between three stools, the Bank of England, the FSA and the government's Department of Industry, with no one in overall charge. Wonderful.

3. IF INTEREST RATES GO UP, BANK DEPOSITS BECOME MORE ATTRACTIVE SO THE STOCK MARKET GOES DOWN...

When the Bank of England raises interest rates bank deposits become more attractive *in relative terms*. For example, if yesterday bank deposits were paying 5% and today they are paying 6% because interest rates have been raised, investors will move money out of the stock market and put it on deposit. This is because, *relative* to the stock market, a bank deposit (which is less risky) is now more attractive.

This has the effect of driving the stock market down – because people are now selling their shares in order to put the money on deposit or are simply putting on deposit money that would have been invested in shares.

4. THE COST OF CORPORATE BORROWING INCREASES, CORPORATE PROFITS ARE HIT, SO THIS TOO DRIVES THE STOCK MARKET DOWN...

Companies are sensitive to interest rate increases because they fund themselves heavily through debt because it is tax deductible. Interest rate increases reduce their profits; worse, it affects the ability of some of them to borrow if their credit standing is already poor. So some companies will go bust if they are already fully stretched.

The future impact of all of this is reflected in the stock market's present price – in short, it goes down since it is a barometer of the health of the corporate sector, now and in the future.

5. STERLING STRENGTHENS AND THE PRICE OF UK EXPORTS IN OTHER CURRENCIES GOES UP...

It's not just UK investors who start to find bank deposits more attractive. Foreign investors do as well. If UK interest rates have gone up, the UK is suddenly a more attractive place to deposit money than, say, the US. So foreign *hot money* as it's called (liquid financial assets that flow

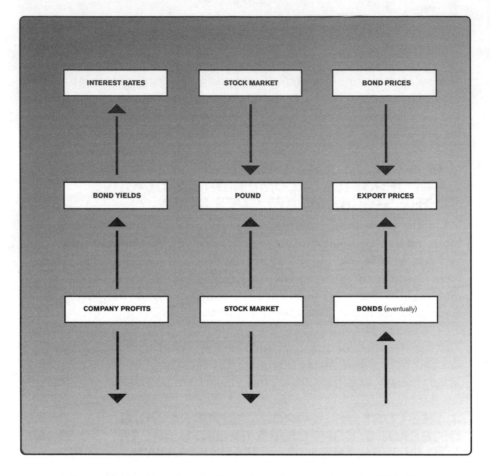

round the world looking for the best return) pours into the UK. Now (remembering the forex market from Chapter 1) this hot money has to be converted into sterling in order to be put on deposit at UK banks. This demand for sterling increases its value against other currencies. Market professionals say that sterling has *strengthened* or *appreciated*.

This is bad for UK companies that export overseas because their products are now more expensive for overseas customers to buy. With sterling stronger, these customers need more of their local currency to buy the same amount of sterling. So they buy fewer of them. This affects the profits of UK companies, so this too drives the stock market down.

6. IN THE MEANTIME, BOND PRICES GO DOWN AND BOND YIELDS GO UP...

As discussed in the previous chapter, when interest rates go up, bond prices go down until their yield is the equivalent of the new interest rate. However, bond markets tend to recover before stock markets because as the stock market falls, the bond market starts to look attractive relative to the stock market, so bond prices start to *rally* (go up). Besides, markets tend to look forward: so if rates have just gone up, the bond markets may soon start discounting – i.e. reflecting – an anticipated interest rate fall.

THE WHOLE STORY

That is the whole story. Test it in reverse. When interest rates go down (to avoid deflation, as has been happening post credit crunch):

- The cost of borrowing goes down, so company profits improve, so the stock market goes up

- Bank deposits become less attractive, which is also why the stock market goes up

- Sterling weakens as the hot money goes overseas and moves into other currencies, so UK exports become cheaper and more competitive in other markets, which is also why the stock market goes up

- Bond prices go up (bonds are now seen to be paying a better coupon than bank deposits, so investors want to buy them) and their yields go down

And on TV:

CUT TO reporter standing in front of the Bank of England: 'Well, I'm standing here in front of the Bank of England which today lowered interest rates by a quarter of a per cent in order to boost the economy.'

CUT TO another reporter standing on a bank's trading floor (with the bank's name prominently displayed on a pillar): 'Here in the City, the reaction to the latest reduction in interest rates was immediate: the stock market rose.'

CUT TO someone representing the corporate sector: 'Employers are cautiously optimistic about this reduction in interest rates, but of course interest rates need to come down a lot further if companies are to feel the real benefits of reduced borrowing costs and improved exports.'

(This last comment is tongue-in-cheek but typical – some people are never satisfied.)

One final point: there has been much discussion in recent months about 'quantitative easing' as a response by the UK government to the worsening recession. This is basically about getting more money into the economy. As a shorthand, people have talked about 'printing more money' which the government could do but which would be inflationary. Another way is by getting banks to lend more. But do already indebted businesses want to borrow more? One solution is for government to buy assets from non-banks (such as corporate debt), which gives the sellers an immediate cash boost. Another is for government itself to borrow from the banks and use that money to buy non-bank assets or use the money to stimulate the economy through public sector spending. The fear in all of this is that in borrowing and spending so much now to get out of a recession, we are storing up trouble for the future. Look at Iceland, whose financial services sector was way out of proportion to its overall economy. Its citizens will be meeting the cost over the next seventy years and living like paupers in the meantime.

A WORD OF WARNING –
WHY THIS DOESN'T ALWAYS HAPPEN

The steps outlined above don't always happen (you will know from the last chapter that markets are unpredictable). Markets hate surprises, as central banks know. So policy makers try to give markets as much warning as possible about likely interest rate moves. If the Bank of England makes it known that it is concerned about inflation and the market is expecting an interest rate rise, the effect can be that when the rise occurs, the markets barely react.

This is because the markets expected it – and in fact wanted it to happen so that the economy didn't get out of control. Because when the economy is out of control it oscillates wildly from boom to bust. Markets don't like that because market professionals can lose large amounts of money quickly. Indeed, if markets felt inflation was getting out of hand but the Bank of England wasn't doing enough, they would react adversely anyway.

One central banker who was a past master at this was Alan Greenspan, Chairman of the US Federal Reserve (the US central bank). For months he would go round the markets telling them that interest rates were going up so that they became used to the idea. Then, when interest rates did go up, the markets would be reassured rather than worried and would react much less unfavourably. By contrast, some UK Chancellors have in the past (when they controlled interest rates) moved interest rates so precipitously that markets have been spooked rather than reassured.

This is what market professionals mean by market *confidence*: confidence that policy makers know what they are doing and are going to do it. In response to the credit crunch, the Bank of England's Monetary Policy Committee (known as the MPC) reduced interest rates rapidly until they were lower than they had ever been since 1694. This was done to enable banks to rebuild their balance sheets (use cheap money to make good the humungous losses they'd incurred in the credit crunch). The problem is that there is nothing else left in the policy makers' armoury to combat depression and deflation, and the speed with which interest rates came down made the markets think that the policy makers feared the economic outlook was catastrophic. This can lead to a self-fulfilling prophecy or a vicious circle (choose your preferred cliché) in that the policy makers' action causes the very thing it was meant to avoid. Because if the markets think that the policy makers can see only disaster ahead, the markets will respond by falling even further – so making that disaster a reality.

IT'S IN THE PRICE

Markets are looking forward all the time and reflecting their expectations in today's prices. Hence the expression, 'The news is already in the market' or 'It's already been discounted in the price.'

This explains another conundrum. When companies unveil a sparkling *set of results* (their annual profit statement), the market often rewards them by marking their share price down – on the basis that there is nowhere to go but down. Equally, when a basket-case of a company reveals yet another cataclysmic loss, its share price may actually go up – on the basis that all of the bad news is now out in the open and things can only get better, making it a good potential investment for future gain.

COVERED INTEREST ARBITRAGE

Finally, there is a trading strategy for exploiting the way in which interest rates affect exchange rates. It's called *covered interest arbitrage* and involves deciding whether to put money on deposit in, say, sterling at the UK interest rate or dollars at US interest rates. It's a good bridge into the subject of derivatives – which are discussed in the next chapter.

Chapter 13

DERIVATIVES, SYNTHETICS AND ALL THAT JAZZ

SPEED-READ SUMMARY

- A derivative is an instrument derived from an underlying security (known as the 'underlying' or 'cash' instrument)

- There are three types: futures, options and swaps (including credit derivatives). Arguably a swap is a type of forward (as is a future) so purists say there are two: forwards and options

- A future is a forward contract – an agreement to take delivery of the underlying on a particular date in the future at an agreed price

- Futures markets allow you to trade on margin (a bit like a deposit), which enables you to command a much bigger market position than if you invested the margin amount in the cash market

- Futures provide unlimited upside and downside

- Counterparty risk is removed through the clearing house

- An option is the right but not the obligation to take delivery of the underlying on a specific date in the future at an agreed price

- Arbitrage is the act of exploiting pricing anomalies between markets, the effect of which is to remove those anomalies

- Swaps originally allowed companies to swap a currency or interest rate. Now swaps are used as the basis for a wide range of risk exchanges

- Credit derivatives are a way of passing on a borrower's credit risk without transferring the loan

- The volume of OTC (over-the-counter) derivatives is far greater than that of exchange-traded derivatives – many OTC derivatives are themselves standardised and can be sold-on

It's appropriate that Chapter 13 is on the subject of derivatives. They can be unlucky for some.

By now you will be familiar with *securities* (shares and bonds). Financial derivatives are instruments that are *derived from* shares and bonds (and a whole lot of other things including commodities and currencies). The securities from which they are derived are referred to as the *underlying* or (confusingly) the *cash market*.

Opinions can differ but there are, broadly, three types of derivative:
- Futures and forwards
- Options
- Swaps

Purists will tell you that there are only two: forwards and options. A future is a forward which is traded on an exchange. A swap is two forwards (the second reverses the first at a future date). Still others call all derivatives swaps (but this is because ISDA, the trade body that provides the industry-wide documentation for OTC derivatives, was originally the International Swap Dealers Association, but is now the International Swaps and Derivatives Association). If this is confusing, don't worry. Read what follows and come back to this only if you want to.

1. FUTURES

The meaning of a future is simple. It's what a future does that is complex. A *future* is simply a *contract to take delivery* of something at a *fixed date* in the future for an *agreed price* (hence a 'future' is short for *futures contract*). Because it's a contract that is delivered and paid at some point ahead of the present, it is a form of *forward contract*: no actual cash changes hands until maturity. The critical point about a future is that it is an obligation to make payment and take delivery whereas an option gives you the right but not the obligation.

ORIGINS – THE CURRENCY AND COMMODITIES MARKETS

Futures have their origin in the foreign exchange and commodities markets. In the forex market, trades are either immediate (for settlement now, called the *spot market*) or for *forward delivery* at some point in the future (known as the *forward* market).

In the commodities markets, especially for soft commodities such as grain, there have been *forward contracts* for centuries. A forward contract enables a producer to lock in a guaranteed sales price, guaranteeing him a return on his harvest (important if he fears a glut which will bring down the overall price and wipe out his profit). It also enables buyers to lock in a cost of purchase (important if they fear a shortage which will drive the overall price up).

An example might be coffee or cocoa where producers want to lock in a profit element (to be able to buy and plant next year's crop) and coffee and cocoa manufacturers want to lock in production at a certain price (so they can provide consumers with a steady supply at a steady price).

Now these producers and manufacturers could spend their time seeking each other out and making individual deals. But a futures market makes it much easier for them to do so.

It offers a *place* where they know they can sell or buy a contract. Second, it offers a *standard* contract in *amount* (one contract is for a specific weight of cocoa), *quality* (of a certain type, such as drinking chocolate) and *time* (futures contracts are for delivery in three months).

These are *exchange traded contracts* as opposed to the one-off, customised contract between a producer and manufacturer which is called an *over-the-counter* (OTC) or *off-exchange* contract.

Exchange-traded contracts provide the enormous advantage that each side isn't required to see out the trade to maturity. If I want to close out my position prematurely I simply sell my holdings in the market.

All of which will attract speculators who will buy and sell such contracts to make a profit, so providing the final, all-important ingredient: *liquidity*. How?

LOCALS

The answer is that every futures market has members who, like broker-dealers and market makers on a stock exchange, buy and sell futures contracts for their own account. These speculators are called *locals*. They are hardened traders who can make vast sums of money or, equally, go bust. Of course, they don't want to take actual delivery of the underlying commodity. What they do at the end of the contract is simply settle up with their *counterparty*. Note that although there is a convention that you don't insist on delivery of the underlying, you can if you want to. This is how the Bunker Hunt brothers tried to corner the silver market in the late 1970s and early 1980s (the Fed rumbled them, sent prices tumbling and they lost $1 billion in the process).

AN ILLUSTRATION

Let's say I am a local and you are a drinking-chocolate manufacturer. You want to lock in a *ceiling* for the price of cocoa, to cap the price you'll have to pay for it so that you don't have to increase the cost of the packs of drinking chocolate that you sell to consumers.

You buy 500 cocoa contracts (where each contract is a sack of standard weight and quality of cocoa) from me for delivery in three months' time at $100 per contract. In three months' time the price of cocoa in the underlying or cash market is $120. Now the market convention is that I don't actually give you the cocoa (although you could insist on physical delivery in which case I'd go into the cocoa market and buy it at $120 and hand it over to you). Instead, I pay you 500 x ($120–100) = $10,000.

You now buy cocoa in the cash market at $120 a sack. But the $10,000 I hand over to you compensates you for the fact that you are having to pay $20 more per sack than you had wanted: indeed, as a result of the $10,000 the *effective cost* to you is still $100 per sack, just as we had bargained. You will be happy.

What about me? The chances are that I have entered into an *offsetting* trade. A producer, worried that he might not get buyers for his cocoa if there is a glut, sold futures contracts to me at $90. In this way he locked in a *floor* below which the price he would get for his crop would not drop. In the event the cash price is $120 (this is what he is able to sell his crop for in the underlying market). So he hands over $30 per contract to me ($120–$90). He has forgone that 'super-profit' on his crop but has had the peace of mind of knowing that he would get $90 for his crop whatever the market price. If in fact the price of cocoa had fallen below $90, I would have had to pay him the difference. So for him the futures trade has provided peace of mind.

You can begin to see that futures enable producers and manufacturers to smooth out spikes in demand and supply. They also enable speculators (locals) to bet on the likely future moves in supply and demand. Locals can enter into a variety of offsetting trades to cover their positions. These are called *trading strategies*. They can be very complex.

You can probably also begin to see that the futures market will bear some relation to the underlying. If the supply of cocoa dries up in the underlying (cash) market, then futures contracts will trade up because the underlying is in shorter supply. As the point nears at which a particular futures contract expires, it will converge in value with the underlying. In recent years, the futures market has been bigger than the underlying in many instruments and at this point what happens in the futures market starts to drive the underlying, making both much more volatile. This has been what has concerned policy makers and regulators and has prompted Warren Buffett, among others, to describe derivatives generally as 'weapons of mass financial destruction.'

ORIGINS IN AGRICULTURE

Modern futures markets have their origins in the US in the 1850s when grain harvests were erratic. By being able to buy and sell grain forward, the effect of these spikes was smoothed out. This is why the major futures markets are in the US, in **Chicago** (which is a natural centre in the US for the distribution and trading of agricultural produce): the **Chicago Board of Trade** (formed in 1848) and **Chicago Mercantile Exchange** (formed in 1874 but renamed in 1898). They, and the European futures exchanges **Eurex** (the combined Swiss and German futures exchanges) and **Euronext.Liffe**, are the biggest futures exchanges in the world. The first financial futures were currency futures, first traded in Chicago in 1972. The Chicago Mercantile Exchange and the Chicago Board of Trade merged in 2006 to form **CME Group**.

OPEN OUTCRY

Futures exchanges have traditionally been *open outcry* with locals and brokers (often in brightly coloured coats) shouting and signing buy and sell orders at each other in *pits* as the various trading areas on a trading floor are called. However, increasingly open outcry is being replaced by on-screen trading. Eurex, for example, has always been an electronic exchange and Liffe (the London international financial futures exchange which merged with FOX, the London options exchange – now part of Euronext) closed its pits in 1999.

Technology enables these markets to trade 24/7 globally. But I'm sorry about the decline in open outcry. Traditionalists argue that having to execute all market trades in the close confines of a pit gives you a palpable sense of the mood of the market and its likely movement. There is nothing more visceral than seeing traders in their brightly coloured jackets like jockeys screaming at each other and gesticulating with hand signals that you see echoed by bookmakers down on the rails at racetracks laying off bets on the horses.

MARGIN – AMPLIFYING YOUR POSITION

So far, a futures contract doesn't seem particularly dangerous. But in inexperienced hands it can be, for two reasons:
- Unlimited loss
- Trading on margin

UNLIMITED LOSS

In the above example, the loss on my trade with you was $10,000. But it could have been much higher. If the cash price had risen to $150, then it would have been 500 x ($150 – 100) = $25,000 in relation to a contract price of just $50,000 (500 x $100). This is one of the downsides of futures: they can expose you to disproportionate losses relative to the price paid.

TRADING ON MARGIN

The other is that futures markets allow participants to *trade on margin*. This means that you don't have to put up the full price of the contract. The closest analogy is with the housing market. People don't put up the full cost of a flat or house. They put up a deposit of, say, 10% and borrow the rest. In effect they buy the house on margin. This has the effect of amplifying any gain or loss.

Let's say you buy a flat for £100,000 with a 10% deposit. In a year's time, prices have rocketed and the flat is now worth £200,000. You sell. You have made £100,000 on a stake of just £10,000 (let's forget the interest you have paid on the mortgage in the meantime). This is a fabulous return.

Now, let's say that over that same year, prices in fact fall. They fall because there's a recession and, because there's a recession, your employer has gone bust, you are out of a job so you have to sell the flat. You sell it for £50,000. Now, we all know that mortgage lenders want all of the loan back. So you have in fact lost not just your £10,000 deposit but a further £40,000. This is a cataclysmic loss of several times your original investment.

What I have described is like a future on the price of property. A future allows you to buy a *market position* or *market exposure* for only a fraction of its cost. You only had to put up £10,000 to command a market position that started at £100,000 and then could have been as high as £200,000 or as low as £50,000. In this way a future, for minimal outlay, *amplifies* or *magnifies* your market position.

Of course, you didn't buy a future. You bought a flat. But let's say that you simply wanted to bet on the price of property without owning it. If so, you could have bought a future: for £10,000 you could have bought a contract worth £100,000 of flat. Then at the end of the year, you don't want the flat. You want the money. In the first scenario, whoever sold you the future pays you £100,000; in the second, you pay him £50,000.

This is exactly how futures work. In practice you never take delivery of

---

Marking-to-market and counterparty risk

When you buy or sell a contract in a futures market you are dealing with another party. What you don't want to have to worry about is whether that party is *creditworthy*: in other words whether they will still be around in three months' time to honour the contract. This *counterparty risk*, as it's called, might put you off dealing in futures altogether.

Futures markets understand this. So, after you conclude a contract with another market participant, the deal is transferred to a *clearing house*, which is part of the structure of the market. The clearing house steps in and becomes the counterparty to each side of the deal: now you have the clearing house on the other side of the deal, not your original counterparty (and the same goes for him too). This also enables the futures market

to do something else that is clever. The clearing house requires market participants to *mark-to-market*. Remember that participants trade on *margin* (they put up just a fraction of the cost of the position). To avoid any nasty surprises at the end of the contract, the clearing house requires each participant to keep that margin topped up if the price of the contract moves against him. So if my contract loses value, the clearing house asks me to *top up* my margin on a daily basis to make good that loss.

Regular users of futures markets maintain *accounts* with the clearing house. As futures fluctuate in value, *margin calls* are made. If my futures positions gain in value, margin is credited to my account and I can withdraw it. If my positions fall in value I have to top it up. Major participants (e.g. banks) are allowed to *cross-margin* between accounts held on different futures exchanges.

the *underlying*. You simply settle up depending on the direction in which the market has gone.

CFDS (CONTRACTS FOR DIFFERENCE)

This is why futures are also known as *contracts for difference* and in their retail guise that is often what they are called (the investor and broker agree to exchange the difference between the price of an asset at the beginning and end of the contract). In this way CFDs can provide exposure to a share without owning it.

SPREAD BETTING

The property example is not quite as fanciful as it may seem. There are brokers offering property-related hedges or 'hedgelets' as one broker calls them. These are based on another retail-oriented derivative trade: *spread betting*. The broker quotes a range or 'spread' for the future price of an index (such as a stock or property index). The investor bets on whether it will end up higher or lower than the spread suggests. For each point that the index moves in the investor's favour, his profit is multiplied by his stake. For each point it moves against, the loss is multiplied by the stake. Say a broker quotes a spread of 4000 to 4100 on the FTSE 100 and the investor bets £10 for every point above 4100. If the FTSE moves to 4200, the investor's return is £10 x 100 = £1000. The investor can also bet the market will fall (shorting it). Returning to property, if you own a house, betting that the market may fall may offset some of the gain you'd make if property prices rose, but will protect you if the market does fall. In this sense, any property owner (whether he or she knows it or not) is betting on property prices going up by being *long* of property: this is called naked risk (unconscious risk). Far better, these brokers argue, that you take that risk consciously and hedge against it.

In practice though you shouldn't worry about whether you have a property future if you have actually bought a flat for £100,000 with a deposit of £10,000. I have a mortgage too. The point is that people need places to live for the whole of their lives. So if you sell your flat you will simply use the money to buy another. If prices have fallen, then the flat you move to will also have fallen. We are long-term investors and over the long term, property – like most financial assets – goes up in value (it's partly a function of inflation – see the previous chapter). We are not worried by *short-term fluctuations* in the market. But a futures contract is for three months: short-term fluctuations are exactly what it is about.

However, the example shows that a future puts you in the same position as if you had owned the underlying *but without actually having to do so*. This is what institutional investors use them for. If I want exposure to the UK stock market (if I want to *buy the market* in the parlance) I can laboriously assemble a portfolio consisting of every share in the FTSE 100. This is time consuming and it costs money – first, to buy the shares, with the broker's turn factored in plus the stamp duty tax; second, because the act of buying the shares will move their price against me; third, because it ties up my money. Wouldn't it be so much easier if I could buy a single piece of paper that says: 'This is the equivalent of every share in the FTSE 100'; and to be able to buy it for just a fraction of its face value? This is what *stock index futures* do.

STOCK INDEX FUTURES

There are all sorts of futures: bond futures, currency futures, commodity futures. But stock index futures (SIF) provide institutional investors with great flexibility in the management of their equity portfolios. A SIF is a single contract that represents an underlying index.

Currency futures

The use of currency futures also helps isolate the risk a money manager is running. So, for example, let's say a money manager has an expert stock selector in the Japanese market. So the actual individual Japanese stocks (shares) in the portfolio are good. But if the money manager likes the US market, it can sell the Nikkei 225 future (which provides the Japanese stock selection without the Japanese market's systemic risk) then go into the US market by selling the yen currency future for dollars to get the US cash to buy the S&P 500 future (the largest, most liquid future on the US stock market). This way the money manager gets the best stock return (Japan) plus the best market return (US) and isolates the currency risk.

If I want to invest in the FTSE 100, I can buy each and every share. Or I can buy a FTSE 100 futures contract on a futures exchange by paying *margin* (the equivalent of the deposit on the flat). Now, on the face of it, the future will give me each of the underlying shares at the end of three months. In practice I simply receive money if the *underlying* market (the *cash* market) has gone up or pay over the difference if the FTSE 100 has over that time gone down.

I can then *roll over my position*: take out a new stock index future for another three months. If I keep on doing this, I have a position in the FTSE 100 without actually owning any of the underlying. This is an artificial position created for me by the future. In short I have a *synthetic* position, which is why these derivatives are sometimes called synthetics (usually only if I am using more than one derivative to create my synthetic position).

Used prudently, SIFs enable institutional investors to:
- Reduce their exposure to a stock market (by selling the SIF) without having to sell the individual shares in their portfolio
- Gain rapid exposure to a stock market (by buying the SIF) without having to buy the underlying shares.

Dynamic hedging

This is a technique that uses stock index futures (SIFs) to provide something called *portfolio insurance* (which has nothing to do with insurance) or *portfolio protection*. By using SIFs, an institutional investor can constantly adjust its asset allocation by adjusting the stock/cash mix of its portfolio in line with movements in the market to give the portfolio maximum exposure to equities (which, historically, give the best return) without taking on the attendant risk.

As the equity market rises, assets are switched out of cash (the risk-free or reserve asset class, usually money market instruments) into equities (the risky or active asset) and as the market falls the reverse is done. If the market keeps falling there comes a point when the portfolio is entirely in cash. This point can be set in advance as a floor below which the portfolio will not fall (even if the market does) because the portfolio no longer has any equity exposure – hence the term insurance.

The 'premium' the investor pays is the loss of upside gain when the market rises because the portfolio is progressively switched into equities in response to the market's upswing and not in anticipation of it. But this is the great attraction, because it does not require any market judgment or forecasting. Just to be complicated, the result is like being fully invested in shares while having a put option whose strike price is the same as the pre-set floor.

Moving in and out of stock markets is cumbersome, the mechanics of which can wipe out the projected benefits. By contrast, commissions or spreads in the futures market are significantly lower than in the cash market and the futures market is more liquid so there is less risk of moving prices against you when you trade.

A money manager's nightmare is wanting to gain exposure to a market – knowing it is likely to move up – but finding the physical act of investing is too slow and inefficient to execute the strategy quickly – meaning that he or she is out of the market just when they want exposure to it. SIFs allow an investor to gain market exposure more rapidly – through a single trade rather than individual trades in scores of stocks in the underlying (cash) market (i.e. on an exchange).

On the other hand, SIFs also enable an investor that holds a substantial share portfolio to keep it while exploiting short-term market declines by selling the future: there's no need to exit the cash market just because you think it may go down, if you need to be invested in that market over the long term (e.g. a UK pension fund investing in UK equities which it will hold for years).

Some money managers maintain global market exposure completely *synthetically* – simply by trading in the relevant SIFs and altering their holdings to reflect their asset allocation decisions (asset allocation has a greater impact on investment returns than individual stock selection; what matters is choosing between particular markets rather than particular shares – see Chapter 9). Futures exchanges have responded by creating contracts on a variety of market indices.

A pension fund that wants to divest itself of a share portfolio (for instance to meet pension liabilities) but fears the market is falling can sell the SIF to fix the value of the portfolio at the current market price, buying itself time to unwind its cash positions at an orderly rate. This – and the act of using SIFs to fine-tune investment performance – is called *dynamic hedging*.

THE LESSON OF LEESON – THE DANGER OF FUTURES

This all sounds jolly splendid. You can begin to see that futures are a superbly efficient way of creating or gaining a position in the market. But the unlimited gain they offer is tempered by the risk of exaggerated loss, which is what makes them dangerous.

Nick Leeson destroyed Barings Bank in 1995 through an overambitious derivatives strategy he pursued on SIMEX (the Singapore futures market). He built up a huge position in the Nikkei 225 (the Tokyo equivalent of the FTSE 100) by buying Nikkei 225 futures on SIMEX. He was betting that the Nikkei 225 would rise. However, what Leeson hadn't foreseen was the Kobe earthquake which sent Japanese markets into freefall. As the Nikkei 225 continued to fall he was required to *mark-to-market* (top up his margin to maintain it in relation to the value of his position). In the end, so great was the market position that Leeson commanded through his holdings of futures, that Barings ran out of capital to enable him to mark to market. SIMEX *closed out* his

---

Speculation and arbitrage

I've described locals (dealers on futures markets) as speculators. The term 'speculator' can have negative connotations. But in the markets speculators are welcome. They provide liquidity.

They also act as *arbitrageurs* (as do hedge funds and market professionals generally). An arbitrageur is someone who exploits a pricing anomaly between different markets or instruments and, by buying the cheaper and selling the more expensive, brings both prices back into line.

In Chapter 1 I mentioned buying bread in a bakery. Imagine for a moment that I discover that the same loaf of bread costs £1 in London, but £2 in Manchester. If I were an *arbitrageur* I would buy lots and lots of loaves in London at £1 and take them to Manchester where I would sell them for £2. Now, initially, I would make a lot of money but three things would happen. First, a lot of other people would start copying me (it's easy money). Next, the demand for loaves in London would be so great that the price would move up. Finally, there would be such a supply of loaves in

Manchester – more than was immediately needed – that the price of loaves would come down. So *equilibrium* would be established between the bread markets in London and Manchester with loaves trading at the same price (say £1.50) in each place.

This is what arbitrageurs do when they scan markets looking for price discrepancies then buy and sell between two markets until there is no gain to be made because the price discrepancy has been *arbitraged away*.

This is especially true of the futures markets, which allow market professionals to exploit *pricing anomalies* between the future and the underlying. If one is higher or lower than the other, an arbitrageur can exploit the difference by selling the high one and simultaneously buying the low one. The act of doing so brings the two back into line while allowing the arbitrageur to pocket the difference. *Index arbitrage* (betting on anomalies between index prices and futures contracts) is regarded as one of the least risky forms of proprietary trading. In an M&A context, a typical arbitrage strategy is to go long of the target while shorting the bidder.

positions (sold them) which crystallised his losses (over £850 million) and the bank was bust.

The shame is that Leeson's long-term bet was right: the Nikkei eventually did recover – but by then it was too late. Leeson was dubbed the 'rogue trader' and went to prison. It's true that he broke rules in concealing his losses. But he wasn't actually trying to derive any personal financial benefit from what he did, other than to enhance his career and, no doubt, earn a big bonus: he wasn't stealing money or dealing on inside information. His was the right bet at the wrong time. In the markets timing is everything. Not everyone shares my sympathy for Leeson. But compared to some of the crooks uncovered since, he doesn't strike me as especially evil.

2. OPTIONS

I hope you can see that futures are devilishly cunning devices but in the wrong hands they can be dangerous. Every so often the regulators have to close down a *boilerhouse* operation which is trying to sell futures to *widows and orphans* (translated this means a dodgy broker, usually offshore, trying to sell futures to retail investors who haven't a clue, in order to take their money off them). Options, by contrast, although they are still derivatives, are much more benign.

An option is exactly what it says: it gives you the *right* to buy something but *not the obligation* – in other words, you don't have to. Let's say that you are thinking of buying a second-hand car. You like mine and I'm asking £1000 for it. You're not sure if the price I want for mine is a good price or not. If it is, you'd feel a fool if you turned my car down only to find it was a very keen price and someone else snapped it up in the meantime. I, for my part, want to sell my car sometime but I'm not fussed when. I'll keep it until I can find a buyer and then I'll buy another, but I'm in no hurry.

So you ask me if I'll keep my car reserved for you at £1000 for a week while you research the market. If I agree, I have given you an option for a week to buy my car at the agreed price. At the end of the week, you don't have to buy my car (you would if it were a future) but if you do, it will be at the agreed price.

What you have done is to *fix the maximum price* you will pay for the car. If you can find the same car at a lower price, you'll buy that instead and let the option *lapse*; if not, you'll come back, *exercise the option* and buy my car.

Derivatives: weapons of mass financial destruction?

Warren Buffett (the Sage of Omaha mentioned in Chapter 9) has gone on record as saying that derivatives (especially futures) have the potential to be 'weapons of mass financial destruction' or words to that effect.

What worries him is this: derivatives provide such an efficient and liquid way of moving in and out of underlying markets and of shorting them, that there is now greater volume in the derivatives markets than in the cash markets. In other words they are bigger. This means that they can drive the underlying markets. Worse still, because they are easy to buy and sell, they can cause massive short-term gyrations in the markets which can be deeply unsettling, like a boat pitching in a storm. Because derivatives have the effect of amplifying movements in the underlying, they can drive downward price moves in the underlying even faster in that direction.

Buffett has been especially concerned with OTC derivatives as being complex, not transparent or disclosed, and difficult to value.

Financial meltdown

In the crash of 1987, futures were blamed for causing more of a collapse in the markets than if the underlying stock markets had existed on their own. As the underlying fell, futures fell further so arbitrageurs started selling each in turn to catch up with the other, like an aircraft in a dive. (This effect can be accelerated by *program trades*, trades in the cash or derivatives market driven by computers that spot when one is out of line with the other.)

Eventually the markets pulled out of the dive. Buffett fears that one day they won't. As communications and technology improve, linkages between markets increase and they become more interdependent, increasing the possibility of global *financial meltdown*. In a sense, with the credit crunch, we've seen it, been there, done that. At least derivatives weren't to blame.

After 1987 regulators tried to restrict derivatives markets. But the markets argued vigorously that they were not at fault. Besides, they have mechanisms for putting the brake on freefalls: they impose daily limits on market moves; if a market exceeds such a limit it is temporarily closed. This can work, or it can stoke up demand for when a market reopens.

PREMIUM

If I'm canny I'll charge you something for that option (called the *premium*) because, first, it's given you an advantage and, second, it prevents me from selling the car during the week even if someone comes along with an absurdly good offer. Let's say I charge you £20 for the option. Now, at the end of the week you may *exercise the option*, in which case I make £1020, or you may walk away, in which case I've got £20 for – well, not doing anything except not selling my car. You, for your part, have paid £1020 rather than £1000 but with that comes the peace of mind of knowing that you still paid less than you would have elsewhere.

By the way, these relative prices are roughly right: an option doesn't necessarily cost very much in relation to the agreed price of the underlying, also known as *the strike price* – in this case, £1000.

Now, let's think about this for a moment. An option is a form of *risk management*. In your case the risk is that the same car may be cheaper elsewhere – but then again, it may not: but at least you have widened the options (no pun intended) open to you.

I for my part have earned a bit of *premium income*. I'm always going to have a car so every week I sell an option on my car – sometimes it's exercised and I go out and buy another; but usually it's not. Of course, when it is exercised, I have to replace my car at a higher price (why else would the option have been exercised?) but over the year, *writing* an option every week (in our scenario I am called an *option writer*) at £20 a week, I am making about £1000 which is almost the price of the car anyway, so over time it's good business for me too. Swings and roundabouts.

AN OPTION EXAMPLE

You can buy options on virtually every type of financial instrument, even futures and swaps (dealt with in the next section: an option on a swap is called a *swaption*). Options are available on indices and on individual shares. There are options on bonds and currencies. An option's own value will go up or down to reflect what is happening in the underlying. In this way options themselves have value and can be traded as standard option contracts on derivatives and stock exchanges (called *traded options*).

Let's say you want to buy a share in a listed company because you think the shares will go up – let's say it's oil company BP and their shares

Options terminology

- *Premium* – the cost of the option
- *Put option* – option to sell
- *Call option* – option to buy
- *Option writer* – someone who sells options
- *Covered option* – where the option writer owns the underlying
- *Naked option* – where the option writer does not own the underlying, so, if the option is exercised, he or she has to go into the market to procure the underlying
- *Strike price* – the price at which the option is exercisable
- *At-the-money* – where the exercise price is the same as the current price of the underlying
- *In-the-money* – when exercising the option will make the option holder a profit (underlying's value is greater than the strike price)

- *Out-of-the-money* – when exercising the option will make the option holder a loss (underlying's value is lower than the strike price)
- *American option* – an option exercisable at any point up to its expiry date
- *European option* – an option only exercisable just prior to expiry
- *OTC option* – tailor-made option that is not traded on an exchange
- *Traded option* – a standardised option that can be bought and sold on an exchange any time up to expiry
- *Covered warrant* – a short-term exchange traded option (call or put) aimed at retail investors which, like a future, can generate great returns with a small premium but where, unlike a future, the maximum that can be lost is the premium

are trading at 300p. Now, you could buy just one share and lock up your 300p. Or you could buy an option (these share options on individual shares are amongst the most common exchange-traded options in the market). Exchange-traded options usually last three months, but option contracts can be quite flexible.

There are three types of option you can buy (and the terminology has got nothing to do with geography): an *American option* is exercisable at any point up to expiry (expiry is the end of the three-month period); a *European option* is exercisable only just prior to expiry; and a *Bermuda option* is only exercisable on certain specified days up to expiry.

Let's say we buy a European option for 10p (which, as I say, is proportionately a realistic sort of price). If over the three months BP's shares never go above 300p (*the breakeven*), your option remains *out-of-the-money*, which means that there's no point in exercising it (it's sometimes called *under water* or *waterlogged*). But if, over that period, BP shares ever go above 300p, you are said to be *in-the-money*. Let's say that at the end of the three months, BP shares have traded up to 320p. This means you have made 10p profit (320p less 300p and the option price of 10p). Now, you can *call for* the BP share (what you have is a *call option*), pay your 300p and keep the share; or sell it in the market and make 10p profit. And over the three months you've been able to use the 300p (or, rather, 290p allowing for the cost of the option) that would otherwise have been spent buying a BP share investing in something else.

The value of the option itself will rise and fall during its three-month life in relation to the price of the underlying. For instance if, during the three months, BP shares shoot up to say 340p, then I could sell my option in the market for maybe 2p or 3p more than the 10p I bought it for, and in that way make a turn of 3p on an outlay of just 10p – a great return! So options can themselves be traded, in which case they are, as I say, called *traded options*.

TRADING STRATEGIES

Clever derivatives traders assemble complex strategies involving interdependent derivatives trades. Impress your friends, colleagues and boss with your knowledge of these:

Straddle = simultaneously buying or selling both a call option and a put option with the same strike price. This strategy works when a market remains within a particular trading range or band. When Nick Leeson broke Barings he was trying to recoup losses on futures contracts on the Nikkei 225 following the earthquake that hit Kobe and Osaka in January 1995 and depressed the Nikkei 225. Leeson bought straddles, hoping the Nikkei would stabilise around 19,000. But it didn't and his losses were compounded.

Strangle = straddle with different strike prices for each option

Strap = a combination of two call and one put option

Bull spread = buying and selling an option at different prices: used where the trader expects only a modest increase in the underlying so gives up part of the potential upside to recoup part of the premium

Bear spread = opposite of a bull spread: used where the trader expects a fall in the underlying but caps the downside risk

Cylinder = buying an option while selling (writing) one at a different strike price – the effect is to offset the two premiums, reducing the cost while reducing the upside

All-or-nothing option = the option holder receives a fixed price if the underlying reaches the strike or goes above it

Butterfly or alligator spread = combination of a bull and bear spread where the premium receipts and payments cancel each other out, so (in theory) it costs nothing

Condor spread or top hat spread = a trading strategy that limits the downside and upside – through buying and selling calls at increasing strike prices. A variation is the *Christmas tree spread*.

It is possible to long or short these – so, for example, to have a long straddle or short strangle. These are all option strategies in relation to equities (shares). They can be combined with bonds, futures and swaps. Complex strategies involve portfolios of different derivatives contracts and glory in names such as *tarantula* and *carousel arbitrage*.

The point is that these strategies enable a trader to take a market position, whether his or her view of the market is bullish, bearish or undecided, while making that exposure *capped* (limited) or *open-ended* (unlimited).

Companies, banks and institutional investors use options to *cap* (in the case of a company) the maximum rate of interest payable on a borrowing, to fix a *floor* below which interest receivable won't fall (in the case of an institutional investor or bank) and to create a combination (a *collar*).

CONVERTIBLE BONDS AND WARRANTS

This is the moment to come clean. I lied when I said at the beginning of this book that equity and debt are the only two forms of money you can get. But it was a white lie. You do get instruments that switch between them: a *convertible* is a bond which allows the holder to switch into equity at a pre-set price; and a *warrant* is a bond that entitles the holder to buy shares in the issuer (or another company). I mention them both here because I hope you can now see that each is really just a bond (a debt instrument) with an option *embedded* in it to buy equity at a certain price. So each is a bond with an *embedded equity option*. A convertible pays investors a lower rate than an equivalent bond, because it gives them the right to convert it into shares if the issuer's share price rises above a certain point. So issuers end up paying less interest (which is good) or issuing cheapish equity (even better).

Triple witching hour

Like bonds, whose market value converges with their face value as they reach redemption, futures converge with the underlying as they reach expiry. But such is their volume that they can drive the price of the underlying. This means there can be twitchy times in the markets when futures, options and options-on-futures are surging towards a common expiry date as their prices and those of the cash market converge, with arbitrageurs working all three (underlying, futures and options). This can send the markets into spikes and freefalls – so much so at times that the point at which these things occasionally come together has been dubbed in Chicago 'the triple witching hour'.

It can be like landing a big plane in a storm – a bumpy ride with massive market gyrations before the plane finally touches down in one piece (you hope).

SYNTHETICS

You can see that futures and options can be used to create artificial positions where you have the same position as if you held the underlying, but without doing so. This is why they are often called *synthetics*, although what market professionals usually mean by the term is a combination of derivatives to achieve a particular position. You may be able to see that if an option can fix a maximum price, it can also fix a minimum price and you can achieve a trading range for an underlying by deploying options. These are called *trading strategies*.

The point is that derivatives take on a life of their own – become an edifice in their own right, piled on top of each other (for instance options on futures) – separate from the underlying but with their own intrinsic value driven in part by what is happening to the underlying in its market. It is this versatility combined with liquidity and low transaction costs that have given derivative markets such volume – and worry people like Warren Buffett who believe that real markets should be driven by economic *fundamentals*.

3. SWAPS

Compared to futures and options, swaps in their original form are hardly derivatives at all.

One reason why they are derivatives is because they enable companies to create synthetic borrowing positions, which is why many swaps are provided by commercial banks and most bond issues these days are made in conjunction with a swap. Another (mentioned earlier) is that ISDA, the trade body that represents swap market participants, originally started as the International Swap Dealers Association (one of its roles is to produce standard legal contracts for deals) and it then spread that role to derivatives in general so that it is now the International Swaps and Derivatives Association.

There were originally two types of swap: *interest rate* and *currency* swaps. An interest rate swap is an agreement to exchange future cashflows for a period; what is swapped is the interest rate in respect of a notional principal amount, not the principal itself. With a currency swap there is (1) an agreement to an initial exchange of currencies at the current spot (cash market) rate and (2) a simultaneous agreement to reverse the swap at a later date but at the same currency rate, regardless of intervening rate changes. The principal amounts do therefore pass between the parties and then back again on termination.

INTEREST RATE SWAPS

With an interest rate swap, two companies agree that each will pay the interest on a loan taken out by the other, where the loans in question are of the same amount. Although the agreement is in respect of the same principal amount they don't actually bother to swap the principal, just the debt service liability in respect of it.

It's as if you and I each had a mortgage of the same amount, yours at a fixed rate, mine floating, and I paid the monthly interest on yours and you did the same on mine. I would now effectively have a floating rate mortgage and you a fixed. Our respective lenders wouldn't know because I would route my interest payments through you and you'd do the same back.

This is exactly how interest rate swaps work – it's why they are similar to *forward rate agreements*. Two companies – one borrowing at a fixed rate and the other at a floating rate – swap a notional amount of principal. All that happens is that each effectively services the other's debt by handing over regularly what the other has to pay by way of interest to its lender.

This creates a synthetic position where a company borrowing at a fixed rate is able to enjoy a floating-rate position and vice versa. So why do companies do this? In markets at different times it may be cheaper to borrow at a fixed or a floating rate (depending on uncertainty over where rates are heading). A company that can borrow more cheaply in its local market (where it is known) at a fixed rate may think interest rates are going to go down; while a borrower that can borrow more cheaply in its local market (where it is known) at a floating rate may want to fix its cost of borrowing so it knows exactly how much it will have to pay over the course of the loan, regardless of interest rate movements. By swapping the debt-service liability each is put in the other's position.

In practice, companies don't have time to look for other companies that want precisely the opposite swap that they want. So each goes through a bank (1) which has enough companies as customers to be able to run a swap book and (for a fee) act as a counterparty to each company's swap or (2) which simply takes on the position (for a fee) and may or may not seek a subsequent offsetting swap.

What companies are doing when they use a swap is *hedging*, which means protecting themselves against the risk of an unwanted market movement.

CURRENCY SWAPS

Currency swaps are like interest rate swaps except that the notional underlying principal is actually swapped because here each company wants the currency the other has. For example, let's say I've been on holiday to the US and have some left-over dollars but I'm planning to go to France. You've just been to Germany and have some left-over euros and want to go to the States. Now we could separately go to Thomas Cook and swap our respective dollars and euros into sterling and then into the currency we want. Or you and I could do a swap between each other. That's all a currency swap is.

The only difference between us and companies is that they will probably be borrowing the money. So all that happens is that a company (Company A, which we'll say is a UK company) borrows in its home market (sterling) and then swaps the proceeds of its loan with a company in another country (Company B, which we'll say is a US company) that has done the same (dollars). Company B wants sterling to set up a factory in the UK and Company A wants dollars to do the same in the US.

Again, it's driven by companies that have cheaper access to their local currency but (in this case) want a foreign currency. Since they are probably also borrowing the money at the same time and may also want to swap interest rates, it is still cheaper to borrow locally and swap the proceeds than to try to borrow in the market of the desired currency.

Again, a bank may stand in the middle or act as counterparty.

At the end of the deal, the principal is swapped back. In the meantime each is servicing its own debt but making a payment across to the other if, under the swap, it would have been worse off and the other better off.

In fact, under both types of swap and in order to reduce counterparty risk, the companies may simply make a periodic net settlement: each continues to service its own debt, then they periodically tot up who would have been worse or better off under the swap structure, and the loser pays the amount of the difference across to the winner.

The important point is that although there is a winner and a loser, each is getting (synthetically) what it wants: the other's position.

OTHER TYPES OF SWAP

The two outlined above are the simplest and oldest. But the term has come to cover any instrument that enables one party to reduce or take on an exposure. So, for example, an equity swap enables an investor to continue to hold its share portfolio while being, economically, in the position of having sold it, at least for the duration of the swap. A credit default swap enables a lender to get rid of its exposure to a borrower or class of borrowers by simply paying a premium to the swap provider. But who might that be? In the case of credit default swaps or credit derivatives (as credit default swaps are now called), the answer is: hedge funds and other investors that can't lend because they aren't banks but which want to enjoy the same position as if they could, and can do so by providing credit derivatives (see below). There are now plenty of other swaps such as *basis swaps*, *pay-fixed swaps*, *forward starting swaps*, *yield curve swaps* and so on. There are even *tax rate swaps* (exchanging one tax position for another).

Swaps can even be combined with other derivatives: a *swaption* (option on a swap) allows the holder to enter into an interest rate swap and is used to swap fixed-rate cashflows that are irregular where one party doesn't want to do the swap unless some market condition (risk) happens. Swaptions are themselves traded. A *Bermuda swaption* allows the holder to enter into a swap on a sequence of dates.

A lot of these swaps are themselves traded in the OTC market (though not sufficiently standardised to trade on an exchange), which is why the total market for swaps is huge. In fact, and it's worth making the point here, the OTC derivatives markets dwarf the futures exchanges in volume, using standard contracts produced by ISDA.

But swaps aren't limited to exchanging liabilities. There are also *asset swaps* where parties exchange the return on assets (e.g. an unlisted equity into a bond), *total return swaps* (where all the cashflows such as interest or dividends are paid to the holder as if it held the bond or share directly) and even *property swaps*.

Property swaps achieve exposure to the property market without transferring the physical property assets. The party that wants to reduce its property exposure (a long-term holder such as an institutional investor) pays part of that return (rent or an amount tied to a property index) to the one that wants to increase its immediate exposure (a property developer that doesn't want to waste months going through long-winded property purchases) which, in return, simply pays annual interest on the notional value of the assets swapped. The developer is betting that property returns will increase at a higher rate than it could get from a bank. If it is wrong the institutional investor wins. Each has avoided the usual property costs (legal, tax and agents' fees) while being able to act on their view of the market much more quickly than if trying to complete an actual property transaction.

This is where swaps and other derivatives start to converge because they simply create a different, synthetic position.

CREDIT DERIVATIVES

When banks lend to companies they don't always want to hold on to the loan, for all sorts of reasons: for instance they may subsequently find a better borrower to lend to; or they may be overexposed to a particular borrower or sector and want to get rid of some of the loan. The problem is that the bank doesn't want to tell the borrower: it will ruin the relationship and banks invest time and effort in becoming a corporate borrower's *relationship bank*.

But bank loans are not especially tradable – they are not like bonds. There are only three ways in which a bank can pass on a loan to another bank (in what is called the *secondary loan market*). But the only way this can be done safely from a legal point of view is by telling the borrower. The three methods are:

Sub-participation – This is generally the most popular way but the least satisfactory from a legal standpoint. Here the bank sells part of its loan to another bank, but that second bank has no direct relationship with the borrower and so is completely reliant on the first bank to pass on its share of the interest and repayments of principal. The borrower doesn't know.

Assignment – This is safer than sub-participation but not quite as safe as novation. The bank simply transfers its loan to the second bank. The borrower knows because it now pays the second bank directly.

Novation – This is, from a legal point of view, the safest way. The old loan is replaced in its entirety by a new loan between the new bank and the borrower. The borrower has to sign the new loan, so it knows all about it.

Credit derivatives overcome these problems. The underlying loan is left in place but the second bank agrees to pay the lender if the borrower defaults. The second bank receives a fee or premium and the lender recovers the amount of any default from it. The borrower doesn't know and the second bank doesn't have to have any direct recourse to the borrower.

In fact credit derivatives can be designed to be triggered by any deterioration in a borrower's credit standing – not just a default which, short of insolvency, is the most extreme. If so, the trigger is by *reference* to the borrower's credit rating, i.e. the *reference company's credit standing*.

The bank providing the credit protection is called the *protection-seller* and is basically writing a put option allowing the lender to 'put' the loan to it or, rather, to recover any loss from holding the loan. A protection-seller may hedge its position by – oddly – buying protection from the borrower which thus earns a fee for not defaulting. This is called a *self-referenced credit default swap*.

TOTAL RETURN SWAPS, CREDIT DEFAULT SWAPS AND CREDIT-LINKED NOTES

So a credit derivative is a contract to transfer the risk of total return on a *credit asset* falling below an agreed level, without transferring that underlying asset. In essence this family of swaps includes:

- *Total return swap* – see above
- *Credit default swaps* (which, however, provide protection only against certain specified credit events whereas the total return swap guarantees the total return)
- *Credit-linked notes* – which combine a credit default swap with a bond (i.e. they have a coupon, maturity and redemption) and are used by investment managers to hedge against rating downgrades or defaults.

This credit derivatives market has grown rapidly with more than $25 trillion outstanding, easily more than the total of all the world's corporate debt. Innovation in this market is constant. A recent development is the constant proportion debt obligation or CPDO which does for an entire index what a credit default swap does for exposure to a company.

The only problem is that banks have been tempted to take on a lot of credit default risk without realising the systemic nature of the risk: if one borrower defaults the chances are that many will because it will be the result of general market conditions (e.g. increase in interest rates or recession).

Which is a good point at which to look at how the capital markets have enabled entire books of loans to be traded – see the next chapter.

Chapter 14

THE ALCHEMY
OF SECURITISATION

SPEED-READ SUMMARY

- Securitisation turns loans that are fixed assets on a bank's balance sheet into securities (bonds) that can be readily traded

- The originator sells the loans to a special purpose vehicle which issues bonds to investors and uses the proceeds from the issue to pay the bank for the loans – money the bank then lends all over again

- There are complex mechanisms to meet early redemptions and defaults and provide credit enhancement and liquidity support

- Any predictable stream of income (receivables) can be securitised – even the receivables of an entire business (whole business securitisations)

- Such issues are also called asset-backed securities

- Existing bonds and loans can be pooled, and fresh securities – called collateralised debt obligations – issued off the back of them

- Securitisation wasn't the cause of the sub-prime credit crunch, but it certainly made sub-prime lending possible

---

So we come full circle. I started way back in Chapter 1 telling you about the causes of the credit crunch and I mentioned something called securitisation and directed you to this chapter. In the last chapter we covered derivatives and in this chapter we look at securitisation – the two types of financial instrument that have had greatest impact on the markets in the last 20 years. And here's the irony: although you can achieve a securitisation the way I'm going to describe it, nowadays you almost don't have to bother because in many cases you can achieve the same effect using a derivative, namely a swap.

Securitisation takes a commercial bank loan and turns it into a bond. What is magic about this is that loans are not tradable but bonds are. So securitisation acts as a bridge between the loan and bond markets: it enables the capacity of the bond markets to be harnessed for the benefit of the smaller loan market.

WHY LOANS BLOCK UP BANK BALANCE SHEETS

Commercial banks need securitisation because loans clog up a bank's balance sheet. Banks lend long but borrow short (funding themselves with deposits repayable on demand and on the short-term inter-bank market – a large contributor to the credit crunch). So central banks insist that the banks they regulate maintain a cash cushion of several percent of their loan book (called *capital adequacy*) to ensure banks always have enough liquidity (free funds) to meet depositors' withdrawals. If a bank couldn't repay deposits on demand, there would be panic amongst depositors, a *run on the bank*, the bank would close and other banks that had lent to it on the interbank market might start to collapse too. This is, in effect, what happened with Northern Rock.

Capital adequacy and the Basel Accords

Central banks from the world's top ten economies (G10) coordinate their regulation of the world's banks through the *Basel Committee on Banking Supervision*.

The committee is based at the Bank for International Settlements in Basel, Switzerland and its successive policy agreements are called the *Basel Accords*. They focus in particular on establishing prudent levels of *capital adequacy* for banks. The latest, Basel 2, was discussed in Chapter 6.

The problem is that capital adequacy is a cost to the bank. The bank is paying interest to depositors and interbank lenders in respect of it. Meanwhile, the bank is prevented from making more loans because it already has a full loan book for the amount of regulatory capital it has. This matters because commercial banks (and at the heart of every conglomerate, universal or integrated bank there is a commercial bank) depend for their profits not just on interest from existing loans but on the arrangement and other fees they charge on new loans. So banks need to continue lending to survive.

Of course, a bank could sell its loan book. But the only people interested in buying a book of loans would be other banks, and they're trying to get rid of their own. This was the conundrum that the brilliant brains at investment bank Salomon Brothers (now part of Citigroup) set about solving almost 30 years ago. How could they find buyers for these loan books? The brilliantly simple solution was to turn the loans into bonds and sell the bonds to the much deeper institutional investor market. Easy to say. Much harder to do, as we shall see.

Thanks to Salomons, a bank can *securitise* its loans (i.e. turn them into *securities*) and get them off its balance sheet (OBS is the term used to describe *off balance sheet finance*).

What happens is that the bank (called the *originator*) sets up a special purpose vehicle (SPV). SPVs are typically off-the-shelf companies (newly formed) with no assets and are based in tax havens like the Netherlands Antilles, British Virgin Islands and so on. This is to ensure they are not subject to tax: any interference with the flows of cash through the SPV (e.g. incidence of taxation on the SPV) would wreck the structure.

The bank *sells its loan book* to the SPV. This removes ownership of the loan book from the bank's balance sheet. The SPV issues bonds to investors, the investors pay the SPV for the bonds and the SPV pays this money to the bank as the purchase price for the loan book (which gives the bank a whole pile of fresh money to make new loans with).

Now, as interest on the loans comes into the bank it simply diverts this interest to the SPV which passes the interest on to the investors. It's important that the bank no longer keeps this interest, otherwise that implies it still owns the loans, which would undermine the structure. The bonds are effectively *backed* by the loans, and investors who buy the

SPV's bond issue do so because they know the interest they receive will come from the loans the bank made.

As loans mature, the repayments of capital are used to redeem the bonds. Investors can buy and sell the bonds in the capital markets in the usual way. Result: an illiquid asset is now tradable; the bank's balance sheet is freed up.

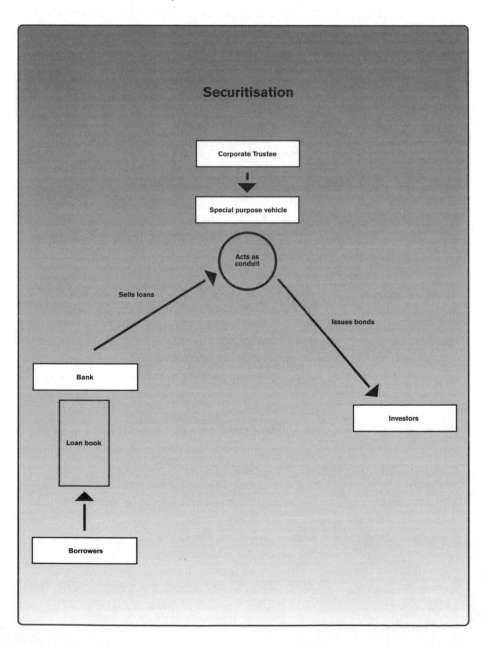

COPING WITH EARLY REDEMPTION

One problem is how to cope with the different maturities of the underlying loans. The answer is to divide the bond issue itself into *tranches*, with some bonds repayable after, say, five years and others after, say, ten. Investors buy the maturity they want. All loans maturing or repaid within the first five years are used to redeem the five-year bonds, and those maturing or repaid between five and ten years are used to redeem the ten-year bonds. In the meantime the proceeds of the loans repaid the earliest in a tranche can be reinvested elsewhere to continue providing bondholders with an interest stream.

COPING WITH DEFAULT

Bondholders would not be amused if there were any hiccup in their receipt of interest or repayment of capital. This risk of delay or default is covered by *credit enhancement* and *liquidity support*.

Credit enhancement can be provided by a *monoline insurer* (which provides insurance against any default; monoline means that it specialises in this business) or – as you were just about to say – a *credit derivative* (see last chapter).

Liquidity support ensures that there is always cash to pay interest due on the bonds. The four main methods of providing liquidity support are:
- Establishment of a *cash deposit* which can be drawn upon to fund a delay in payments. The cash deposit would be funded out of either the proceeds of issue of the bonds or money advanced under a subordinated loan. A bank that agrees to accept the SPV's cash deposits in return for a specified rate does so under a *guaranteed investment contract* (or 'gic')
- *Liquidity facility* – i.e. a committed loan facility provided by a suitably rated entity (such as a stand-by credit from another bank)
- A *second tranche of bonds subordinated to (i.e. coming behind) the main issue* which will receive interest only if and to the extent that there is sufficient liquidity to pay
- *Overcollateralisation* – i.e. having a pool of assets of $120 million to service securities of $100 million.

The point is that any delay or default is really the originator's (that is, the lending bank's) fault – it made the loans in the first place. So the cost of any delay or default and mechanisms to avoid them is ultimately routed back to the originator.

Historically, the structure works only if it makes the original loans OBS. Therefore the SPV must not be owned by the originator (instead it is usually vested in an independent corporate trustee) and the interest from the underlying loans must be routed away from the originator (though the bank is usually appointed by the SPV to administer the loans so the borrowers aren't aware of the securitisation). The bondholders for their part can sue only the SPV.

The earliest securitisations were of US household mortgages (sound familiar?), which is why securitisations are also called *asset-backed securities*. The reason why Salomons chose home loans for the first securitisations was (1) the last thing people stop paying is their mortgage and (2) in the US many such mortgages are federally guaranteed so these loans were backed by the US government. Good thing it wasn't trying to do that now. Up until the credit crunch, mortgage-backed securities still dominated this market and in their earliest guises were called *pass-through certificates*. But nowadays, securitisations have become completely acceptable to bond investors and anything that offers an income-stream can be securitised. Examples of receivables that have been securitised include: car loans; credit card debts; hire payments under hire purchase agreements; and rentals under equipment leases (asset finance). You may have heard of Bowie bonds – bonds issued on the back of David Bowie's future stream of royalties (which was a way for him to enjoy as a lump sum now earnings stretching decades into the future after his death.

But, even more exciting, securitisation has been harnessed in M&As and venture capital deals: a business's future income-stream can be securitised to raise capital (this is called *whole business securitisation*) – almost using the business to buy itself (where allowed: under UK company law, there are rules against *financial assistance* which is when a company uses its own money to buy its own shares).

COLLATERALISED DEBT OBLIGATIONS (CDOs)

The idea behind any *asset-backed bond issue* is to package up revenue-producing assets then launch a bond issue off the back of them, using the revenue-stream to pay the interest on the bonds. CDOs do this: loans or bonds payable by various borrowers are pooled and new securities (CDOs) are issued that pay out according to the performance of the pool. The term 'collateralised' simply means the new securities are underpinned by the underlying loan and bonds. I

Structured finance

This is a loose term used to describe any *repackaging* of an existing security or the attaching of a derivative to it, such as a bond with an option attached.

One example is stripping coupons from bonds and selling them separately (the original bonds become *zero-coupon* or *deep discount* bonds while what were the coupons become a set of bonds with different maturities). These are sometimes called *STRIPS* (separately registered interest and principal securities).

Another is *securitising trade finance* receivables (remember factoring, discounting and the à forfait market?).

Structured notes are bonds whose cashflows depend on one or more indices and/or that have embedded forwards or options.

---

mentioned earlier that SIVs were set up by banks to hold pools of CDOs including sub-prime home loans. SIVs were themselves meant to be OBS but some did so badly that the sponsoring bank felt obliged to stand behind it – this is what did for US investment bank **Bear Stearns**, amongst others.

Like securitisation in general (of which they are an example), CDOs take loans off commercial banks' balance sheets. Because they pool the debt of various borrowers, a CDO issue can – like any securitisation – be packaged into tranches but here each tranche has a different level of risk (rather than maturity) with the top slice representing triple-A borrowers where risk of default is lowest. The bottom slice (representing the worst credits in the pool) takes the first losses and for this reason is called (confusingly) the *equity tranche* (since it bears a level of risk closer to equity) or, more colloquially, *toxic waste*. One problem with CDOs is that the toxic waste often ended up with the bank selling the CDO, because no investors were prepared to buy it, although the upside was supposedly that the toxic waste also carried the potential for the highest return. It comes as no surprise that hedge funds were big buyers of CDOs.

Just to recap, in case you came in late or have been half asleep or have been chatting at the back of the class: the recent sub-prime crisis was exacerbated by exactly this consequence. What happened was that loans (usually mortgages) were made to sub-prime credits (which in plain English means people who are the least likely to be able to repay). These were then securitised and sold off, with the banks which packaged these securities pocketing chunky fees. Many were shoved into SIVs (structured investment vehicles) which were funds set up to invest in these instruments. When the US housing market started to collapse in 2007, it meant that the real collateral behind these securitised loans – mortgaged property – was worth less than the debt incurred to buy it. So the value of the instruments created by securitising sub-prime loans plunged too. This in turn meant that banks holding the toxic waste were sitting on huge losses as indeed were SIVs (many of them managed by the same banks). This in turn led to the credit crunch (inability to borrow money) because banks were unwilling to lend to each other since no one knew who else might be bust. Result: gridlock in the financial markets, huge declared losses, battered balance sheets and banks running cap-in-hand to governments and sovereign wealth funds to bail them out by buying their shares.

Some CDOs are synthetic, made up of pools of credit derivatives. Others, called *Russian dolls*, contain investments in other CDOs.

This idea of slicing or 'tranching' levels of risk is being applied to the credit default swaps market and these techniques are beginning to converge. Having different levels of risk is an insurance concept – as we will see in the next chapter.

Chapter 15

LLOYD'S OF LONDON & THE REINSURANCE MARKET

SPEED-READ SUMMARY

- Lloyd's is the centre of the world's insurance and reinsurance industry. It is part of the City but is not regarded as part of the financial markets

- It is made up of managing agents, members' agents, Names and brokers

- Managing agents are underwriters and they run syndicates which specialise in marine, motor, aviation and non-marine risks

- Syndicate capacity is provided by Names who used to be individuals but are now companies

- Members' agents look after Names and advise them on which syndicates to join

- Brokers bring risks to Lloyd's to be insured or reinsured

- In the 1980s, Lloyd's was brought to a standstill but after Reconstruction & Renewal in the early 1990s, old liabilities were hived off into Equitas

- Catastrophe bonds and alternative risk transfer are means of using the capital markets to fund reinsurance risk

And now for something completely different. Lloyd's of London is most certainly part of the City. It's in Lime Street at the eastern end of the City, the part that's historically and geographically closest to London's old docks. But Lloyd's is not regarded as part of the financial markets. Instead it is at the heart of the insurance and reinsurance world.

Insurance and shipping are intimately connected. The one was spawned by the other: people with maritime interests – captains, shipowners and merchants with cargoes – would gather in Edward Lloyd's coffee shop in the 1690s to make deals and share information about the fates of vessels and their cargoes. Wealthy individuals would share the risk of insuring a ship and its cargo. They became known as underwriters and had unlimited liability: they had to meet a claim even if it bankrupted them. Eventually the insurance market outgrew the coffee shop and moved, taking the name with it. (The shipping market itself – which trades ships' capacity to carry cargo, called *charters* – is separate and is known as the *Baltic Exchange*.)

MANAGING AGENTS, MEMBERS' AGENTS AND NAMES

Lloyd's was therefore a club – like the stock exchange – and made its own rules. The stock exchange had jobbers and brokers. Lloyd's had *managing agents*, *members' agents* and *Names* (always written with a capital 'N'). Managing agents ran *syndicates* and were the modern-day underwriters. Each syndicate had capacity to underwrite risk. This capacity was provided by Names. Names were not active members of the market (although most managing agents were also Names and were called *working Names*); they were individuals who were essentially investors. Members' agents acted for Names, putting them on syndicates and managing their affairs.

SYNDICATES AND BROKERS

Each of the 66 syndicates specialised in certain types of risk: *marine, motor, aviation* and *non-marine* (everything else). The managing agent would accept risk on behalf of the syndicate. His expertise lay in pricing risks, the price being the *premium* paid to the syndicate for underwriting the risk. *Brokers*, acting for clients with risks, placed those risks with syndicates by going round managing agents who would accept a slice of the risk, which went on the underwriter's *slip* (bit of paper).

BECOMING A NAME

It was always regarded as a social and professional coup to be invited to be a Name at Lloyd's.

Membership was by invitation only. All a prospective Name had to show was liquid assets of £250,000 (later put up to £500,000) but – and this is the key to understanding why people wanted to become Names at Lloyd's – you didn't hand the money over (as you would if you were making an investment). No, instead, a Name simply had to keep the money in fairly liquid assets – cash, a bank deposit or shares would do (not a house or an Old Master painting) – in order to meet any claims if necessary.

In practice, unless the syndicates in which a Name participated had a really bad year, the Name would never have to produce the money. So this money could be invested elsewhere while providing the Name with underwriting capacity at Lloyd's. Like any long-term investment, good years at Lloyd's outnumbered the bad over time. So to be a Name was a guaranteed path to wealth, especially since that £250,000 was earning a double return.

Until the 1980s, that is.

HOW THE MARKET REACHED MELTDOWN

Three events coincided which bankrupted 1500 Names (out of 34,000), caused some to commit suicide and changed the market forever:

- **Long-tail asbestosis liability** It was in the 1980s that the risks to health of asbestosis became widely known. In the US, those affected (many of whom were retired) sued their former employees and these companies claimed on policies in existence at the time, going back decades. US courts awarded triple damages (as they do for egregious tortious liability) and much of this massive liability ended back at Lloyd's. Names who'd been invited to join in the 1980s alleged that Lloyd's knew of this impending liability and recruited them to share the burden. This was always denied by Lloyd's and never proved.
- **Baby syndicates** Names discovered that working Names (the managing agents) were running *baby syndicates* within their actual syndicates. These were mini-syndicates into which managing agents invited each other and into which they siphoned off the best business of the syndicates they ran. This was not at the time against the rules (parliament later legislated against it) but Names regarded it as a breach

of trust. Working Names responded that since it was their underwriting expertise that made the profit for Names, the latter shouldn't mind if working Names kept some of the cream for themselves.

- **LMX spiral** This was the practice of sending the same risk round the market, enabling each syndicate to book some of the premium before passing the risk on. It inflated syndicates' income and meant that when a claim was made it hit the whole market. In short, the LMX spiral concentrated risk in the market, rather than spreading it.

New Names had good grounds for complaint. But the position was exacerbated by:
- A succession of poor underwriting years caused by a coincidence of major claims – earthquakes, hurricanes, plane crashes, oil rig disasters, terrorist acts
- The fact that members' agents didn't put new Names on the best-performing syndicates (since, by definition, they weren't the ones needing capacity) but on either new syndicates without experience or track record or old ones that had had bad years and needed additional capacity; in other words, syndicates less likely to perform well.

By the early 1990s Lloyd's was in a mess. The market was at a standstill with Names suing members' agents and managing agents, and syndicates suing each other, not to mention the LMX spiral. The whole market was gridlocked by litigation. Only the lawyers did well.

RECONSTRUCTION & RENEWAL

So Lloyd's instigated an enormously complex process called R&R (Reconstruction & Renewal) out of which emerged an entity called Equitas to meet all these claims. Equitas was capitalised at $14 billion, making it the largest reinsurer in the world at the time. Lloyd's drew a line under all that had happened and essentially started again as a brand new market, with all the old residual risks hived off to Equitas to meet those claims as they came in. As a condition of R&R, all litigation was stopped.

CORPORATE CAPITAL

And – a decision that still rankles with some Names who hoped to trade out of their losses – Lloyd's decided that it would switch to corporate capital: instead of syndicate capacity being provided by individuals, 80%-plus is now provided by corporate capital – companies that provide syndicates with their underwriting capacity. Think of these companies as investment trusts: they 'invest' in syndicates, and people who want to invest in Lloyd's can do so by investing in these companies (although investors tend to be insurance companies, insurance brokers and institutional investors rather than individuals).

You might argue that companies have limited liability (which they do) so that syndicates now have more limited backing than with old-style Names. Not so. In the old days, individual Names could and did go bankrupt. But the mutualising effect of having syndicates backed by Names meant that no syndicate would have all of its Names go bankrupt at once, so it could always meet claims. So it is with corporate capital. No syndicate will be faced with having all of its backers go bust at the same time.

REINSURANCE

Mention of Equitas (above) as a reinsurer is a reminder that Lloyd's is principally a *reinsurance* market.

Insurance companies don't just take in the premium and sit on the risk. They take in the risk from the insured (you and me) in return for a premium, then place the bulk of that risk with other companies called *reinsurers* and pass on a slice of the premium. These reinsurers aren't household names because they don't deal with the retail market (people like you and me). But they can be big companies and they often have the word *Re* in their name, such as **Munich Re, Swiss Re** and so on. These companies that take on primary insurers' risk are called *retrocessionaires*. They in turn may lay off part of the risk to further reinsurers who in turn may lay some of it off at Lloyd's.

In fact Lloyd's is the largest reinsurance market in the world, partly because it has never failed to meet a claim and partly because its underwriters are expert at pricing new and novel risks. For example, the first space satellites were insured at Lloyd's. An underwriter (managing agent) at Lloyd's will always quote a price no matter how strange or new the type of risk in question – for example terrorist risk. Someone once obtained cover against seeing a ghost.

ALTERNATIVE RISK TRANSFER

A related area of finance is called *alternative risk transfer*. It's basically about harnessing the capacity of the capital markets (which are huge) to help the insurance market (which, surprisingly, is much smaller). Sound familiar?

CAT BONDS

At its simplest, you take a risk of a catastrophe (say a hurricane or an earthquake) and you securitise it by turning it into a bond. In other words, an insurance company insures the risk then buys a reinsurance contract from an SPV (special purpose vehicle) which issues catastrophe bonds to institutional investors. The bond, as usual, has a specified maturity, which can be anything from short- to long-term. Now, this is where it gets interesting. If, during the life of the bond, the catastrophe occurs, the investors can lose interest on the bond and even part or all of their principal – depending on the terms of the bond and their own risk appetite: this is because the risk is tranched (sound familiar?) into different levels of risk to suit different investor appetites. Yet cat (catastrophe) bond issues total almost $2 billion a year: hedge funds are big buyers, surprise, surprise.

To understand this, you have to understand how insurance works. Essentially, insurers offer cover in layers. So, for a catastrophe, the first layer might be $1 billion: any losses up to $1 billion are within that layer and met by the insurer or insurers *on line* for that layer. But if the losses spike up through that layer, then any *excess* which pushes the losses into the next layer is met by the insurers of the next layer. So, as a pension fund, you might buy a bond that is only at risk if losses hit more than, say, $10 billion. Now, that would require a heck of a catastrophe, so in the context of risk, it's not as much of a gamble as it may sound.

A more sophisticated version may make the trigger not so much the catastrophe itself but the level of the insurance company's own loss, or the level of industry losses. And the bond may be structured not only in loss tranches (as above) but in terms of whether the bondholder loses principal or simply forgoes interest and recovers the principal at the end of the bond's term.

If so, the investor is actually doing nothing more foolish than making an interest-free loan (of course, if the trigger event doesn't happen, the investor still receives interest – usually at a high rate to reward it for the risk). Now, an interest-free loan is exactly what is required when a catastrophe occurs: money to put things right, money that in due course can be paid back or refinanced. This is sometimes called a 'stand-by

Cat bonds and weather derivatives

The very first catastrophe bond to be concieved, in the mid-1990s by the **California Earthquake Authority**, was never in fact issued. Ironically, the layer of insurance it was intended to cover was in fact provided by – you guessed it – Warren Buffett's Berkshire Hathaway. He weighed up the risk of loss against the rate of return and thought it so attractive he bought the lot. There wasn't an earthquake.

One of the first successful cat bond issues was made by Swiss insurer **Winterthur** in the late 1990s to cover it against the risk of hailstone damage to cars (a major source of claims in Switzerland). Investors' capital was not at risk and they obtained conversion rights into Winterthur's stock on the bond's maturity. If a single event (hailstorm) damaged more than 6000 insured cars, the bond's coupon would be forfeit that year.

Various attempts have been made over the last ten years to create markets in catastrophe and related products (e.g. *weather derivatives*) where – just like the futures markets – such risks can be transferred efficiently through a deep and liquid market. **CATEX**, an electronic exchange for the trading of catastrophe risks and weather derivatives, was launched in 1994 and they are now also traded on the CME.

Generally, such attempts have been hampered by low volumes (making it relatively poor business for brokers and locals) and lack of benchmark indices. Without sufficient volume, it's hard to create a viable index. Without an index, a broader range of non-specialist investors will be less likely to participate because they will have no way of knowing how well their investments are doing in relative terms.

Farmers can insure against the risks of poor weather, tourist resorts against loss of earnings. Energy companies use *heating degree days* contracts which work like options, paying out a set amount where the temperature falls below the strike.

capital commitment'. So *catastrophe bonds* can be structured to provide, effectively, a *stand-by facility* (like an overdraft) just at that point when money may be otherwise difficult to raise. Insurance gives you the money to cover your losses; a stand-by capital commitment lends it to you.

HOW IT WORKS IN PRACTICE

For example, take an oil company. This company uses a lot of offshore oil rigs. Occasionally one of these goes down in stormy weather. The company could insure against that loss. But insurance contracts are annual (syndicates at Lloyd's are, technically, 'annual adventures' that disband and re-form every year). The company insures for a year and if it doesn't suffer a loss, it loses the whole premium. Then as soon as it does lose a rig, the premium goes up – because whichever insurer was holding the contract that year has suffered a total loss just for one year's premium.

Now, statistically the company reckons to lose one rig every ten years. So it could do one of two things:

- It could take out a ten-year contract where – if there is no loss – it gets a proportion of the insurance premiums back (this does happen but there aren't a lot of insurers providing that cover – besides which, the company is taking a credit risk on an insurer being around for that long!); or
- The company could issue a bond for ten years and specify that if during that time it loses a rig, the bond will not pay interest for, say, three years. What this gives the company is interest-free money for a period when it needs it most – when its credit standing has been impaired because of the loss of a rig so that the cost of funds to replace the rig will be at their most expensive. In essence, the company is issuing a bond instead of paying an insurance premium. Clever, eh?

Don't forget that institutional investors would only commit, at most, a tiny part of their portfolios to catastrophe bonds in the hope of earning a high reward. But loss of interest will not damage the portfolio overall (the effect of diversification). And the benefit of bonds is that they can be held by a wide spread of investors; whereas a reinsurance contract may be held by fewer insurers. Hedge funds were amongst the first investors to spot the opportunities.

So what happens is that: (1) capital markets' capacity (roughly $20 trillion) is used to top up reinsurance capacity (roughly $150 billion) and (2) the risk is spread more widely amongst investors than it might have been if it had remained concentrated in the insurance and reinsurance markets.

A fitting final note about Lloyd's and the insurance and reinsurance markets: it was thought that Equitas (see above) would run out of money. But in the event, in 2006 Warren Buffett's Berkshire Hathaway fund agreed to buy $5.7 billion of reinsurance cover from Equitas with a further $1.3 billion in 2009.

Which reveals what, I think, is one of the most interesting facets of the financial markets: how it all connects.

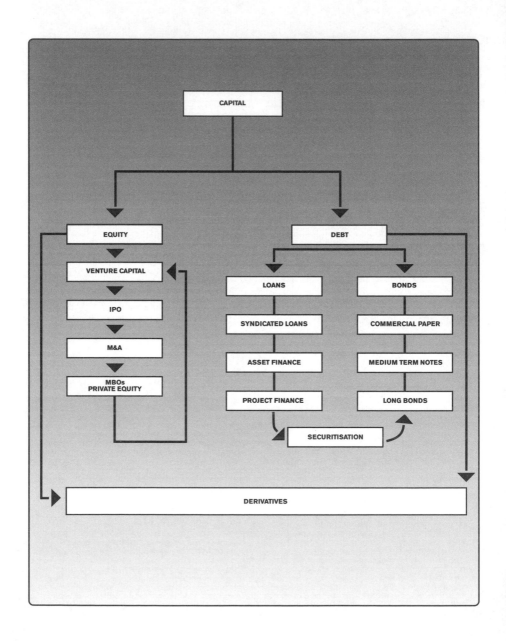

AFTERWORD & BIBLIOGRAPHY
– WHERE NEXT?

Congratulations on getting this far. I started this book by saying that I keep a simple framework in mind when thinking about who does what in the City (companies/banks/institutional investors/brokers).

If it helps, I also use another one (see opposite). What this does is to show the two types of capital (equity and debt) and then to place much of the contents of this book under each heading. So venture capital, IPOs, M&As and MBOs are under equity (with the link from MBOs/private equity back to venture capital). Then I divide debt into loans and bonds. Under loans are other types of commercial banking transaction. Under bonds I put the different maturities from commercial paper up to long bonds. The reference to securitisation is a reminder that it is used to turn non-tradable bank loans into tradable securities. Finally, I put derivatives at the bottom because they cover both equity and debt instruments. This picture doesn't cover everything (for instance convertible bonds which can flip into equity; or acquisition finance) but I hope it helps.

WHAT NEXT
Now, this book should have:
- provided you with a framework into which to slot whatever else you learn about the City, finance and the international capital markets and the institutions active in them
- given you the confidence to ask questions to further your knowledge, however simple or stupid you may think those questions are
- sparked in you sufficient interest to go on and sample other books by real experts. If so, here are the ones I recommend.

OVERVIEWS
You can't go wrong with the three titles in the Economist Books series. If this book is a basic guide, they are definitely the next step up. They are:

The City: A Guide to London's Global Financial Centre by Richard Roberts published by Economist/Profile, London (2004)

Wall Street: The Markets, Mechanisms and Players also by Richard Roberts published by Economist/Profile, London (2003)

Guide to Financial Markets by Marc Levinson published by Economist/Profile, London (2002)

They are particularly good on recent history and provide extensive statistical information. Roberts in *The City* devotes a whole chapter to scandals. Juicy.

A good round-up of recent developments that also ties in government policy is *City State* by Richard Roberts (who wrote two of the Economist series above) and David Kynaston (who wrote the history detailed below) published by Profile, London (2001).

FINANCE AND BANKING

A fine collection of essays originally published as articles in the *Financial Times* is *Mastering Finance: The Definitive Guide to the Foundations and Frontiers of Finance*, ed. Tim Dickson and George Bickerstaffe and published by FT Pitman Publishing, London (1997).

The Business of Banking: An Introduction to the Modern Financial Services Industry by Geoffrey Lipscombe and Keith Pond and published by Financial World Publishing, Canterbury (2002) is a good primer.

INSIDE AN INVESTMENT BANK

Two books that give you some idea of what investment banking is really like are *Goldman Sachs: The Culture of Success* by Lisa Endlichs published by Little Brown, New York (1999) which gives a fascinating insight into what makes Goldman Sachs different; and *Liar's Poker* by Michael Lewis, published by Hodder & Stoughton, London (1989) – the first true account of life as a trader in a bank which reads at times like a Marx Brothers' slapstick.

COMMERCIAL BANKING / LENDING

How to Negotiate Eurocurrency Loan Agreements by Lee C Buchheit published by IFLR/Euromoney Institutional Investor, London (2000) This thin volume is a must-read for all bankers and corporate borrowers.

Buchheit learned his craft as a partner in major US law firm C
Gottlieb and became the legal doyen of the debt-rescheduling n
the 1980s and 1990s. This book sets out typical clauses and wha
lender's and borrower's negotiating arguments are. It is also – I kid y
not – one of the funniest books I have ever read. Indispensable.

IPOs

The London Stock Exchange produces a great deal of useful
information and publications. In particular its *Practical Guide to Listing*
published in conjunction with law firm DLA Piper is very clear and
explains the underlying business considerations as well as the process.
Visit the LSE's website at: www.londonstockexchange.com

MARKETS

The classic book is *Reminiscences of a Stock Operator* by Edwin
Lefèvre, first published in 1923, which is the fictionalised biography of
ace speculator Jesse Livermore. The edition on my shelf was published
by Wiley, New York (1994).

There are also numerous books on Warren Buffett and his value
approach to investing. The one I have is *Benjamin Graham on Value
Investing* by Janet Lowe, published by Pitman, London (1995). Graham,
sometimes described as the father of financial analysis, lived through
the 1929 crash and his approach is the basis of Buffett's. The book is
based on interviews with a number of value investors including Buffett.

You may want to keep by your armchair *The Financial Times Guide to
Using the Financial Pages* by Romesh Vaitilingam published by FT
Pitman Publishing/Pearson (1996).

ECONOMICS

Free Lunch: Easily Digestible Economics by David Smith published by
Profile, London (2004) is a concise, readable guide by the economics
editor of the *Sunday Times*.

RISK

If you're interested in risk, read *Seeing Tomorrow: Rewriting the Rules
of Risk* by Ron S Dembo and Andrew Freeman published by John
Wiley, New York (1998). It bridges psychology and maths in a
wonderfully readable way.

DERIVATIVES

One of the best books on derivatives is actually a legal text book, *Derivatives Law & Documentation* (Sweet & Maxwell), by Simon Firth, a top derivatives partner at Linklaters. The opening chapter is a masterly summary of derivative types and the derivatives market.

LAW

The multi-volume *Law and Practice of International Finance* by Philip Wood published by Sweet & Maxwell, London (1995) is without parallel. Wood spent his career at Allen & Overy and was the pre-eminent banking lawyer of his generation, synthesising common law and civil law precepts.

HISTORY

There is nothing new under the sun. What goes round comes round. Everything the City does now was first done three thousand years ago by the Hittites, or something like that. Read David Kynaston's splendid and definitive four-volume history to see how and why: *The City of London* by David Kynaston published by Chatto & Windus/Pimlico (1994 onwards).

JARGON BUSTERS

There are numerous on-line research sources. Two good jargon-busters are:
www.wikipedia.com
www.investopedia.com

I also use *A-Z of International Finance: The Essential Guide to Tools, Terms & Techniques* by Stephen Mahony published by FT Pitman Publishing/Pearson (1997) which is a dictionary of financial terms and trades.

FINANCIAL PRESS

I try to keep up-to-date by scanning the pages of the financial press regularly. The ones I like are:
- The *Financial Times* – the daily paper known as the 'pink 'un' because of the salmon-pink paper it's printed on. See the box on how to read it in a way that looks knowledgeable
- *The Economist* – a weekly current affairs newspaper (it calls itself a newspaper but is a magazine): its business and finance sections are a must-read.

I also dip into *Euromoney* magazine, which has all of the gossip and analysis about what is happening in the world's capital markets.

How to read the *Financial Times*

1. The FT comes in two parts, the main section and the companies & markets section. There may also be supplements – e.g. the investment management supplement and various surveys that are country- or sector-specific (e.g. Zaire or the Motor Trade). The first thing to do is to bin the supplements (many of them are advertising driven) unless you happen to be interested in the subject (the FT's supplements, it has to be said, are better than most).

2. Next, read the Lex column, on the back page of the first section. It is written by the FT's bright young writers and is read by captains of industry, bankers, politicians and other opinion formers. After a while you detect a pattern. If they are commenting on X plc, a company that has just unveiled sparkling results, the piece will be along the lines of 'how much longer can they keep this up – must be heading for a fall'. If it's on Y plc, a bombed-out stock, the word will be 'can only get better from here'.

3. Next, read the first few pages of the second section (Companies & Markets) – you'll know when to stop because halfway through the words run out and it turns into figures, reporting stock, commodity and currency markets globally.

4. So put the second section to one side and read the first section – glance at the front page, then read it from back to front. Unless you're fascinated by geopolitics and the latest round of trade talks, it gets progressively more boring the closer you get to the front.

5. Next, turn back to the remaining pages of the second section (the ones covered in numbers) and scan this with a serious look on your face. This stage is optional and depends on whether you want your fellow commuters to think you really have an investment portfolio.

JARGON BUSTER

If you can't find what you want here, try:

- www.wikipedia.com
- www.investopedia.com
- *A–Z of International Finance: The Essential Guide to Tools, Terms & Techniques* by Stephen Mahony

A forfait	The *trade finance* market where *letters of credit* are traded
ABS	Asset-backed security – a bond backed by collateral such as a pool of mortgages
Accelerate	The act of a lender in having a loan repaid early, usually because of an event of *default*
Agent or agent bank	The bank that gets the mandate from a borrower to arrange a syndicated loan for it and collects the repayments from the borrower during the life of the loan to distribute to the other *syndicate* members
AIM	Alternative Investment Market – the junior market to the London Stock Exchange, designed for younger companies with short trading histories (usually because they are in hi-tech fields that require substantial initial investment)
Alpha	The most traded shares ('alpha stock') on the stock exchange, or the difference between the expected return of a portfolio and the actual return achieved
Amortisation	Paying a loan back in a series of instalments
Arbitrage	The act of simultaneously buying and selling in two separate markets to gain from pricing differences between them
Arbitrageur	Someone who practises arbitrage – either professionally or over the internet from home in their pyjamas
Asset finance	Tax-favoured way of funding an asset where a bank (lessor) buys the asset and leases it to the borrower (lessee) for the

	asset's useful economic life in return for regular payments (rental) paid by the lessee over the life of the lease to reimburse the lessor for the capital cost of the asset plus interest. Also known as finance leasing
Balloon repayment	Used in loans and finance leases where the final instalment to be paid by the borrower under the financing is much larger than earlier instalments
Bank	An institution that is licensed to conduct banking business – see *Commercial bank* and *Investment bank*
Basis points	Hundredths of a per cent (0.01%) – so bankers will talk about a bond being priced at 25 basis points over Treasuries, meaning 0.25% over what US government bonds are paying
Basis rate	The rate on which interest under a loan or bond is based, e.g. LIBOR, EURIBOR
Bear	An investor who thinks the market will fall
Bells and whistles	*Swaps* and *options* attached to a bond issue
Bid/Offer	Brokers quote two prices for securities – the price at which they will buy from you (bid) and the price at which they will sell (offer) to you. The difference or 'spread' is their 'turn' (profit) since, obviously, they will bid for less than they will offer
Block trade	Where a bank buys or sells an entire portfolio of securities, usually on behalf of an institutional investor
Bond	An IOU issued by a corporate or bank (the terms 'bond' and 'note' are virtually interchangeable)
Book building	A means of syndicating a financing by soliciting indicative bids from prospective syndicate participants (banks)
Book running	The role taken by a bank in arranging and syndicating a loan or bond issue
Bridge financing	Temporary financing used before the long-term funding is put in place – for instance, a loan taken out by a bidder in an M&A transaction which will then be refinanced by a share or bond issue once the takeover has been completed
Broker	Intermediaries that buy and sell securities as agents for institutions or on their own account, including 'broker-dealers' (market makers) and 'inter-dealer brokers' (brokers that specialise in intermediating between dealers that want

anonymity when trading in the markets)

Bull	An investor who thinks the market will rise
Bullet	Bank loan, the principal of which is repayable in one tranche on its maturity (i.e. no amortisation)
Bunny bond	A bond where the coupon allows the holder to take more bonds instead of interest – leading to a proliferation
Buy side	That part of the market that buys securities – i.e. institutional investors
Cable	The $/£ trade in the foreign-exchange market
Cap	An upper limit or ceiling on the interest payable under a loan
Capital adequacy	A minimum amount of money (capital) that a bank is required to maintain as a ratio to the loans it has made (assets), for prudential reasons to ensure it is able to repay depositors; it is now based on an internationally accepted framework (the Basel Accord) that assigns risk weightings to bank assets and minimum capital ratios
Carry trade	Borrowing at a low rate to buy high-yielding investments
Cashflow	The strength of revenue or income flowing through a business; a business can be very profitable (i.e. make a large margin between its sales and its cost of production) but still go bust because its income lags its cost of sales; equally a business can have strong cashflow but only marginal profitability and still go on year after year
CDO	Collateralised debt obligation – a bond issue backed by a pool of bonds or those which provide the income stream to pay interest to investors
Central bank	A government entity that may have a regulatory function (regulating local banks) or an economic policy function (e.g. controlling inflation) or both
Chapter 11	Named after the US legislation that allows an insolvent company to seek protection from its creditors, so enabling it to restructure and resume trading on a solvent basis
Clearing house	Usually used in the context of a *derivatives* market (*futures* and *options*), this provides the offsetting trade which ensures market participants are not exposed to their *counterparty credit risk*

Collar	A lower limit or floor on the interest payable under a loan
Collateral	The security provided by a borrower for repayment of a loan
Collective investment scheme	A pooled fund that enables investors to invest in shares and bonds indirectly
Commercial bank	A bank that takes in deposits and borrows in the wholesale market in order to make loans. The difference between the interest it receives and the interest it pays is the bank's margin. High street clearing banks are commercial banks
Commercial paper	A type of bond with a very short maturity – usually three months (called '90-day paper')
Commitment	The amount of a loan agreed to be lent by a bank
Committed facility	A loan that a bank is obliged to make up to an agreed maximum and that is available to a borrower for a specified period
Convertible	A bond that gives the holder the right to switch it into equity (shares)
Corporate finance	The banking activity of advising a company on how to raise money and/or an M&A deal
Corporate social responsibility	A movement that requires companies to do more than make profit, but to have regard to their stakeholders (employees, customers, suppliers, local citizens) and their wider position in society as a whole
Counterparty	The other side in a securities or *derivatives* trade
Countertrade	A part of *trade finance* involving the barter of goods and services, often in emerging markets that lack hard currency. For example, a New York law firm was once paid by a government in turkeys and denim. Countertrade specialists act as brokers in such deals
Coupon	The rate of interest paid on a bond – traditionally bonds (other than debentures) were bearer so the issuer would pay interest only to the person bearing the coupon.
Cov-lite	Used to describe a loan agreement or bond which imposes obligations (covenants) on the borrower that are less onerous than usual (this occurs in a toppy bull market where banks are chasing borrowers or issuers)
Credit agreement	The main document under which a loan or other debt-based funding is made

Credit crunch	The term used to describe the collapse in lending from 2007 onwards (especially in the US home loan market) that prompted a global recession from mid-2008 onwards
Credit risk	The risk that a borrower or counterparty may default
Custodian	A bank that holds securities on behalf of an institutional investor
Dark market	A private market where cross-trading occurs without traders or prices being revealed
Dawn raid	M&A term where a bidder builds up an unexpected stake in a target by scooping up shares quickly in the market – a long-standing ban has recently been lifted
Debenture	A corporate bond listed on the London Stock Exchange, often secured on the issuer's assets
Debt	Any form of finance where the borrower agrees to repay the principal amount of the debt and in the meantime to pay interest on it (also known as 'servicing' the debt) which is tax-deductible; the only other form of finance is *equity*
Debtor-in-possession	A company trading out of Chapter 11 insolvency to which senior-ranking loans can be made
Default	Failure to repay a loan or part of a loan on time – usually because the borrower is bust
Dematerial-isation	The electronic record of securities ownership, replacing paper or hard-copy certificates (enabled for the London Stock Exchange by the Uncertificated Securities Regulations 2001 which set out the legal framework for CREST, specifying the conditions on which companies can allow their securities to participate in CREST by allowing shares to be dematerialised and providing for their transfer without a written instrument)
Depositary receipts	Where securities are held on deposit by a bank, acting as depositary, which issues other tradable securities (depositary receipts) in respect of them
Derivatives	Instruments that are derived from shares or bonds and are either *OTC* or exchange traded, such as *futures* and *options*
Disinter-mediation	Borrowers (companies and governments) tapping the capital markets (investors) directly rather than via banks. Banks loathe this idea – it cuts them out – but whenever banks are less creditworthy than their borrowers the latter may bypass them
Drawdown or drawing	The point at which a corporate borrower gets the money it is borrowing

Due diligence	A detailed review of a borrower's financial position, made by a bank or lead manager in a bond or share issue, to satisfy lenders or investors of the borrower's credit standing
Equity	The form of finance where shareholders put up risk capital in return for the prospect of dividend payments and capital growth on their shares; dividends are paid out of the company's taxed income
EURIBOR	Like LIBOR: the interbank offered rate for the euro sponsored by the European Banking Federation
Eurobond	The traditional name for an international bond – i.e. issued by a corporate outside its domestic jurisdiction in a currency other than its domestic currency (note: here, 'euro' has nothing do with the euro currency)
Event of default	One of the events entitling a lender to terminate a credit agreement and ask for the borrowing to be repaid immediately
Exit route	The way in which an investment is realised – e.g. in *venture capital*
F9 model monkey	Slang for a trader who, before doing a trade, consults a spreadsheet using the F9 key
Finance lease	See *Asset finance*
Financial covenants	Promises made by a borrower in a loan or credit agreement about the continued state of its business that, if broken, allow the lender to accelerate the loan
Financial Services Authority (FSA)	The UK's financial watchdog or regulator responsible for supervising banks, fund managers, insurance companies and for the rules governing listings on the London Stock Exchange
Flotation	The point at which a private company is listed on the London Stock Exchange and offers its shares to the public; also known as 'listing' or 'going public' or an 'initial public offering' (IPO)
Forex	Foreign exchange – the largest money market in the world
FRN	A 'floating-rate note' – i.e. a bond whose coupon varies in line with a benchmark interest rate (as opposed to fixed-rate bonds)
FTSE 100 FTSE 250	FTSE is the Financial Times Stock Exchange set of leading market indicators – FTSE 100 is the index of the top 100 UK listed companies by market capitalisation and the FTSE 250 the next 250

Fungible	Two or more securities that in terms of issuer, interest rate, par value and maturity are interchangeable
Future	A derivative that allows the holder to command a market position without actually holding the underlying security, by putting up a margin (a small percentage of the total exposure) and which is settled on expiry by payment or receipt of the difference between the future price and the underlying. Unlike an option which gives the holder the right but not the obligation, a future imposes the obligation which – together with the ability to trade on margin – is what makes futures so dangerous to novices
Gearing	The ratio of a company's debt to its equity capital
Gilts	UK government bonds
Global bond	Nowadays issuers issue just one paper bond, the global bond, which is deposited with a securities *custodian* which then keeps electronic records of individual bond holdings
Hedge fund	A *collective investment scheme* that takes high-risk positions in derivatives and currencies and uses short positions to generate high returns; the manager is usually on a performance-related fee
Hedging	The use of derivatives to protect an investment or market position against market fluctuations
High-yield bonds	See *Junk*
Institution or institutional investor	The ultimate buyers of securities (equities and bonds) – insurance companies, pension funds and investment managers (who run *unit trusts, investment trusts* and *OIECs*)
Interest rate swap	An agreement to exchange a floating-rate liability for a fixed rate or vice versa – the two parties notionally swap an underlying principal amount then pay each other interest as if they had made the swap; in practice the amounts arc netted so that only one payment passes from one to the other; the effect is to give each party a *synthetic* position as if it had borrowed at the swapped rate
In-the-money	An option that, if exercised, would produce a profit as opposed to one that is out-of-the-money ('under water'), which would normally be allowed to expire without being exercised
Intra-day	Within the trading day

Investment bank	Not really a bank at all, but an institution that underwrites the issue of securities by companies, makes a market in them and trades them for its own account. Mostly American
Investment trust	A listed company that invests in the shares of other companies. Also called a closed-ended fund because (being a company) it has a set number of shares in issue
Investment grade	Securities that are rated as such by rating agencies (BAA and above by Moody's or BBB and above by Standard & Poor's), enabling pension funds to buy them
ISDA	The International Swaps and Derivatives Association, a trade body representing market users that provides standard legal documentation for these trades
Islamic banking	Forms of financing in accordance with sharia law which forbids interest (riba) and gambling (maisir) but allows participation in profit
Issuer	A company, bank or government that issues bonds or equities
Junior debt	Debt that ranks behind senior debt so is the last to be paid out on a borrower's insolvency
Junk	Below-investment grade bonds which most pension funds are not permitted to buy. Also called high-yield bonds
LBO	Leveraged buyout – like an MBO but where the ratio of debt funding to equity is high
Lead manager	The bank that leads a syndicated bond issue, liaises with the issuer and puts together the *syndicate* of other underwriters
Letter of credit or L/C	Used extensively in trade finance, a document issued by a bank at the instructions of the buyer in a transaction to pay the seller (called the beneficiary) a stated sum within a prescribed time limit – by being drawn on a bank, the L/C becomes a tradable instrument that the beneficiary can sell in the market, usually at a discount to its face value
Leverage	Gearing or borrowing
Liar loan	A sub-prime loan where the borrower self-certifies their income
LIBOR	London Interbank Offered Rate – the rate at which creditworthy banks will lend to each other in the wholesale market

Limited recourse	Used in *project finance* where the lenders do not look principally to the borrowing entity for repayment but to the cash-generation of the project itself
Liquidity	A measure of the tradability of a company's *shares* – affected by free-float of shares held by outside investors – and of the ease with which a security can be traded on the market
Loan book	A *commercial bank's* portfolio of corporate loans
Long	To have a position in the market – i.e. to have bought a share or bond
M&A	'Mergers and acquisitions' – i.e. the activity where companies take each other over
Mandate	The appointment by a borrower or issuer of a bank to arrange a syndicated loan or bond issue
Margin	The deposit required by a derivatives market to hold a *futures* position
Market risk	The risk that general market movements – for instance in interest rates, shares or currencies – will affect a particular investment
Mark-to-market	The daily requirement to recalculate the current value and increase margin as a *futures* position deteriorates
MBO	Management buyout where the managers of a business (usually a division or subsidiary of a large public company) agree to buy it from the company, usually using *venture capital* to pay for the bulk of the purchase price
Merchant bank	A UK term for a bank that traditionally provided *corporate finance* advice to companies raising money and/or involved in *M&A*. Some also provided investment advice through a fund management arm. Most have been absorbed into *commercial* or *investment* banks. Called 'merchant' because they assisted UK exporters/importers when Britain was a trading empire by providing letters of credit
Mezzanine finance	Found in *venture capital* deals (e.g. *MBOs* and *LBOs*) where the capital is part-equity, part-debt, and ranks behind *senior debt* but ahead of *junior debt* and *equity*. Also used to describe debt that can flip into equity (e.g. convertible bond or loan)
Microcredit	Providing small loans to poor people in third world countries to stimulate economic activity

Microfinancing institution	A lender that provides *microcredit*
Monoline	Specialist insurer that back-stops complex securitisations and project financings by providing a credit guarantee or completion bond
Mortgage-backed	A bond issue collateralised by a pool of mortgages
MTN	Medium term note – a bond; usually part of an 'MTN programme' where a panel of banks provide a wide range of financings to a corporate, ranging from loans to bond issuance
Netting off	Where two parties owe each other a number of payments and only a single net amount passes from one to the other in settlement
Ninja loan	A sub-prime loan extended to a borrower said to have 'no income, no job, no assets'
Non-recourse finance	An absolute version of *limited recourse*, where the lenders do not look to the borrower for repayment but to the income generated by the assets being financed
OEIC	Open-ended investment company – a form of collective investment scheme
Ofex	An off-exchange share matching and trading facility for companies that do not want to join the London Stock Exchange or AIM. Appeals to illiquid or family stocks
Office	Part of a bank or institution: front office is the client-facing, fee-earning part; back office is the administrative part (e.g. settlement of trades); middle office means those parts that are not fee-earning but are crucial to a bank's well-being such as IT, compliance, HR and legal
Option	A derivative that gives the holder the right to buy (call) or sell (put) an underlying security, but not the obligation. 'American' options are exercisable at any time up to expiry; 'European' options are only exercisable immediately prior to expiry
Origination	The *investment bank* activity of advising borrowers on the issue of *bonds*
Originate-to-distribute	A form of securitisation where loans (especially home loans in the US) are made specifically to be sold on (a principal cause of the sub-prime credit crunch)
OTC	Over-the-counter: a security or transaction that is not traded

	on an exchange but is bought bespoke from a bank. Also used to refer to virtual markets where trading is between participants without the structure of a regulated market, such as the foreign exchange market
Piggyback loan	A sub-prime loan where a second mortgage is taken out to provide the deposit for the first
PIKS	Payment in kind securities, used in an M&A where the return accrues over their term and is often guaranteed by the target
Placing	Where a broker or *investment bank* places an issue of shares or bonds with a small group of institutions – this means the issue is not public and less disclosure is required. Also known as a 'private placement'
Plain vanilla	A financing that is straightforward, e.g. a *bond* issue without any 'bells and whistles'
Poison pill	An M&A term meaning a defensive tactic employed by a company to prevent itself from being taken over – generally frowned upon as protecting the incumbent management
Portfolio	A holding of different investments
Precipice bonds	Bonds linked to equity market returns that offered some protection in declining markets but huge exposures if shares fell off a cliff
Price/earnings ratio	A measure of the company's rating by the stock market – calculated by dividing the share price by the last published annual earnings per share (net profit divided by the number of ordinary shares in issue)
Price or pricing	The interest rate at which a loan is made
Principal finance	The activity of an *investment bank* in buying and selling businesses for its own account, using its own capital, to generate a profit for itself
Privatisation	The term covering the many ways in which public sector activities are transferred to the private sector
Program trade	A computer-driven trading activity that is triggered by discrepancies between the price of *bonds* or *shares* and their related *derivatives*
Project finance	Also known as 'limited recourse' or 'non-recourse' finance because the lenders have recourse only to the project itself; often used to finance third-world infrastructure projects where the state buys the output (e.g. hydro-electricity) which funds

	the lending, and the lenders have rights of 'step in' if the borrower (the project company) defaults
Property investment fund	A *collective investment scheme* that holds a pool of underlying property investments, allowing investors to move in and out of property more quickly (by buying and selling units in the fund) than if they held the underlying assets directly
Quantitative easing	Techniques open to governments and central banks to increase the money supply (for instance by buying corporate assets and debt) in order to stave off recession
Rating	The rating conferred on a *bond* issue by a *rating agency* that indicates the likelihood that the issuer will repay it
Rating agency	Independent agencies (Standard & Poor's, Fitch and Moody's are the best known) that assess an issuer's ability to service and repay a *bond* and provide a credit rating (triple A is the highest) to enable institutions and brokers to assess a bond's creditworthiness quickly
REIT	Real estate investment trust: a type of *property investment fund*
Repo	Repurchase agreement – a method of providing a secured loan, usually for a three-month period, where institution A sells a bond to institution B for price X and in the same agreement agrees to buy the bond back from B for price Y: the difference between X and Y is the carry-cost or implied interest rate; the loan is secured since if A defaults, B has legal title to the bond and can sell it. Repos are one of the techniques used by central banks to control liquidity in the markets
Rescheduling	Where the banks agree to spread the repayment of a loan over a longer term to enable the borrower to repay it at all
Retail	Where the customer is an individual
Retiring debt	Paying off a loan or other debt funding
Revolver	Revolving credit facility – i.e. a bank loan that works like an overdraft: any principal repaid can be drawn again
Rights issue	A further issue of shares by a listed company – called a 'rights' issue because existing shareholders have a right to the new shares in proportion to their existing holdings so that their stake in the company is not diluted
Search for yield	Attempts by investors to seek higher-yielding instruments when interest rates are low
Securitisation	Financial engineering that turns an income-stream (for

	instance from a book of loans) into tradable securities, by selling the income-stream to an *SPV* which then issues bonds. Also described as repackaging predictable cashflows from an asset class (such as mortgages) and refinancing them by issuing securities in transferable form
Security	Lawyers use this term to mean security for a loan but markets use it to mean an *equity* or a *bond*
Sell side	That part of the market that sells *securities* – i.e. bond issuers such as companies and governments, as well as *investment banks* and brokers that underwrite, distribute, sell and trade them
Senior debt	Loans that rank ahead of *junior debt* and shareholders on a company's insolvency
Share	Evidence of *equity* ownership in a company
Short	To have sold a *share* or *bond* without owning it (in the expectation that the price will go down so that the broker can buy it in at a cheaper price when required to deliver the security) – hence 'shorting the market'
SIV	Structured investment vehicle – a fund dedicated to investing in securitisations such as *CDOs* and *ABSs*
Sovereign wealth fund	An investment fund owned by the country whose assets it invests (aka SWF)
Specific risk	Risk particular to a bond or share. The opposite of *systemic risk*
Spread	The difference between a broker's bid and offer for a security – i.e. its turn or margin; the less liquid a market, the wider the spread
SPV	Special purpose vehicle – a shelf company used to make a *bond* issue, usually incorporated in a low-tax jurisdiction to reduce fiscal drag on the deal
Square book	A term used by brokers and investment banks to mean that their positions in the market are completely offsetting
Stretch loan	A sub-prime loan where more than half the borrower's gross income will be required to service the loan
Structured finance	A loose term that covers various activities from the repackaging of securities to the linking of derivatives to securities, preferably with a degree of complexity
Sub-prime lending	A fancy term for lending to poor credit risks

Swap	A way of changing a floating-rate loan into a fixed-rate and vice versa; also a way of changing a loan into a different currency by swapping interest-streams but not the underlying principal, enabling each of the two counterparties to obtain a better rate or currency position than they would in their respective markets
Swaption	An option to enter into a *swap*
Syndicate	A group of *commercial banks* (lending to a single borrower) or *investment banks* (underwriting a bond issue)
Syndicated loan	A loan to a single borrower made by a group of banks on the same terms – often used where the sum borrowed is more than a single bank would wish to lend
Syndication	The banking activity of creating a syndicate for a loan or *bond* issue; usually done by the lead manager
Synthetic	The use of *derivatives* to replicate a market position
Systemic risk	Market risk – i.e. not risk that is specific to a particular security
Teaser loan	A sub-prime loan at an artificially low rate of interest, designed to be refinanced at a later date
Technical analysis	Using historic data about market movements to predict the future – practitioners are also known as chartists because they plot such movements on graphs
Term loan	A loan with a fixed drawdown period, schedule of repayments and specified end-date
Tick	Technically, the smallest price movement by which a *future* can go up or down; usually used to describe a bond, share or general market movement – it 'ticked up' or 'down'
Tombstone	The rectangular advert or lucite ornament announcing the successful *syndication* of a loan or *bond* issue, listing the borrower/issuer and syndicate members (so called because it looks like one)
Toxic tranche	The riskiest slice of repackaged debt, often left with the bank originating the repackaging
Trade finance	A method of ensuring that exporters get paid and buyers pay only when they have the goods; uses *letters of credit* (drawn on creditworthy banks) that are then discounted in the 'à forfait' market
Tranche	A slice of a loan or *bond* – may apply to a particular part-repayment

Treasuries	US government *bonds* – the US government is the largest borrower in the world and is regarded as the safest (if it goes bust we might as well all pack up) so it commands the finest pricing of its *bonds*, which is the benchmark off which all international bond issues are priced
Trustee	Some *bonds* are issued with a trust structure allowing a corporate trustee to act on behalf of bondholders
Underwriting	Most issues of *bonds* or *equities* are underwritten by investment banks, which guarantee that the issuer will raise the intended amount of money even if, on the day of issue, market sentiment means that take-up of the issue is less than expected
Unit trust	An open-ended collective investment scheme, i.e. where the investment manager can issue as many units as necessary to meet demand
Value-at-risk (VAR)	Computer-based risk analysis that enables a bank to gauge and manage its aggregate exposure to markets – done by devising models based on historic data of market movements, price volatility and correlations between markets
Vendor placing	Linked to *M&A*, where the target's shareholders are paid in the bidder's shares which are then sold in the market to give them what they really want – cash
Venture capital	Equity finance provided by specialist 'venture capitalists' in return for a shareholding in the business (usually a relatively new and small one); they realise their investment when the company floats or is sold in a 'trade sale'; note that they also finance *MBOs*
Vulture funds	Think of these as investment funds run by arbitrageurs
Warrant	A *bond* or *derivative security* that allows the holder to buy *shares* in a company
White knight	An M&A term for a third company that comes to the target's rescue in a bid – usually by bidding for the target itself
Whole business securitisation	A *securitisation* where the entire income of a business is securitised
Wholesale	Where the customer is a business or government

INDEX

If what you're looking for is not here, look in the Jargon Buster (this index excludes the Jargon Buster and the Bibliography)

LONGTAIL